Dogan Keles

AF239095

Uncertainties in energy markets and their consideration in energy storage evaluation

PRODUKTION UND ENERGIE

Karlsruher Institut für Technologie (KIT)
Institut für Industriebetriebslehre und Industrielle Produktion
Deutsch-Französisches Institut für Umweltforschung

Band 4

Eine Übersicht über alle bisher in dieser Schriftenreihe erschienene Bände
finden Sie am Ende des Buchs.

Uncertainties in energy markets and their consideration in energy storage evaluation

by
Dogan Keles

Gefördert vom Bundesministerium für Wirtschaft und Technologie aufgrund eines Beschlusses des Deutschen Bundestages.
Die Verantwortung für den Inhalt dieser Veröffentlichung liegt bei den Autoren.

Dissertation, Karlsruher Institut für Technologie (KIT)
Fakultät für Wirtschaftswissenschaften, 2013
Referenten: Prof. Dr. Wolf Fichtner,
              Prof. Dr. Stefan Nickel, Prof. Dr. Dominik Möst

Impressum

 Scientific
Publishing

Karlsruher Institut für Technologie (KIT)
KIT Scientific Publishing
Straße am Forum 2
D-76131 Karlsruhe

KIT Scientific Publishing is a registered trademark of Karlsruhe Institute of Technology. Reprint using the book cover is not allowed.

www.ksp.kit.edu

Print on Demand 2013

ISSN 2194-2404
ISBN 978-3-7315-0046-9

Uncertainties in energy markets and their consideration in energy storage evaluation

Zur Erlangung des akademischen Grades eines
Doktors der Wirtschaftswissenschaften

(Dr. rer. pol.)

von der Fakultät für Wirtschaftswissenschaften
des Karlsruher Institut für Technologie (KIT)

genehmigte

DISSERTATION

von

Dipl. Wi.-Ing. Dogan Keles

Tag der mündlichen Prüfung: 10. Mai 2013
Referent: Prof. Dr. Wolf Fichtner
Korreferent: Prof. Dr. Stefan Nickel, Prof. Dr. Dominik Möst
Karlsruhe, 2013

Preface

Considering the expansion rates of the renewable energy sources in Germany in recent years, the goal of the federal government to cover a share of 35% of electricity demand from renewable energies by 2020 seems to be rather exceeded. In the past few years, a strong expansion of electricity supply systems based on wind power and photovoltaic (PV) could be realized in Germany. At the end of 2012, about 31 GW of wind power and about 33 GW of PV were installed. The fluctuating feed-in of electricity from these resources leads to situations in which almost the entire load can be covered by these sources, but also to situations in which these resources provide almost no electricity to serve the load. This development significantly increases the uncertainty in energy markets, especially regarding the wholesale prices of electricity. The players in the energy sector have to take into account the uncertainty during their decision making process. This is where the dissertation of Dogan Keles attaches. He analyses uncertainties in energy markets and develops appropriate modeling approaches for their consideration particularly in investment decision models. Exemplarily, he implements them to assess energy storage technologies under uncertainty.

In this book, Dogan Keles successfully illustrates his work on the modeling of electricity prices with the help of stochastic processes. In this context, he focuses also on the relatively new phenomenon of negative prices. The integration of the fluctuating feed-in from wind power plants in his models is also very innovative. This approach helps to simulate electricity prices in order to take adequately into account the so-called "merit-order effect of renewable energy". Finally, he illustrates the practical relevance of his models by using them for the techno-economic evaluation of pumped storage hydropower plants and compressed air energy storages.

The studies of Dogan Keles were carried out within various projects at the Chair of Energy Economics, Institute for Industrial Production (IIP), KIT. Thereby, he also used his experiences gained during his research stay at the Department of Industrial Engineering and Operations Research, University of California, Berkeley. His models and his new findings have encountered widespread interest and have made Dogan Keles a much sought-after expert concerning the modelling of uncertainties in energy markets. His high reputation in energy economics is also reflected in an excellent list of publications.

Karlsruhe, 2013 *Wolf Fichtner*

Abstract

Due to the liberalization of electricity markets, electricity wholesale prices must be regarded as an uncertain parameter within models for investment planning in the energy sector. Another uncertain parameter is the fluctuant generation of renewable power due to the uncertain availability of wind or solar energy. Both parameters play an important role if energy storages are dispatched and evaluated based on market prices. And, as energy storages represent an important option to cope with the increasing share of fluctuant power production, new methods are necessary to evaluate the economical feasibility of different storage types and the effect of support policies for them.

Before new evaluation methods incorporating uncertainty can be developed, the stochastic and deterministic characteristics of the uncertain parameters have to be analyzed and modeled adequately, so that simulation data can be produced for the evaluation models. This work concentrates initially on the analysis and modeling of electricity prices and wind power, which contributes the major share within fluctuant generation of renewable power. A combined modeling approach is developed and used for the generation of a large number of time series. The combined modeling of both parameters has the advantage that simulated series contain the so-called "merit order" effect of wind power feed-in on prices. The consideration of this effect is especially important, if integrated plants, consisting of wind power plants and energy storages, are economically evaluated.

In the main part of this work, a variety of models are developed for the evaluation of energy storages under uncertainty. These models are then applied to the investment evaluation of a compressed air energy storage (CAES) and pumped storage hydropower (PSHP) plant. The results show that the model, based on stochastic dynamic programming (SDP), delivers the best annual return and thus the highest internal rate of return (IRR) amongst the methodologies which consider electricity prices as uncertain.

Finally, an extended version of the SDP model is used for the investment evaluation of an integrated plant, consisting of a CAES and wind power plant. The model results indicate that such a plant is not economically feasible, although a flexibility premium is applied as a further support mechanism. The flexibility mechanism of 15 €/MWh appears sensible in order to achieve a coordinated operation between the energy storage and wind power plant, but it does not increase the IRR to the level of current PSHP investments. A short analysis with other support mechanisms, such as capacity payments, for flexible power plants shows that the desired IRR level can be achieved for investments in Germany, if the quantum of capacity payments is similar to ones currently paid in Spain.

Acknowledgment

First and above all I wish to acknowledge the supervision of my adviser, Professor Wolf Fichtner. I am very thankful to his useful hints and encouragements during the completion of this work. Especially his feedback during the doctoral seminars and colloquia helped me to improve the quality of my studies. I am also very thankful for the friendly work atmosphere that is established by Prof. Fichtner at the Chair of Energy Economics at the Karlsruhe Institute of Technology (KIT) and that contributed to the success of this work.

I wish also to express my special thanks to the co-advisor of this work, Prof. Dominik Möst from the Technical University of Dresden. His suggestions helped me to define and to develop the topic of this work. Many thanks also to Prof. Stefan Nickel for co-reviewing my dissertation. Futhermore, I want to thank Prof. Shmuel Oren from the University of California, Berkeley for hosting me for a couple of months at his department and for discussing in detail the stochastic optimization model developed in this dissertation. I appreciated also the support of Oren's doctoral students, especially that of Anthony Papavassiliou, who is now a professor at the Catholic University of Louvain. Anthony's crtitical feedback and his review of parts of this dissertation improved both, the stochastic models used in this work and the dissertation itself. Thanks also to Chris Henderson from Queensland University of Technology for also reviewing parts of this dissertation. Special thanks also to Prof. Christoph Weber and Mr. Oliver Woll from the University of Duisburg-Essen. They hosted me for several days in Essen and gave me a clear introduction to modeling with recombinig trees, which are applied to the stochastic dynamic optimization model within this work.

I want to acknowledge also the "Young Investigators Group" program of the KIT for funding my research about stochastic modeling in energy economics and enabling the execution of this dissertation. I am also very thankful to the Karlsruhe

House of Young Scientists (KHYS) of KIT for funding my research visit to UC Berkeley and contributing to the success of this dissertation.

Für die angenehme Arbeitsatmosphäre und die angenehmen Gespräche und Aktivitäten auch außerhalb der Dienstzeiten möchte ich mich bei meinen Kolleginnen und Kollegen am Insitut für Industriebetriebslehre und Industrielle Produktion (IIP) sehr bedanken. Ganz besonders möchte ich mich bei meinem ehemaligen Gruppenleiter Dr. Massimo Genoese bedanken, der sowohl für Diskussionen über die in der Arbeit verwendeten Modelle als auch am Ende für eine kritische Durchsicht der Arbeit zur Verfügung stand. Ich möchte auch meinen Kollegen Christoph Nolden, David Balussou, Martin Schönfelder, Frederik Trippe, Alexandra-Gwyn Paetz und Lutz Hillemacher sowie meiner derzeitigen Arbeitsgruppe (Robert, Lea, Rupert, Philipp und Andreas) für die Überprüfung von Teilen dieser Arbeit und für die Unterstützung bei der Prüfungsvorbereitung bedanken.

Ayrica, degerli ailemin bütün üyelerine, özellikle annem ve babam Huri ve Ahmet Keles'e, kardeslerim Fatma ve Samil'e, dedem Ali hocaya ve esim Elife bana verdikleri destek icin cok cok tesekkür ediyorum. Nilgün Yaren ve Nesibe Yade icin ve tüm egitime destek verenler icin...

Karlsruhe, 06th July 2013   *Dogan Keles*

Contents

Preface   iii

Abstract   v

Acknowledgment   vii

1 Introduction   1
   1.1 Background   1
   1.2 Investment decisions under uncertainty   2
   1.3 Scope and structure of the work   4

2 Uncertainties in liberalized electricity markets   9
   2.1 Liberalization of electricity markets and structural changes   9
      2.1.1 Liberalization process in Germany   10
      2.1.2 Markets for electricity   12
      2.1.3 Structural changes in the German energy sector   16
   2.2 Electricity price characteristics and uncertainty   20
      2.2.1 Characteristics and volatility of electricity prices   21
      2.2.2 Price peaks   23
   2.3 Uncertain commodity prices   25
   2.4 Volatile renewable power generation   29
   2.5 Other uncertainties in electricity markets   33
   2.6 Conclusions   36

3 An overview of stochastic modeling approaches for liberalized electricity markets   37
   3.1 Stochastic processes for modeling uncertainties in electric power generation   39

	3.1.1	A brief survey of electricity price models	39
	3.1.2	Commodity prices	44
	3.1.3	Other uncertain parameters	47
3.2	Scenario generation and reduction	49
	3.2.1	Analytical scenario generation	49
	3.2.2	Simulative scenario generation and scenario reduction	50
3.3	Optimization models applied to power production and investment planning	53
	3.3.1	Short- and mid-term power production planning and portfolio management	53
	3.3.2	Long-term system optimization	59
	3.3.3	Investment decision models	62
3.4	Conclusions	65

4	**Modeling electricity spot prices considering negative prices**	**69**
4.1	Negative electricity prices at the EEX	71
4.2	Modeling approaches for electricity price simulation	74
	4.2.1 Modeling approach for deterministic components	75
	4.2.2 Modeling stochastic components with financial and time-series models	79
		4.2.2.1 Mean reversion model	80
		4.2.2.2 ARMA and Integrated ARMA (ARIMA) models . .	81
		4.2.2.3 GARCH process	84
		4.2.2.4 Regime-switching approach	85
	4.2.3 Modeling negative electricity prices	90
4.3	Evaluation of the different stochastic models	92
	4.3.1 Estimated parameters and simulation results	93
	4.3.2 Importance of the regime-switching and deseasonalising approaches	95
	4.3.3 Model results with versus without negative prices	100
4.4	Critical reflection of the electricity price models	101
4.5	Conclusions	103

5 Modeling wind power feed-in and its impacts on electricity spot prices   **105**

5.1 Impacts of wind power feed-in on electricity prices 106

5.2 Integrated approach for modeling WPF and electricity prices 110

    5.2.1 Overview of the modeling approach 111

    5.2.2 Wind power feed-in model 113

        5.2.2.1 Modeling seasonality of wind power feed-in 115

        5.2.2.2 Stochastic component of capacity utilization 119

    5.2.3 Simulation of electricity spot prices under consideration of wind power feed-in 124

5.3 Wind and electricity price simulation results 128

    5.3.1 Results of the WPF simulation 128

    5.3.2 Results of the electricity price simulation with and w/o wind power impacts 129

5.4 Conclusions and future research 134

6 Evaluation of energy storage and wind portfolios under uncertainty   **137**

6.1 Evaluation of bulk energy storage plants considering electricity price uncertainty 137

    6.1.1 Large scale power storage plants 139

        6.1.1.1 Pumped storage hydropower plants 139

        6.1.1.2 Compressed air energy storage power plants 141

    6.1.2 Models and strategies for dispatching energy storage power plants under uncertainty 144

        6.1.2.1 First strategy: perfect foresight optimization with Monte-Carlo simulation 146

        6.1.2.2 Scenario tree for strategies under uncertainty 151

        6.1.2.3 Second strategy: simple model under uncertainty . . 153

        6.1.2.4 Third strategy: day-by-day optimization 155

        6.1.2.5 Fourth strategy: stochastic dynamic programming . 158

    6.1.3 Evaluation of CAES power plants under uncertainty 161

    6.1.3.1 Results based on 2011 prices 162

    6.1.3.2 Results for the scenario year 2020 166

   6.1.4 Evaluation of PSHP plants under uncertainty 170

  6.2 Mark-to-market evaluation of wind power plants under uncertainty . 172

   6.2.1 Evaluation method 173

   6.2.2 Evaluation of a wind power plant based on the
market premium mechanism 175

  6.3 Combined evaluation of energy storage and wind power plants . . . 177

   6.3.1 Model extensions for portfolio evaluation 178

   6.3.2 Market-based evaluation of an integrated plant 181

    6.3.2.1 The impact of net charges on storage value 183

    6.3.2.2 Changing the configuration of the integrated power
plant 185

   6.3.3 Discussion of alternative policies 187

  6.4 Conclusions 188

7 Conclusions and outlook   **191**

  7.1 Conclusions regarding modeling uncertainty 191

  7.2 Recommendations concerning the viability of energy storage 194

  7.3 Critical reflection and future research 196

8 Summary   **201**

A Appendix   **205**

  A.1 Equations 205

  A.2 Tables 206

  A.3 Figures 208

B Abbreviations   **211**

C List of Figures   **213**

D List of Tables   **217**

E Bibliography   **219**

1. Introduction

1.1. Background

Liberalization of electricity markets started in the 1990ies. At this time electricity prices were regulated by public authorities (see Stoft (2002)). Power production and investment planning in the electricity sector were exposed to only a few limited uncertainties, such as primary energy prices and the development of the demand curve. Among the primary energy prices, oil or coal prices were subject to limited long-term fluctuations, as these commodities were already traded on widely liberalized markets. Investment planning and decisions could be made under conditions that were usually known a priori. Peak load could be reliably forecast and primary energy prices could be fixed with the help of long-term contracts (see Olsina et al. (2007)).

However, since the liberalization of energy markets and the establishment of new trade centers for electricity, such as the European Power Exchange (EPEX), electricity has been increasingly traded on spot markets, where demand and supply determine the equilibrium price in each hour. Although the majority of electricity is traded via bilateral contracts, electricity spot prices remain the main driver for power plant dispatch or electricity trade in general, as traders balance their position with the help of liquid spot markets (see Konstantin (2009)).

Electricity spot prices are very volatile due to various reasons and their future development is highly unpredictable. They describe a strong uncertainty not only for power production planning, but also for investment evaluation based on the cashflows resulting from the optimal power production plan. Investment decisions in power plants or in any other technology, which is dispatched in the spot market, have to be made considering uncertain electricity prices. Therefore, investment decision methods have to be designed in such a way that they can appropriately capture this uncertain parameter.

In parallel with electricity prices, renewable power generation describes another important source of uncertainty, if decisions on power plant dispatch, portfolio optimization and on investments in energy technologies are made. Since the establishment of support mechanisms for renewable power generation, such as the Renewable Energy Act in Germany and other European countries, the proportion of fluctuant power generation has significantly increased. The residual load, which describes the difference between the total electrical load and the delivered fluctuant renewable power, has therefore become highly volatile (see Spliethoff et al. (2011) and Maurer et al. (2012b)). The residual load and fluctuant renewable power generation directly influence the dispatch of flexible conventional power plants. Thus, uncertain renewable power generation also plays a key role for investment evaluations, which are completed based on volatile cash flows resulting from power plant dispatch.

However, the growth of the share of renewables not only affects the power plant dispatch and investments in power plant technology, it also necessitates new investments in additional energy technologies, such as transmission lines or energy storages, to transport and distribute the produced renewable power adequately, and to balance the fluctuations of power generation. Importantly, energy storages should be introduced into the market in a bulk quantity (see Gatzen (2008)), if the electricity system is transformed to one which is almost completely based on renewable power production. But as investments in energy storage face the same uncertainties as power plant investments do, this raises the question of how to carry out a proper evaluation of these investments and how to analyze the impacts of possible support policies on investment activity in this uncertain environment.

1.2. Investment decisions under uncertainty

The evaluation of investments in the energy sector has not been traditionally carried out applying a sophisticated modeling approach for uncertain parameters. Prior to the liberalization of energy markets, the number and distribution of uncertain parameters was limited to a specific range, so that perfect foresight strategies and models were predominantly applied in the past. Sensitivity analyses were additionally carried out to analyze the impacts of different developments of the less predictable parameters. To capture uncertain developments in the long-term, scenario analysis is still the most common methodology. With particular regard to primary energy prices, a variety of assumptions are made for each scenario within perfect foresight models. The goal is to achieve decision support based on the overall analysis of all scenarios (see Keles et al. (2011)).

Due to novel market conditions, however, investment decisions now have to be made in a significantly more uncertain environment. Perfect foresight strategies are less appropriate, especially if very volatile parameters, such as electricity prices or renewable power generation, have to be considered within the decision process. New methodologies that can cope with these uncertain parameters have to be developed. One of these methodologies is stochastic optimization, which tries to find robust solutions, although one or a group of the parameters are uncertain.

To incorporate uncertain parameters into stochastic optimization models, their distribution has to be estimated and described. One of the methods describing their distribution is to model them with the help of stochastic processes and to generate scenario trees based on the simulation results of the stochastic processes (see Gröwe-Kuska et al. (2003)). However, this method requires the probability distribution of the uncertain parameters based on historical data. Alternatively, expert knowledge regarding the probability distribution can be also used to describe possible future developments of uncertain parameters.

The probability distribution, generally represented by a stochastic tree, can then be used within stochastic optimization models to find an optimal solution over all possible developments of the uncertain parameter(s). The solution can contain the optimal values for power plant dispatch or the optimal amount of investment in a specific technology.

As the stochastic optimization represents an appropriate method, the question arises, how to apply this methodology to evaluate necessary investments in energy storages, considering very volatile parameters with fine time resolution, such as electricity spot prices and renewable power generation. Therefore, the focus of this study targets the description and modeling of these uncertain parameters and their incorporation into the developed stochastic optimization models.

1.3. Scope and structure of the work

The intention of this thesis is to develop an appropriate modeling approach for the main uncertainties on liberalized energy markets, such as electricity prices and renewable power generation, and to analyze their impacts on energy storage evaluation. The focus is firstly set on the modeling of short and mid-term developments of uncertain parameters with the help of stochastic processes. The simulated price and wind power generation paths are then used within different models, such as stochastic optimization models. These models evaluate not only energy storages under uncertainty, but also combined power plants consisting of an energy storage facility and a power generation technology based on a fluctuant source, such as wind power. The main research question that this part of the study focuses on is whether an energy storage is economically feasible under current or 2020 electricity price levels and structures or not. The analysis continues with which legislative regulations and support mechanisms can have a positive effect on the economic value of energy storages and of the combined power plants mentioned above. It is expected that the support mechanisms will lead to an income improvement of energy storages, but the question is: will these improvements lead to a positive evaluation of energy storage investments, if a return rate of 8-10% (common for energy investments) is applied? Last but not least the study concentrates also on the effect of sophisticated strategies for energy storage dispatch based on stochastic dynamic programming (SDP). Thereby, the target of the analysis is how much the economic result of the storage dispatch can be improved with the help of an SDP strategy compared to simple dispatch strategies.

To carry out this overall analysis and modeling approach, the work has been structured as follows: Chapter 2 describes the main uncertain parameters and the latest developments causing uncertainty in the electricity sector. The seasonal patterns and the volatility of the uncertain parameters are analysed and described in more detail in this section. The core findings of this detailed analysis will help to determine the most relevant uncertain parameters for energy storage evaluation. Furthermore, these findings will be used to develop consistent approaches for modeling of relevant uncertainties.

Chapter 3 provides an overview of stochastic modeling approaches for liberalized electricity markets. Initially the most common methodologies for the modeling of uncertain parameters are introduced, following with some established methods to incorporate uncertain input parameters into optimization models. This chapter widely relies on the author's own contributions to the paper Möst and Keles (2010).

In chapter 4, the developed modeling approaches for electricity prices are described in detail. Various modeling approaches for deterministic patterns and stochastic residuals are developed and applied for electricity spot prices. As the stochastic residuals can be modeled via different time-series and financial models, these approaches are implemented and used in a software environment to make simulation runs for the residuals. Afterwards the outcomes of the different models are compared to find the most appropriate approach for electricity price residuals. Furthermore, the focus is also set on new modeling approaches, which are developed to capture negative electricity prices and price processes switching between base and jump regimes. Finally, the importance of different model components, that are developed to describe a specific characteristic of electricity prices, is analyzed based on a range of error measures that are calculated for model runs with and without each component. This analysis of a range of possible model components describes the most appropriate modeling approach. This chapter is based on the author's contributions to the paper Keles et al. (2012).

Chapter 5 introduces a modeling approach for another important uncertain parameter in the electricity sector, i.e. fluctuant wind power generation. This parameter has become more and more important recently due to its increasing share within the gross power production of Germany and other European countries. The modeling approach for wind power generation consists of an autoregressive time-series model, which uses historical wind power feed-in values to calibrate the model parameters and to simulate wind power feed-in paths with an hourly resolution for a whole year. The second issue, which is analyzed in this chapter, is the impact of wind power feed-in on electricity spot prices. As electricity spot prices are directly affected by the amount of renewable power feed-in due to the merit order effect, the price reduction effect should be incorporated into the electricity prices, especially if the simulated electricity prices and wind power feed-in paths are jointly accounted for in further analyses.

Chapter 6 describes different strategies and modeling approaches for the optimal dispatch of energy storages on the day-ahead spot market and minute reserve power market, as well as the calculation of the maximal annual return that can be earned due to each strategy. Based on maximal annual returns the investment evaluation is then carried out in the next step. The models maximizing the annual return contain not only a perfect foresight strategy, but also several modeling approaches to optimize the energy storage dispatch under uncertainty. The results of the models based on uncertainty are compared with the results of the perfect foresight strategy to detect the best strategy for energy storage dispatch under uncertainty.

Examined methodologies are then applied in the evaluation of different bulk energy storages, such as compressed air energy storage (CAES) power plants and pumped storage hydropower (PSHP) plants. The economic feasibility of investments in these technologies is assessed for different interest rates and economic lifetime assumptions.

In the second part of this chapter, the combined implementation of an energy storage facility and a wind power plant is also modeled and various policy mechanisms are discussed. These policy mechanisms could be introduced to make these kinds of integrated power plants financially viable and to achieve a more coordinated operation of energy storages and wind power plants. A coordinated operation could shift wind power produced in off-peak hours to peak hours. The evaluation of a standalone wind power plant is also carried out in this second part in order to have a complete overview about all related investment possibilities.

Chapter 7 lists all of the conclusions derived from the research results. Initially all conclusions regarding modeling aspects of uncertainties and their incorporation into optimization models are discussed. Following which the main conclusions and recommendations for investors and policy makers are presented. The chapter ends with, a short outlook on future research topics and on further extensions of the developed models. The study concludes with a short summary in chapter 8.

2. Uncertainties in liberalized electricity markets

Actors in electricity markets are facing new challenges and uncertainties driven by the liberalization of the electricity markets, the introduction of new instruments and markets, such as the carbon market, and structural changes in the energy sector caused by the intensive financial support for renewable energies. While the liberalization of the electricity markets replaced regulated producer prices for electricity with volatile wholesale prices, which make earnings and profits uncertain for power plant operators, the establishment of the carbon market lead to an uncertain cost component among the electricity generation costs. The uncertainty increases, if the operated power plant is based on a fluctuant power source, as it is the case for wind power plants or photovoltaics, and if the produced electricity is directly sold on the spot market[1]. Besides, the volatile power generation also leads to an uncertain amount of electricity that has to be produced from conventional sources to serve the so-called "residual load".

It is important to understand these new sources of uncertainty and their characteristics. This is neccessary for an appropriate consideration of uncertainties within models, which are applied to evaluate investments in new power plants and energy storages. Therefore, the characteristics and impacts of the main uncertainties, such as electricity prices, fuel prices and volatile renewable power generation, are analysed in this part of the work. As the liberalization process is one of the main sources of uncertainty, this process is firstly focused in the following.

2.1. Liberalization of electricity markets and structural changes

In 1996 European authorities started the liberalization of the European electricity market (see Parliament (1996)) to allow free market access to participants on the

---

[1]In this case a quantity risk is added to the price risk.

power generation as well as on the power consumption side. The liberalization provides generators with the opportunity to sell the produced electricity on energy markets or bilaterally to private energy suppliers, instead of selling it to public suppliers or distributors via regulated prices. On the other hand consumers are now free to choose their electricity supplier.

The former regulation of the electricity sector was criticized by companies from other sectors, which disclaimed the existence of natural monopoly in the electricity sector. Especially the so-called "economies of scale" caused by large-scale power plants are less and less significant, as technological development leads to a more decentralized electricity system with smaller power generation units (Schulz (1996)). Also the argument of large irreversible costs, which justified the regulation of the sector, is today mainly limited to investments into transport and distribution grids. Irreversible costs are existent, if new competitors in the market have to build up a large infrastructure, such as transmission lines, which cannot be used for any other application (see Wietschel (2000)). Therefore new investments have a low liquidity value, so that new investors are not competitive against existing market players. However, as these costs are generally limited to the transmission and distribution system, the regulation of the sector should cover only these parts of the electricity sector, but not the electricity generation and trading areas. Hence, the EU parliament passed a EU directive to push the liberalization of the electricity markets in the member states (see Parliament (1996)) and to deregulate at least the electricity generation and trading sector.

Policy makers in Germany followed this EU directive and started the stepwise liberalization and privatization of the energy sector in the late 1990ies. This process led to an increased uncertainty in the energy sector. Hence, the liberalization process in Germany is described in detail in the following.

2.1.1. Liberalization process in Germany

In Germany, the EU Directive was legally implemented by the law for the new regulation of the energy sector (EnWG (1998)) and it was updated by the second law, i.e. EnWG (2005) law. The aim of the new EnWG was to ensure a secure, well-priced and environmentally friendly electricity and gas supply of the country. These characteristics of energy supply were extended by the attributes "consumer friendly" and "efficient" to set consumers into the focus of energy supply. Thus, the lawmakers achieved a more cost competitive electricity generation and distribution system, which in turn should lead to lower electricity prices for consumers without loosing the security of supply.

To achieve these aims, the liberalization was continued by the new EnWG prescribing the unbundling of the electricity sector. Due to the new legislation energy companies were separated into their main parts: generation, transmission and distribution. At the beginning of the unbundling process, the transmission and distribution branches of the former regional energy suppliers were transformed to seperate companies. Generation companies were also founded based on the corresponding branches of the former integrated companies. Together with transmission and distribution companies, they belonged to the same holding. More precisely, the accounting and the operation of generation and transmission companies as well as newly founded trading companies were completely seperated from each other. Each of these companies was then self responsible for its economic operation, even if they were belonging to the same holding company. After the disposition of the main transmission companies by the energy holdings in the last years[2], the unbundling of the transmission system can be seen as completed.

Today, the unbundling process enables new market participants to produce and to feed in their electricity into the grid of transmisson and distribution companies. Due to the EnWG the grid access has to be offered by system operators to all energy suppliers applying the same conditions. However, the market access is subject to charges for all market participants. Trading companies have to pass through the same net usage charges, which are paid by their customers, to the transmission and distribution companies. The height of net charges is determined by transmisson and distribution companies and it is to be permitted by the Federal Network Agency (see BMWI (2008)). Therefore the transmission part of

---

[2]In 2013 only the TSO TransnetBW GmbH is still within the organization of one of the major energy holdings in Germany.

the electricity system remains a regulated sector, as it still constitutes a natural monopoly.

2.1.2. Markets for electricity

The liberalization of the electricty sector lead to an important growth of electricity trading on energy exchanges. The main markets for electricity in Europe are currently the exchanges Nordpool, the Intercontinental Exchange (ICE), the Amsterdam Power Exchange (APX), the European Power Exchange (EPEX) and European Energy Exchange (EEX). The EPEX Spot exchange is the merger of the electricity spot market of the EEX and the French electricity exchange Powernext. While EPEX is a market for spot trade, the EEX provides the trade of electricity via derivative contracts, such as futures or options.

On electricity *future markets* derivative contracts are mainly financially settled and do not contain the physical delivery of electricity. They are used for hedging price risks by energy suppliers. The main contract types are futures, which are offered as monthly, quarter yearly and yearly contracts. They contain the financial balancing of payments, which would occur from the sale or purchase of a constant volume of electricity during the period of validity, e.g. one month in the case of monthly futures. The buyer of such a contract, i.e. the long side, gurantees the purchase of electricity for the actual future price and is no longer affected by growing spot prices in future. In contrast, the seller hedges his position against falling spot prices (see Hull (2008)).

As the future market generally contains the financial settlement of the contracts, its volume is a multiple of the amount of electricity physically consumed in the EEX region. Another derivative product, the so-called "option", does not prescribe its holder the purchase or sale of electricity, but the option to exercise the contract. Consequently the holder of the option will only exercise it, if he expects a positive cash flow. On the other hand, the seller of an option contract has to fulfill the contract, if its buyer exercises it. Although options are further instruments energy suppliers can use for hedging, they are still less important in electricty trade due to the trade volumes at the EEX.

Beside the derivative markets, the major markets for electricity trade are *spot markets*, which enable the physical trade of electricity. The EPEX Spot market covers the electricity trade for the middle European countries Germany, Austria, Switzerland and France. The EPEX day-ahead market had a total turnover of 296.3 TWh in 2011 with a growing tendency (see Figure 2.1)[3], so that the EPEX Spot is meanwhile the largest market for day-ahead spot trade followed by the NordPool ElSpot, whose trade volume made up 294.4 TWh in 2011.

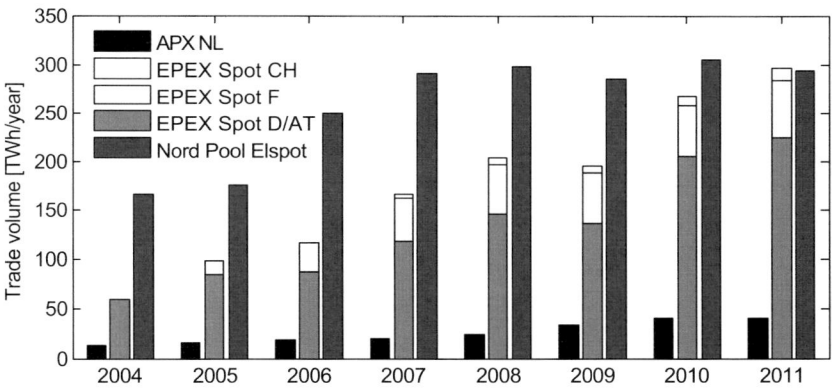

Figure 2.1.: Development of the trade volume at the main electricity spot markets (data source: EPEX, NordPool, APX)

The physical trade of electricity at the EPEX takes place at two different spot markets. The major market is the day ahead spot market, at which buy and sell orders are possible until 12 noon for each hour of the following day. Beside the hourly orders, it is also possible to trade block contracts, e.g. base or peak contracts, which ensure the delivery of a constant amount of power during the delivery block, i.e. the whole day for base contracts and the time between 08:00 am and

---

[3]The overall electricity consumption in the EPEX countries added up to 1155.5 TWh in 2011 (see ENTSOE (2012)). That means that about 25.6 % of the total electricity consumption of these countries was served via the day-ahead spot trade.

08:00 pm for peak contracts. At 12 noon the day-ahead auction is closed and the auctioneer clears the market determining the equlibrium price between demand and supply curves as the system price for each hour of the following day (see EPEX (2012b)). The physical and finacial settlement of the trades are then carried out by the clearing house of the EPEX on the next day.

However, in some cases the market is seen as unbalanced, e.g. supply and demand curves do not meet at a price scale defined by given thresholds (see Table A.1 in the appendix). Due to the latest "Operational Rules of the EPEX Spot", a second auction is then initiated by the EPEX Spot, for which the traders are encouraged to send new purchase or sale orders or to adjust earlier orders for single or a couple of hours. Thereby only orders are considered which reduce the imbalance in the system. The second auctioning is also carried out, if the market conditions seem to be unusual, e.g. if one or several hourly prices strongly differ from the other prices of the same day or from prices of the same hours of a comparable day (see EPEX (2012a)). The second auctioning takes place soon after 12 noon for all regions of EPEX except Switzerland[4], so that finally the day-ahead results can be published at 12:40 pm.

As already mentioned the day-ahead auction is the main spot market at the EPEX and other exchanges. However, if after the orders on the day-ahead market, the traders still have a surplus or shortage of electricity amounts in their portfolios, they can sell their surplus or buy their required amounts at the other spot market, the so-called *intraday market*. However, traders can also follow the strategy to act mainly in this market. The main characteristic of the intraday market is that electricity can be sold and purchased every 15 minutes for time slots of the same day, but only until 45 minutes before delivery starts. If electricity suppliers need power in the more short term, e.g. if the load of their consumers differs from their registered schedule, they have to purchase and pay for balance power. To make sure that there is enough available balance power in the system, the transmission system operators (TSOs) buy reserve power on the markets established for reserve energy.

---

[4]For Switzerland all the mechanisms are applied one hour earlier.

Three different types of *reserve power* are purchased by the European TSOs: the primary and secondary reserve power, which are mainly spinning reserves, and the minute reserve power, which is a non-spinning reserve power. Spinning reserve power is delivered by increasing or reducing the turbine output of the power plants that are already online, while non-spinning reserve is delivered by generators which are offline, but can be started within a few minutes. There are also some so-called fast generators, which can also deliver secondary reserve as a non-spinning reserve, e.g. pumped storage hydro power plants. But the non-spinning reserves usually deliver minute reserve power, which has to be available within 15 minutes after the request of the TSOs. Fast generators, like gas turbines or pumped storage hydro power plants, are suited for that function, so that operators of these power plants have to decide whether they offer their generator capacity on the spot market or on the minute reserve power market.

In contrast, the primary reserve has to be delivered within 30 seconds after it is requested. This power can be only delivered by power plants, which are already online during the determined delivery period of primary reserve power. Secondary reserve power has to be available within 5 minutes after its activation. It is usually also delivered by power plants that are online. As mentioned above some energy storage plants, such as pumped storage hydropower plants, can start within five minutes and deliver secondary reserve power. Other energy storage types, such as compressed air energy storages, need longer starting time (up to 15 minutes). They can therefore offer only minute reserve power.

Different reserve power markets are established in Germany to fulfill the requirements and specifications of each reserve power. The main difference in the market design is the bidding and delivery period. While primary and secondary reserves are auctioned weekly and the delivery period covers also a week[5], the minute reserve power is traded day-ahead for six 4-hour-blocks of the following day. The minute reserve power is distinguished as positive and negative minute reserve (see Regelleistung.net (2013)). Furthermore, each reserve power market

---

[5]Secondary reserve is traded for two different blocks within a week. While the high tariff block covers the time between 8:00 am and 8:00 pm on working days, the low tariff block covers the remaining time. For both blocks two different products, positive and negative secondary reserves, are traded.

is characterized by different minimum order sizes, different number of time slots per day for which the orders have to hold, and different payment schemes (see Table 2.1).

Table 2.1.: Main properties of the German reserve power markets (source: Bundesnetzagentur (2011a) and Bundesnetzagentur (2011b))

	Primary reserve	Secondary reserve	Minute reserve
Minimum order size	+/-1 MW	+/-5 MW	+/-5 MW
Order increment size	1 MW	1 MW	1 MW
# of time slots per day	1	2	6
Payments for reserve	power	power & energy	power & energy
Delivery period	1 week	1 week	4 hours
Activation time within	30 seconds	5 minutes	15 minutes

2.1.3. Structural changes in the German energy sector

Beside its liberalization, the energy sector is affected by other regulatory mechanisms that also cause significant changes. This mechanisms are listed as follows: the introduction of the CO_2-emission trading, the final decision about the phase out of nuclear power plants after the Fukushima Daiichi accident, the introduction of the Renewable Energy Act and the Combined Heat and Power Act.

The first mechanism, the *emission trade* via CO_2-certificates, the so called European Union Allowances (EUA), was established in 2005 as a Europe-wide market to fulfill the Kyoto target to reduce the annual CO_2-emissions by 8 % until 2012 compared to 1990[6]. To achive its target, the European Union signed the "EU

---

[6]The European Union strengthened its target with a self-commitment to 20 % reduction.

Burden Sharing Agreement" that splits the EU targets to fifteen member states[7]. The member states developed the so-called "National Allocation Plans (NAP)", which contain caps for the number of certificates. The NAPs also allocate CO_2-certificates to different emission sources.

The European Commision decided the allocation of 95 % of the certificates free of charge in the first period (2005-2007) of the emission trade and 90 % of the certificates in the second period (2008-2012) (see Parliament (2003)). Thus, only 5 % of the certificates were auctioned by the member states in the first period. The price of CO_2-certificates declined to almost zero during the second half of the first period, when information spread suggesting the system was overstocked with certificates (see Öko-Institut (2010)).

In the second phase the cap for CO_2-emissions is significantly reduced due to the actual NAPs[8]. For Germany 452 million tons CO_2-emissions per year are allowed for the plants, which are affected by the emission certificate system, while in the first period the cap amounted to 499 million tons CO_2 per year. The German NAP allocates CO_2-certificates to existing power plants that have been in operation before 01/01/2003 based on the average historical emissions of each power plant and a technology based benchmark. That means that the amount of emissions of a power plant e.g. from the period 2000-2005 is considered as basic quantity for the number of allocated certificates. This basic quantity is then adjusted by the benchmark and is multiplied with the number of years in the second phase of emission trade (see ZuG (2011)). The allocation of CO_2-certificates to new power plants only depends on the technology-based benchmark for the appropriate technology. For each technology a different benchmark is defined: 365 g/kWh for gaseous fuels and 750 g/kWh for other fuels (see BMU (2006)).

Beside this new allocation plan, the cap for CO_2-emissions and thus the total number of CO_2-certificates are reduced by more then 10 % in the second phase. Together with the so-called "banking" enactment, which allows the use of certificates from the second phase also in the third phase, the new cap has lead to more

---

[7]Due to this agreement, Germany was obligated to reduce its CO_2-emissions by 21 % compared to 1990 (see Commission (2000))

[8]The NAPs need the permission of the European Commission.

or less stable CO_2-certificate prices in the second phase. It can be concluded that the development of the CO_2-certificate prices will be one of the main parameters for structural changes in the electricity sector rather in the mid- and long-term than in the short-term.

The *nuclear phase out* is another regulatory mechanism, which changes the constitution of power plant capacity in Germany. The nuclear phase out, which was firstly decided in 2000, was delayed by the current government in October 2010 extending the operation time of the existing nuclear power plants. However, after the Fukushima Daiichi nuclear disaster, the German government revised the extension of the operating times and decided the immediate shutdown of eight nuclear units, while the remaining nine units have to be shut down until 2022 (see Bundestag (2011)). The nuclear phase out will lead to the planning and construction of new power plants based on coal and gas, if the gap after the total shutdown of nuclear power plants cannot be closed by renewable energy technologies (see Umweltbundesamt (2011)).

The increase of renewable capacity and thus the structural change of the German electricity sector was boosted by the *Renewable Energy Act (in German: "Erneuerbare Eneergien Gesetz EEG")* and the *Act on Conservation, Modernisation and Extension of Combined Heat and Power (CHP)*[9]. The latter act provides bonuses and incentives for the installation of especially small-scale CHP plants to push decentralized electricity generation. However, the more effective act is the EEG, which ensures fixed feed-in tariffs (FITs) to investors for each unit of electricity produced from renewable energy sources (RES). The German EEG was first established in 2000 and then updated by the amendments in 2004, 2006 and 2009. The amendments adjust the height of the fixed tariffs depending on the costs and the market penetration of each renewable technology. The dynamic adjustment of the feed-in tariffs for renewable power lead to a strong growth of especially wind power and photovoltaics (see Figure 2.2). The boost in photovoltaics (PV) and thus the increase of necessary financial resources lead to the last amendment of the EEG in June 2012, which significantly reduced the feed-in tariff for PV elec-

---

[9]orig.: "Gesetz für die Erhaltung, die Modernisierung und den Ausbau der Kraft-Wärme-Kopplung (Kraft- Wärme-Kopplungsgesetz, KWKG)

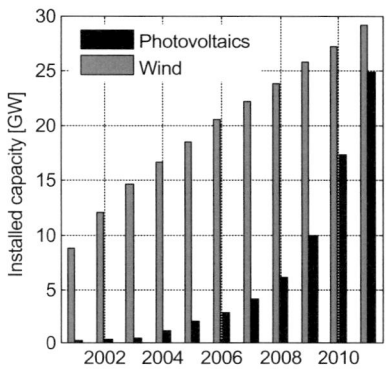 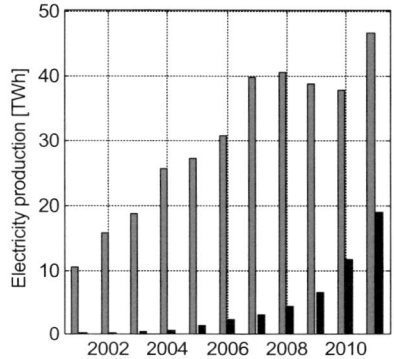

Figure 2.2.: Installed capacity and electricity generation of wind power plants and photovoltaics

tricity and limited the funding for photovoltaics to a maximum total capacity of 52 GW[10]. If this limit is reached, the feed-in scheme for PV shall completely be removed.

The FIT system is funded by the so-called EEG charge that is paid by all electricity consumers, except energy intensive companies. Due to the high usage of FIT (see Table 2.2), the EEG charge had to be raised in 2011 and in January 2013 to guarantee the financing of the RES power. The FITs vary for each renewable energy technology and size and their height is annually reduced by a specific degression rate for new installations. Beside the feed-in tariffs, the EEG guarantees the primary feed-in of renewable electricity to the grid at any time. It can be stated that the German EEG is a successful regulation to increase the share of RES power. The feed-in tariff system is now applied by other European countries, e.g. in France, whose RES funding was initially based on a certificate system.

The structural changes in the electricity sector caused by the EEG and other energy policies, such as the establishment of different electricity markets, has lead to new sources of uncertainties. These uncertainties have to be adequately

---

[10]Some 25 GW photovoltaics capacity was already installed at the end of 2011 (cp. in 2010 17.3 GW, see BMU (2011)). The PV capacity exceeded the 30 GW mark in August 2012.

[11]Difference costs are the gap between total RES funding and the income for RES electricity on the wholesale market. These difference costs has to be covered by the EEG charge.

Table 2.2.: EEG funded electricity and funding quantities (source: BDEW (2012))

Year	2007	2008	2009	2010	2011
EEG funded electr. [TWh]	67.1	71.2	75.1	80.7	99.9
Average FIT [ct./kWh]	11.76	12.67	14.36	16.35	17.15
Total RES funding [bill. €]	7.9	9.0	10.8	13.2	17.1
Difference costs [bill. €][11]	4.6	5.1	5.6	9.8	12.8

considered within the decision making process in the electricity sector. The main uncertainties and some of their characteristics are described in the following.

2.2. Electricity price characteristics and uncertainty

Electricity wholesale prices, especially spot market prices, have become very volatile since the liberalization and the establishment of electricity trade on energy exchanges, such as the European Energy Exchange or NordPool in Europe or PJM and CAISO markets in the USA. Thereby electricity is generally traded via hourly or block contracts on day-ahead spot markets[12], while on future markets electricity can be bought with monthly and (quarter) yearly contracts (see EEX (2011)). The hourly trade of electricity on spot markets leads to prices which can strongly vary for different hours of the day depending on the main driver, the actual electricity load (demand). The hourly varying prices are caused by the fact that electricity is not or only in small quantities storable. Therefore the prices result from the marginal costs of the most expensive producing unit adjusted by a scarcity premium, which is driven by the supply and demand situation.

---

[12]On the main US electricity markets (PJM, CAISO), the intraday electricity price settlements are done every five minutes.

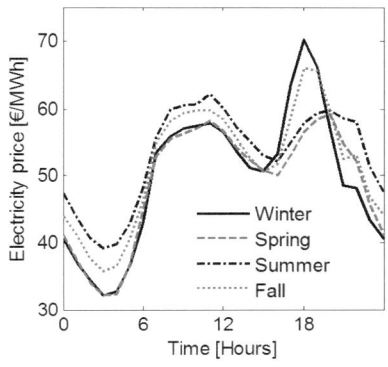 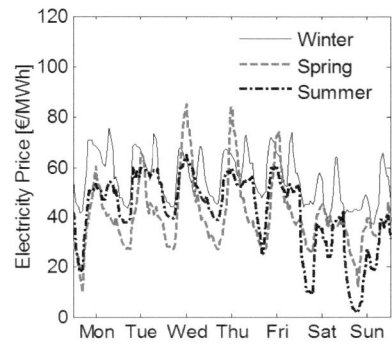

Figure 2.3.: a) Average daily price curves b) Weekly price curves for different seasons (based on 2011 EPEX day-ahead prices)

2.2.1. Characteristics and volatility of electricity prices

Electricity prices at the EPEX display the characteristics of the system load, so that price peaks occur at the same time periods as load peaks (see Weron (2006)). The electrical load is higher in the midday hours on summer days or in the evening hours on winter days. As the demand for electricity and thus the load is low at night, electricity prices usually reach their minimum in this so-called offpeak time (see Figure 2.3).

The EEX spot prices possess also a weekly pattern, which is caused by the lower load at weekends or on holidays. The lower load at weekends is again directly displayed by the lower electricity prices for the same time period[13]. A further deterministic cycle determined for electricity prices is the annual seasonality, which results from the different demand for electricity during each season of the year. Beside the seasonal cycles, electricity prices are characterized by a long-term trend, which corresponds to an average growth of the annual mean price by 2.80 €/MWh between the year 2002 to 2011[14]. However, the price means of the

---

[13]The load-price relation is driven by the merit order of the power plant technologies that take part in the EEX spot market (see Genoese (2010)).

[14]The growth of the annual average prices is determined as the growth rate of the linear regression line fitted to the curve of the annual price means.

Table 2.3.: Some basic statistics of electricity prices (data source: European Energy Exchange (EEX))

[€/MWh]	2002	2003	2004	2005	2006	2007	2008	2009	2010	2011
mean	22.55	29.48	28.55	45.93	50.83	37.95	65.76	38.98	44.48	51.07
std	15.94	26.49	10.80	27.25	49.40	30.37	28.73	18.70	13.97	13.68
skewness	7.78	32.03	0.50	4.86	25.08	6.86	1.16	-1.13	-0.07	-0.66
SPE	71%	90%	38%	59%	97%	80%	44%	48%	31%	27%

single years can significantly vary from the regression line. As it can be observed from Table 2.3, some annual means are clearly lower than the total mean (41.66 €/MWh), while others, such as the price mean in 2008, are distinctly above it. But not only the annual price level is volatile, but also the inner-year distribution of the prices varies strongly. This can be observed from the high standard deviation (std) of the electricity prices for each year. The "normalized" standard deviation, which is called standard percentage error (SPE) in the following, even reaches values over 90%, which is a sign for high inner-year volatility of electricity prices. But as the SPEs and standard deviations vary each year, it can be stated that the volatility is not constant over the years and that electricity price series are heteroscedastic.

The high volatility can also be determined by drawing the boxplot of the electricity prices for the last years. The boxplot shows that the medians significantly differ for the last six years. This issue highlights the different price levels before, during and after the economic crisis in 2009 (see Figure 2.4).

Finally, the different quantile distances for each year indicate that the inner-year volatility is not constant over the analysed time period. The quantile distances of the years 2006 and 2008 are twice than the ones of the years 2009 to 2011. The varying quantile distances are again a sign for heteroscedastic behaviour of electricity prices.

2.2.2. Price peaks

As it is visible from Figure 2.4, there are many prices beyond the whiskers of the boxplot, especially beyond the upper whisker. These prices represent price peaks, which occur in times when the difference between available power plant capacity (excluding system reserves) and the system load becomes very small. This can happen e.g. in cases of power plant outages at times of a high system load. Therefore, these prices can be seen as scarcity prices, which are not explainable by the marginal cost of the price setting power plant, as it should be the case in times of non-scarcity due to the merit order pricing theory.

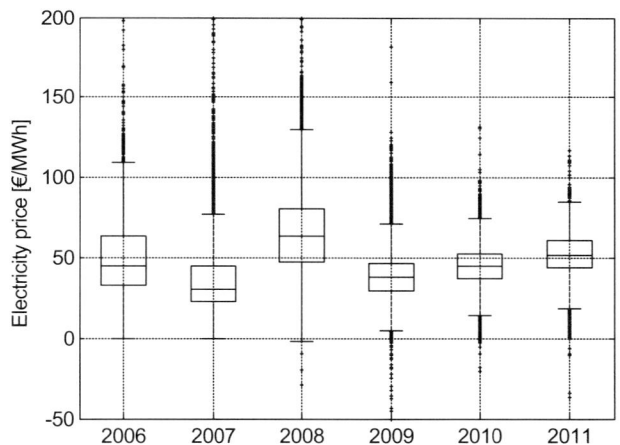

Figure 2.4.: Boxplot of the electricity prices between 2006 and 2011 (data source: EEX, EPEX)

The price peaks or price changes into an upper price level are causing the typical left-skewed distribution of electricity prices. The higher the positive values for the skewness (see Table 2.3), the more left-skewed is the distribution. However, the left-skewness does not exist in the last three years. The prices seem to be equally distributed around the mean. The small negative values for these years even indicate that the prices are slightly right-distributed.

One reason for the change in the distribution is the new design of the EEX day-ahead market, which allows negative prices since September 2008. Negative prices are balancing the positive price peaks, which in turn leads to the more or less non-skewed distribution of electricity prices in the last four years. Another reason is the change in market mechanism, i.e. the introduction of a second auction, which can be initiated by the EPEX Spot, if e.g. equlibrium prices are not found between -150 €/MWh and 500 €/MWh for one or a couple of hours (see section 2.1.2). The second auction can result in the reduction of peak prices far beyond 500 €/MWh, which in turn reduces the left-skewness of the distribution of electricity prices.

The second auction seems to change also the amount and height of price peaks determined by applying the Grubbs' test for outliers (see Table 2.4). The test is separately carried out for the electricity prices of each year[15]. The first analysis of the outliers shows that their number as well as their mean considerably differ for each year. It can be noticed that the number and the mean of outliers are lower for the years 2010 and 2011. In 2011 only two values are determined as outliers and their mean is slightly higher than the 100 €/MWh level, while the mean value of the price peaks was close to 400 €/MWh in 2006 (see Table 2.4). This can be seen as a result of the secondary auction introduced in 2011 in the day-ahead spot market, but also as a result of better forecast tools for renewable electricity feed-in, which enables more precise offers on the spot market.

The reduction of price peaks does not automatically equal to a reduction of the volatility of the non-peak prices. For example, nearly the same standard deviation can be notified for the years 2010 and 2011 (13.85 €/MWh and 13.55 €/MWh respectively). Thus, it can be stated electricity prices will stay volatile and the

---

[15]One of the requirements of the Grubbs' test for outliers is that the analysed series is normally distributed. As the price logs are rather normally distributed than the prices themselves, the test should be applied for the logs. However, the logarithmisation transforms all peak values to values which are closer to the mean of the series, so that almost all positive outliers are eliminated. Therefore, the Grubbs' test is still applied for the prices itself roughgly assuming a normal distribution for them.

Table 2.4.: Mean and number of outliers determined with the Grubbs' test

	2006	2007	2008	2009	2010	2011
# positive outliers	58	105	21	14	4	2
mean of the outliers [€/MWh]	390.60	208.73	234.19	126.80	125.51	115.67

volatility can even increase, if more renewable generation capacity is installed without building up additional energy storage capacity.

2.3. Uncertain commodity prices

As electricity is still mostly produced from fossil primary energy sources, the uncertainty of electricity prices depends on uncertain prices for fossil energy carriers. The main price among the fuel prices is the crude oil price. As many contracts for other fossil fuels are linked to the oil price development, the crude oil price can be seen as the "lead currency" for different energy prices (see Villar and Joutz (2006) and Jones et al. (2004)). Therefore, the development of the oil price is mainly followed by other fuel prices. However, as the price development of other fuels is also affected by other factors, e.g. outages of production facilities, gas and coal prices do not fully correlate with the oil price (see Figure 2.5).

Although the trend of the oil prices was generally positive corresponding to an annual growth of 7.51 $/barrel (10.14 %/a) in the last eight years (2004-2011), the prices were subject to strong fluctuations resulting from different factors, such as global economic development, global demand for oil and the supply situation in the producing countries. For example, the global economic crisis in 2009 lead to oil prices which equaled to only one third of that which were observed in the time of strong economic activity, such as briefly before the economic crisis as well as after the recovery of the global economy in 2011. Furthermore, analysing the oil

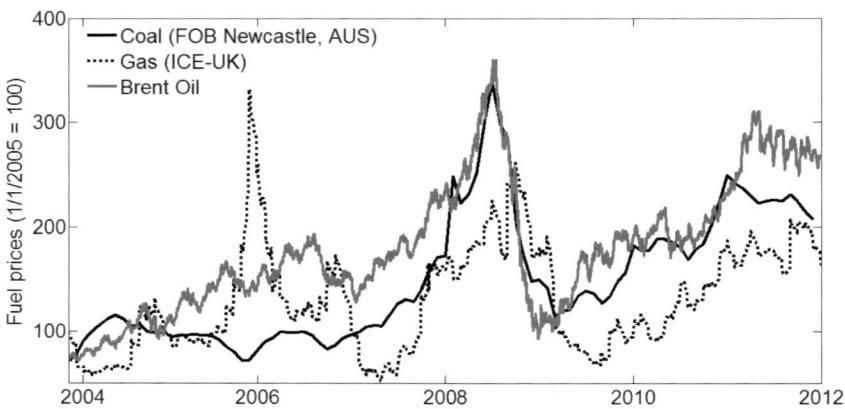

Figure 2.5.: Development of the fuel prices between 2004 and 2012 (data source: Intercontinental Exchange ICE)

prices of a single year, it can be noticed that they possess also a strong inner-year volatility. For instance, the price curve of the Brent crude oil varied between 92 and 125 \$/barrel in 2011.

Taking a closer look at the oil price volatility, it can be noted that the volatility σ_Δ^{oil} of the period 2004 to 2011 amounts to $1.83\%/\sqrt{d}$ or $29.05\%/\sqrt{a}$. The standard deviation σ^{oil} of the daily price settlements for Brent crude oil is equal to 25.13 \$/barrel for the same whole period. For the single years, however, σ^{oil} varies strongly: A high daily σ^{oil} is noted in 2008 (28.25 \$/barrel), when world economy was exposed to disturbances due to the global financial crisis. However, σ^{oil} was considerably lower (e.g. 5.52 \$/barrel in 2006 or 6.96 \$/barrel in 2011) in years with a smooth running of the global economy.

The gas price follows the oil price process with a delay of a few months, which can be especially noticed from the price development from 2007 on. Figure 2.5 shows that the up and downs of the Brent oil price since 2007 influence the UK natural gas price, which shows similar up and downs, but a few months deferred to the oil price. Besides, the gas price curve possesses a further strong peak in the winter 2005 and 2006, which was caused by the outages of several important gas production facilities in the Gulf of Mexico after the Hurricane Katrina. Therefore, the volatility σ_Δ^{gas} of gas prices ($53.81\%/\sqrt{a}$) is even higher than the oil price volatility. Contrarily to the volatility, the growth rate of the gas prices adds up to "only" 6.73 %/a for the last eight years and thus it is lower than that of the oil price.

Among fossil fuel prices the coal price curve has the highest growth rate equal to 15.31 %/a. The "Newcastle free on board (FOB)" coal price nearly tripled in the last eight years reaching values far beyond 100 $/ton in 2011. The strong growth of the coal price can be explained by the extremely high increase of global demand for coal caused especially by developing countries, such as China and India (see IEA (2007)). In contrast to that strong growth, the volatility of coal prices (about $30\%/\sqrt{a}$) is not as high as that of gas prices and it exceeds only slightly the oil price volatility (see Table 2.5). Finally, it should be noted that coal price indices are mainly monthly noted, so that for short-term analyses the coal price volatility is irrelevant.

Table 2.5.: Trend and volatility of fuel prices between 2004 and 2011 (data source: ICE)

Price	Brent oil	UK natural gas	Newcastle FOB coal
Trend	$7.51\$/bl. \cdot a$	$0.27£/therm \cdot a$	$10.08\$/ton \cdot a$
	$10.14\%/a$	$6.73\%/a$	$15.31\%/a$
Volatility σ_Δ	$1.83\%/\sqrt{d}$	$3.39\%/\sqrt{d}$	$8.92\%/\sqrt{m}$
	$29.05\%/\sqrt{a}$	$53.81\%/\sqrt{a}$	$30.90\%/\sqrt{a}$
std σ	$25.13\$/bl.$	$0.17£/therm$	$32.78\$/ton$

Beside fuel price uncertainties, the CO_2-certificate prices describe another important source of uncertainty. This uncertain parameter influences the electricity generation costs and has to be regarded within economic evaluation of power

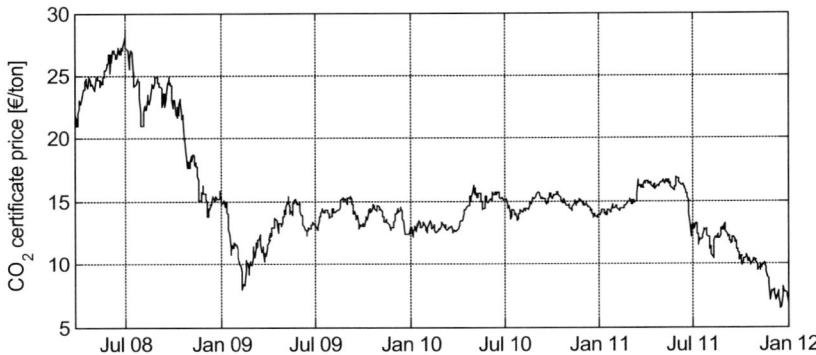

Figure 2.6.: CO_2 price development in the second phase of EU emissions trading (2008-2012) (data source: EEX)

plants. However, the determination and modeling of CO_2-certificate price uncertainty is a very challenging task. The CO_2 prices are not only driven by liberalized market mechanisms, but also by political decisions, which cannot be quantified with a reasonable probability value. The uncertain regulatory environment is also one of the reasons for the irregular process of the CO_2 price curve. The irregularity of CO_2 prices can be espcially noted in the price drop in 2006, caused by the oversupply of certificates and the regulation at that time. This regulation did not allow the banking and use of certficicates in the second period.

In the ongoing second period, the oversupply is avoided by more strict emission caps and the actual political framework that allows the use of certificates of the second phase within the third period. However, prices remained volatile also in the second period, as the global economic crisis lead to a strong price decline at nearly all commodity markets. While during the economic crisis in 2009 the CO_2 price fell to 8 €/ton, the price dropped in the financial crisis in 2011 below 8 €/ton (see Figure 2.6). Between both crises the CO_2 price recovered and reached even values beyond 16 €/ton. This fluctuation of the CO_2 prices can be also observed from the high volatility value $\sigma_{\Delta}^{CO_2}$ for the whole period, which equals to $2.2\%/\sqrt{day}$ or $40.4\%\sqrt{a}$.

The "market uncertainty" of CO_2 prices in the second phase seems to be extended by regulatory uncertainties in and after the third phase. Although the amount of certificates that will be auctioned in the third period (2013 and 2020) is already decided and increased to 50 % (see Defra (2008)), it is unclear whether or how the prices will react to this auctioning level. Besides, it is difficult to predict how CO_2 prices will be affected by new national emission caps. Emission caps will be adapted to reach the EU wide reduction target of 20 % of the annual CO_2 emissions until 2020 compared to base year 1990[16]. CO_2 prices will therefore remain uncertain, depending on the latest political regulation for CO_2 emissions. The probability of political decisions about emissions and thus of CO_2 prices are very difficult to capture within investment evalaution or energy models. It could be incorporated into that models applying different scenarios for several price levels.

2.4. Volatile renewable power generation

The price uncertainties mentioned above are one of the main uncertainty types that have a strong impact on the electricity sector. Further uncertainty types are related to electricity demand and supply. Especially the supply of electricity has become more and more volatile due to strong expansion of electricity generation from renewable energy sources (RES), such as wind power and photovoltaics (PV). The short-term fluctuation of RES complicates the dispatch of conventional power plants, which deliver the residual load[17].

The residual load has become very volatile, particularly due to the feed-in of electricity from wind and solar resources. Thereby, the feed-in of e.g. wind power can be very high throughout a day, while it is nearly zero on the following day. On October 2009 4th wind power feed-in (WPF) firstly exceeded 40 % of the electrical system load in Germany, which in turn lead to negative electricity spot prices at about -500 €/MWh at the EEX (see EEX (2012)). However, the WPF came down to almost zero on the next day, which lead to a residual load around 60

---

[16]This target equals to a reduction of 21 % until 2020 compared to 2005.

[17]The residual load is the difference between system load and fed-in RES electricity.

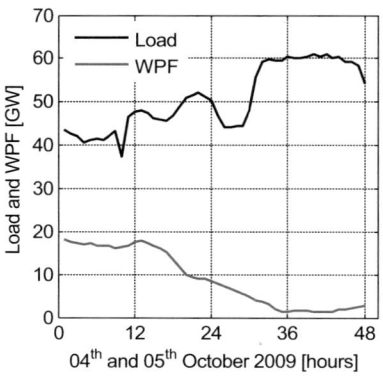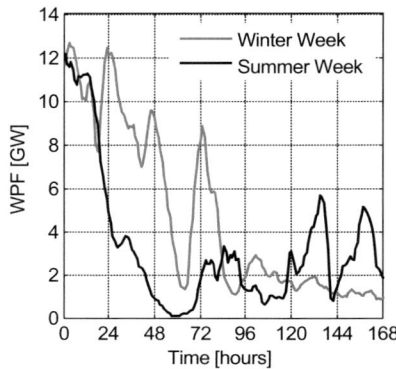

Figure 2.7.: a) Wind power feed-in and system load on October 4th and 5th 2009 in Germany b) Exemplary weekly wind power feed-in (data source: German TSOs)

GW (see Figure 2.7). It can be stated that more than 60 GW conventional power plant or energy storage capacity is still required, although only some 20 GW can be dispatched on days like October 4th.

The high volatility is also displayed by the WPF curve of exemplary weeks. The strong up and downs of the WPF curve leads to the very high short-term volatility of $15.2\%/\sqrt{h}$ in 2011 (and $14.7\%/\sqrt{h}$ in 2010 respectively).

However, wind power is not the only volatile RES power. In the last years the feed-in of electricity from PV-modules has become more and more important. Due to high feed-in tariffs, the PV capacity in Germany grew to more than 30 GW in 2012, which counts to more than one-sixth[18] of the total electricity generation capacity of the country almost catching up with the onshore-wind capacity. Similar to wind power, the PV electricity generation is also directly affected by the current weather conditions. The cloudiness and duration of the sunshine period within a day influences the amount of generated PV electricity. Although this amount is also stochastic due to weather conditions, it follows some basic patterns. In contrast to WPF, which seems to be totally stochastic, despite weak daily and annual cycles (see section 5.2.2.1), the PV electricity feed-in follows sinusoidal patterns. The stochasticity of PV electricity lies in the height of the daily amplitude of the

---

[18]The total installed capacity of Germany corresponded to 167.8 GW in 2011 (see BDEW (2013)).

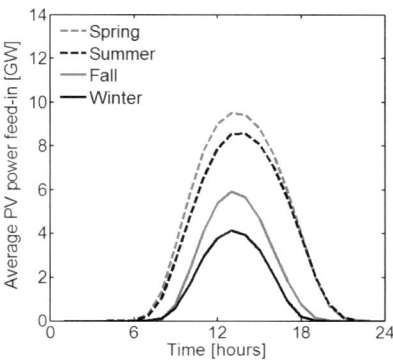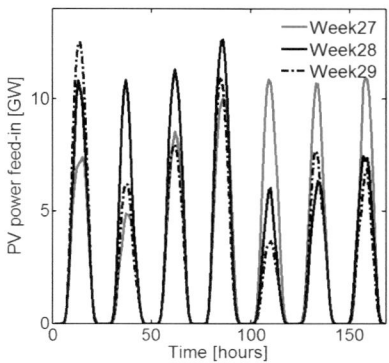

Figure 2.8.: Average daily PV power feed-in and exemplary feed-in for summer weeks in 2011 (data source: German TSOs)

feed-in curve. It can be observed that the feed-in curve possesses multiple times higher peaks on non-cloudy days than on cloudy ones (see Figure 2.8).

The height of the daily cycles and peaks can considerably vary even for days of the same week. Figure 2.8 visualises that the PV feed-in peaks are higher for some days of a week than for the other days of the same week. And as the process of the peaks is totally irregular (see Figure A.1 in the appendix), the height of the feed-in peaks can be seen as a stochastic parameter driven by uncertain weather conditions. The only pattern, which could be determined for the PV feed-in peaks, is that the peaks are on average higher in spring and summer months than on winter days. This can be explained by different off-axis angles of the solar radiation. Finally, a high volatility (about $57\%/\sqrt{d}$) could be determined for the curve of the daily feed-in peaks, which makes it again clear that the main stochasticity of PV power feed-in lies in the height of the daily peaks.

Beside the height of the daily cycles, the duration of the PV power feed-in within a day differs for each season of the year. As it can be also observed from Figure 2.8, the day period, in which PV electricity is generated, is much smaller in the winter (about eight hours) than in the summer. The daily cycle of the PV electricity feed-in is almost sixteen hours long in the summer months.

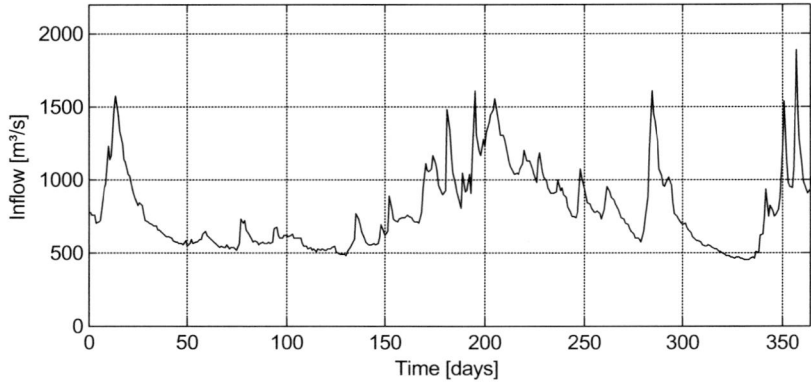

Figure 2.9.: Daily inflow quantities on the Rhine river at the Rheinfelden hydropower plant (data source: BAFU (2012))

The last RES source, which leads to a volatile power generation, is hydropower. Although the output of hydrostorage power plants can easily be adapted to actual demand, the output of run-of-river hydropower plants are exposed to the uncertain inflow rate, as these plant types possess only a very small storage capacity[19]. Thus, their ouput goes along with the inflow rate, which indeed shows a strong seasonal pattern, but is still subject to a strong stochastic component. The analysis of the inflow volatility at the Rheinfelden run-of-river hydropower plant illustrates that even the daily inflow quantity varies significantly throughout the year (see Figure 2.9). σ_Δ of the inflow is determined as $10.2\%/\sqrt{d}$ at the location of this run-of-river power plant, which is one of the biggest plants of this type at the Rhine river. Finally, it can be stated, that although the volatility of the inflow quantitiy is considerably high, it plays a minor role compared to the volatility of PV and wind power production.

---

[19]Hydropower plants with a large storage capacity are exposed to the uncertain flow rate, but their power production is only affected by the long-term fluctuation of the inflow rate.

2.5. Other uncertainties in electricity markets

The availability of power plants is another uncertainty at the electricity supply side. While planned revision and maintenance periods cannot be seen as a uncertain reduction of power plant availability, outages are unpredictable and thus a main source of uncertainty regarding the availability of power plants. Especially lignite, coal and oil burning power plants are affected by power plant outages, so that their availability decreases about 3-4% (see Table 2.6).

Table 2.6.: Stochastic non-availability of power plants (source: EWI et al. (2004))

Power plant technology	Non-availability
coal power plant	4.2%
lignite power plant	3.2%
CHP power plants	2.0%
oil/gas condensation power station	4.2%
nuclear power plants	3.0%
gas turbines	5.0%
(pumped) storage hydropower plant	0.0%

Power plant outages and their non-availability are one reason for the activation of reserve power. The main reason for the activation of reserve power, however, are load and RES power prognosis errors, which have to be balanced with the help of reserve power. As these errors are totally stochastic, the activation of reserve power illustrates another short-term uncertainty. Schmoeller (2005) demonstrates the correlation between activated reserve power and load as well as wind prognosis errors.

Beside these short-term uncertainties, which affect especially the dispatch of power plants and the trade at the spot market, there are long-term uncertainties, which have an impact on the structural development of the electricity sector. The long-term uncertainties are inter alia technological developments, political regulatories and the long-term demand development.

The technological development is pushed by different policies, which support not only the research of new technologies, but also their market introduction. Some of these technologies, such as the different RES technologies, are supported to introduce them into the market in large-scale, while others are still at an early phase of market introduction and need research funding. For both cases, the final aim is to bring the specific costs of these technologies down to a level at which they can compete against conventional power plants without receiving any funding. However, the time at which the costs of a funded technology will decrease to the market parity is difficult to predict. The same goes even for wind energy that already holds a big share within the German electricity generation. Although there exist learning curves for the development of cost degression of new technologies, the learning rates are spread within a wide interval, so that uncertainties regarding the cost degression and market penetration rate of single energy technologies still remain (see Weber (2005)).

Regulatory uncertainty is another uncertainty type, which influences the electricity sector especially in the long-term. Although one major uncertainty, i.e. the role of nuclear power, seems to be eliminated in the German case, others remain. One of these is the further development of the EU CO_2 emission certificates market within and after the third phase (2013 to 2020) and the uncertain height of emission caps for the European countries (see section 2.3).

Another important regulatory uncertainty lies in the further funding policy, especially concerning the Renewable Energy Act (EEG). The EEG is amended every three years adjusting the feed-in tariffs (FIT) for each RES technology. The adjustment of the FIT follows the cost development of the renewable energy technologies. However, sometimes the FIT are also adapted to the market expansion of the single technologies. If e.g. a technology enters the market in large amounts and the EEG electricity costs for consumers seems to get out of control due to the high quantity of electricity for which FIT has to be paid, the FIT rates are reduced not only by the planned degression rate, but also by extra reduction rates. That is why, due to the amendment of the German EEG in 2011, the FIT for PV power was lowered by applying an extra reduction of more than 15 % in 2011[20]. A further extraordinary reduction of about 15% was arranged in the latest adjustment of the EEG in March 2012, which has been applied to installations after April 1st, 2012. The application of the extra reductions lead to a significantly decreased FIT for 2012 compared to that which was originally planned (see Table 2.7).

PV is not the only technology, which was affected by the amendments of the EEG in Germany. Wind power as well as bioenergy were also subject to different new regulations established by the EEG amendments. Especially, the development of the FIT system and the introduction of funding possibilities for direct sold RES power substantially influences the development of RES technologies. As future regulations regarding RES electricity cannot be foreseen, regulatory and political uncertainties have to be considered within decisions in the electricity sector. However, as they can hardly be quantified, the only plausible way to incorporate them into decision tools is applying scenario analyses.

The last long-term uncertainty is the future development of the electricity demand. Depending on different energy efficiency, fuel price and climate protecting scenarios, it is expected that electricity demand will decrease in the upcoming decades in Germany. However, the reduction rate varies in each scenario due to the applied energy effciency and fuel price assumptions (see Keles et al. (2011)).

Table 2.7.: Planned FIT for PV on roofs due to the different German EEG amendments

Act	FIT 2012 [€-ct/kWh]	FIT 2014 [€-ct/kWh]
EEG 2004	38.08	34.37
EEG 2009	32.06	26.54
EEG 2012	26.15	21.65
EEG 2012 adjusted[21]	19.50	15.31

---

[20]Originally an annual degression rate of 5 % was decided for the FIT of PV power. The extra reduction was necessary after the boost of PV in 2010 by more than 7 GW.

2.6. Conclusions

The number and volatility of uncertain parameters in liberalised markets increased in the last years. The main sources for new uncertainty are liberalization of the electricity sector, CO_2 emission trading, support policies for renewable energies and other structural changes in the energy sector. Important uncertainties in energy markets can be listed as follows: electricity prices, fuel prices, CO_2-certificate prices, renewable power generation, power plant outages and political decisions on energy market regulation.

Although all of the uncertainties mentioned above play an important role for the development of the electricity sector, only the electricity spot price and the renewable power feed-in of the next 24 hours are decisive for the short-term power plant dispatch. These parameters possess also the highest volatility values as presented above. If an investment evaluation is carried out based on the cash flows resulting from the power plant dispatch, the uncertainty of these parameters should be considered in any case. Therefore, electricity prices and WPF are considered as uncertain parameters within the evaluation models described evaluation in chapter 6.

The PV power feed-in also plays an important role for the short-term power plant dispatch in the meantime and thus for investment evaluations. However, as up to now there is not enough data for a stochastic simulation of PV power generation, this parameter is not modeled and included into the evaluation models described in chapter 6. Before the investment evaluation and electricity price models as well as their results are presented, an overview of existing stochastic modeling approaches, that cope with uncertain paramters, is introduced in the following.

---

[21] Due to the Renewable Energy Act that is currently in force.

3. An overview of stochastic modeling approaches for liberalized electricity markets

Energy companies are strongly affected by uncertain conditions, as they are exposed to the different risks from liberalized energy markets in combination with huge and to a large extent irreversible investments. Uncertainties that generation companies are facing include the development of product prices for electricity as well as for primary energy carriers, technological developments, availability of power plants, the development of regulation and political context as well as the behaviour of competitors (see chapter 2). Thereby, the need for decision support tools in the energy business, mainly based on Operations Research models, has significantly increased. Especially to cope with the different uncertain parameters, several stochastic modeling approaches have been developed in the last few years for liberalized energy markets.

This section aims to give an overview and a classification of stochastic models especially dealing with price risks in electricity markets[1]. The diversity of these approaches makes it difficult to get a comprehensive overview of the field of stochastic models and thus this survey should guide the way through the process and describe the state-of-the-art in this research area, especially focusing on price risks in electricity markets. A lot of stochastic energy models currently deal with fluctuating feed-in of renewable energies. However, the stochasticity of feed-in of wind and other renewable energies are not fully covered, but a short description of the main approaches will be given in the following.

Furthermore, the approaches for coal, gas and oil price modeling are not described in detail, but general approaches for electricity markets are considered in

---

[1] Beside stochastic models, deterministic models have been successfully used to give decision support in liberalized energy markets. A good overview of electricity market modeling trends with deterministic models can be found in Ventosa et al. (2005).

this section. Thereby the focus is set on stochastic methods developed in Operations Research and financial mathematics with practical relevance and applicability. Electricity markets are characterised by some technical features which determine the complexity of such models (see chapter 2). Electricity market modeling usually requires the representation of the underlying characteristics and limitations of the production assets. As these models take the technical characteristics of the production system and the fundamental data into account, they are often called fundamental models. Beside these fundamental models, sophisticated financial and economic models can be used for modeling uncertain commodity prices in the short term. In this survey, the various modeling approaches in the energy business are classified as follows:

- stochastic models for electricity prices, commodity prices (primary energy carriers) and other uncertain parameters (hydro inflow and wind distributions) (see section 3.1)

- scenario generation and reduction (see section 3.2), which is important for the practical relevance and applicability in energy markets due to the need for a structured handling of large data amounts, as well as

- stochastic optimization models for investment decisions, for short- and mid-term power production planning as well as for long-term system optimization (see section 3.3).

As the three fields cannot be examined separately from one another, they are illustrated by selected integrated models which represent a complete approach. Thereby the practical relevance of the different methods and their applicability to real markets is of crucial importance. In a conclusive summary, shortcomings of existing approaches and open issues that should be addressed by operation research are critically discussed (see section 3.4).

3.1. Stochastic processes for modeling uncertainties in electric power generation

The first step of stochastic modeling is the analysis of the time-variant process of the uncertain parameters. Whereas forecasting the uncertain load was the main challenge before liberalization (for load forecasting see Hahn et al. (2009)), now new uncertain parameters have to be considered in energy modeling, which are inter alia electricity prices, commodity prices (e.g. fuel, CO_2-certificates), fluctuant inflow to hydro reservoirs and uncertain wind power generation. These parameters are analysed using different stochastic processes, such as mean-reversion processes. Thereby historical data, which is available at the power exchanges, is necessary for the estimation of the main stochastic parameters, e.g. mean and volatility. In the following section, some of these stochastic processes applied to different uncertain parameters are described and some selected models are listed in Table 1.

3.1.1. A brief survey of electricity price models

Different theoretical methods can be applied for electricity price simulations. However, the various methods are also used for different research questions or planning tasks. Thus, the different methods cannot directly be compared with each other as each method has its strengths for a special planning task and also corresponding weaknesses. In general, these methods can be classified into fundamental models, game theory models[2], financial mathematical models, statistical and econometric time-series models as well as the technical analysis or expert system (Weber (2005)).

Fundamental models preferably use a comprehensive modeling of the whole electricity system with all suppliers, whereas each single power plant or technology classes are described separately in the modeling approach. Detailed knowledge of electricity demand as well as capacity use and maintenance hours of power plants can be also incorporated into this kind of models. These models are often

---

[2]Ventosa presents a survey of electricity generation market modeling, distinguishing fundamental models, equilibrium models and simulation models (see Ventosa et al. (2005)).

used to develop energy scenarios for long-term view (see Möst and Keles (2010)) and for middle- to long-term planning tasks and price forecasts, where especially structural changes have to be taken into account.

Game theoretic approaches consider the strategic behaviour of different market stakeholders. These models simulate competitive electricity markets and analyse long-term equilibriums on the wholesale market in general based on a Cournot-Nash framework (Hobbs (2001), Lise et al. (2006)). This kind of models is preferably used to test different market design options and to analyse the behaviour of market participants.

Beside these equilibrium-focused models, the other two model types, financial and time-series models, concentrate on price simulation based on historical prices with an hourly or daily resolution. These models are especially used in risk management and for short-term price forecasts. The financial and time-series models can be also grouped to the so-called stochastic models.

While some of these stochastic models separate stochastic and deterministic parts (i.e. trend and seasonality) of the price process (see Karakatsani and Bunn (2008)), others consider both in a single closed approach (see Lucia and Schwartz (2002)). However, in some models, electricity prices are described only with a stochastic process (regardless of any deterministic component). But considering both deterministic and stochastic components delivers a more detailed and appropriate approach.

Electricity prices p_t or their logarithms X_t can be seen as a mathematical composition of deterministic and stochastic components.

$$X_t = X_t^{trend} + X_t^{season} + X_t^{residue} \qquad [3.1]$$

The deterministic components of the price logs are the trend X_t^{trend} and annual seasonality X_t^{season}. Besides, there are models which simulate the power prices multiplying all components with one another (see Schmoeller (2005)). In this case the stochastic residues of historic price logs series form a weak stationary process, if the original price logs are divided by their deterministic components. A stationary process in turn is necessary, if the stochastic residues $X_t^{residue}$ are modelled by an autoregressive moving average (ARMA) process.

Table 3.1.: Stochastic electricity and commodity price models - Overview

	Uncertain Parameter	Stochastic Process	Trend/Seasonality	Correlation
Tseng and Barz (2002)	electricity and fuel prices	MR Process	considered	between electricity and fuel prices
Weron et al. (2004)	electricity prices	MR Process with regime switching	considered by sinusoid function	no correlation
Barlow (2002)	electricity prices	nonlinear OU Process	considered by trigon. function	dependencies from demand
Karakatsani and Bunn (2008)&Bunn	electricity prices	AR process with fundam. components	considered via demand curve	dependencies from demand
Muche (2007)	electricity, coal and CO_2-prices	MR-/ARMA- process with jump diff.	not considered	between CO_2 and electricity prices
Schwartz (1997)	electricity and fuel prices	MR Process	deterministic function	not considered
Weber (2005)	electricity and fuel prices	MR Process	by longterm equilibrium prices	between oil and other fuel prices

Table 3.1.: Stochastic electricity and commodity price models - Overview

	Uncertain Parameter	Stochastic Process	Trend/Seasonality	Correlation
Schmoeller (2005)	electricity and fuel prices, inflow to hydro	ARIMA Process and peak regime	considered by trigon. function, not for coal	between coal and gas prices

But before a stochastic process can be applied to the stochastic residues of the price logs, they have to be determined removing the deterministic components trend and seasonality from the original data series.

The first component, the trend can be calculated via an exponential function, assuming a constant annual growth rate for electricity prices. Alternatively, a linear function can also be chosen for the trend component (see Schlittgen and Streitberg (2001)), if the modelled time steps are discrete.

The model for the other deterministic component, seasonality, is a more complex one, as it should consider load variations and thus price variations within a day or on different day types, also according to specific load on these days. A possible classification of day types, for example in four categories, can be made as follows:

- Monday or working day after holiday

- Working day (Tuesday, Wednesday, Thursday)

- Friday or day before holidays

- Weekend day or holiday

The seasonality component can be modelled via different trigonometric functions. There are sinusoidal oscillation functions which consider the basic and the first harmonic oscillation (see Seifert and Uhrig-Homburg (2007)).

$$X_{d,h} = \alpha_{d,h} + \sum_{i=1}^{2} \beta_{d,h}^i cos\left(2i\pi\frac{t-\tau}{8760}\right) + \gamma_{d,h}^i sin\left(2i\pi\frac{t-\tau}{8760}\right) \qquad [3.2]$$

Other approaches use daily and monthly dummies representing the daily and annual seasonality respectively. These approaches and the modeling methods for the simulation of the stochastic component, such as ARMA-processes and mean-reversion processes are implemented and applied on data from the German electricity market (see chapter 4) and will not be described in detail here.

3.1.2. Commodity prices

In the electric power industry, modeling of commodity prices focuses on the price path simulation of prices of fuels, such as coal, gas and certainly oil. Some models (e.g. Muche (2007)) consider also CO_2-certificate prices, since CO_2-certificate trading is established in electricity markets. However, one of the main uncertainty for electric power producers is fuel prices. Different stochastic models have been explored in the last few years, to handle uncertain fuel prices. Again, they use mean-reversion processes and ARMA processes to describe the stochastic development of the commodity prices. Some of the commodity price models consider trend and seasonality of the price development similar to electricity price models (see Heydari and Afzal (2008)). And some financial models include a second factor, the convenience yield[3], which also follows also an MR Process (see Schwartz (1997)). These models contain the correlation of the convenience yield and the commodity prices. But more interesting is the correlation between different fuel prices. Thereby the dependency of other fuel prices on the oil price plays a key role. Analogue to electricity price simulations, the logarithms of the primary energy prices are generally modelled instead of the prices themselves ($X_f = ln p_f$). Thereby f represents the index of fuel (primary energy carrier PEC) types. More precise approaches (e.g. Weber (2005)) model the derivatives of the price logs with the help of a mean-reversion process.

$$d(dX_f) = \kappa_f(\mu_{dX_f} - dX_f) + \sigma_{dX_f}dW_f \qquad [3.3]$$

whereas $dW_f = \varepsilon_f\sqrt{dt}$ is a Wiener Process. Thereby the error term ε_f of the Wiener process dW_f is standard normal distributed. For estimation purposes, the continuous model is again changed into a discrete one based on discrete time periods for the fuel price simulation; i.e. the marginal time interval is replaced by a discrete time period $\Delta_t = 1$. Based on the discrete approach, the oil price is modelled firstly, as oil is still the most important world energy carrier. The oil

---

[3]The convenience yield can be defined as the surplus of holding the commodity itself instead of a future contract. It plays a major role in times of scarcity of resources.

price simulation is followed by the simulation of the other fuel prices considering correlations based on the oil price.

$$\Delta(\Delta X_{oil}) = \kappa_{oil}(\mu_{\Delta X_{oil}} - \Delta X_{oil}) + \sigma_{\Delta X_{oil}}\varepsilon_{\Delta X_{oil}} \sim N(0,1) \qquad [3.4]$$

For other energy carriers the mean-reversion model is extended by a term for the difference to the long-term equilibrium oil price $(X_{Oil} - \theta_f X_f)$ and oil price changes $(\Delta\Delta X_{Oil})$ as further explanatory variables, considering correlations and dependencies on the oil price:

$$\Delta(\Delta X_f) = \kappa_f(\mu_{\Delta X_f} - \Delta X_f) + \beta_f(X_{Oil} - \theta_f X_f) + \gamma_f \Delta\Delta X_{Oil} + \sigma_{\Delta X_f}\varepsilon_{\Delta X_f} \qquad [3.5]$$

The new parameters represent the tendency to the oil price β_f, the price ratio θ_f between the specific fuel price X_f and the oil price and at last a factor γ_f describing the dependency on the oil price change. After estimating these parameters from historical data via the least-squares method, the extended mean-reversion process can be applied for different fuel prices.

However, these mean-reversion models for fuel prices do not take deterministic components as trend and seasonality into account. But as mentioned above, there are models considering these components similar to electricity price modeling. The trend function again generally contains a constant growth rate, whereas the seasonality is described by again a trigonometric function (see 3.2). However, as coal prices are noted quarterly, there are no significant seasonal effects noticeable, so the models for coal do not include seasonality functions. In contrast to coal prices, gas prices possess strong seasonal effects, which can be described by a trigonometric functions.

After removing the deterministic components trend (and seasonality), the received stochastic residues of fuel prices are modelled via ARMA processes. But the ARMA model can only be applied to a stochastic process, if the process is at least a weak stationary one and the error term (see 3.6) follows a White noise process (see Hackl (2008)). The residual series of the detrended coal prices form a strong stationary process, so the an ARMA process can be applied to the stochastic series. If the a stochastic series is not stationary, it can be transformed into a stationary one using a filter (see Box et al. (2008)). This filter can be the differences of two sequent residues forming a new residue series.

Sometimes a filter has to be applied d-times to receive a stationary process. The composition of filtering the stochastic price series d-times and the proper ARMA(p,q) process is also called autoregressive integrated moving average process (ARIMA(p,d,q) process). For example, coal prices are modelled by Schmoeller (2005) with the help of a ARIMA(1,1,0) process, while the gas prices are described by an ARIMA(2,0,1) process.

These approaches describe independent models for coal and gas prices. But in fact there is a correlation between both price processes. Therefore the ARIMA (1,1,0) process for coal is extended, taking into account the correlation of the coal price in t with the average gas price in $t - \rho$:

$$X_{coal,t} = \alpha X_{coal,t-1} + \gamma \bar{X}_{gas,t-\rho} + \varepsilon_t \qquad [3.6]$$

As mentioned above, coal prices are noted quarterly, so the coal price logs are not modelled on the basis of daily price changes. However, if future expected prices are required, e.g. for real option models (see 3.3), the AR(1) process for electricity prices can be formulated also for coal prices (see Eq. 3.19), based on the expected value from the perspective of today's price logarithm X_0. As the risk-neutral process is required for real options, the AR(1) process is extended by a term $\lambda \cdot \sigma / \kappa$, representing the market price of risk (see Hull (2005)).

$$E(X_{RN,t}) = e^{-\kappa t} X_0 + \left(\alpha - \frac{\lambda \cdot \sigma}{\kappa} \right) (1 - e^{-\kappa t}) \; ; \; Var_0(X_{RN,t}) = \frac{\sigma^2}{2\kappa} (1 - e^{-2\kappa t})$$
$$[3.7]$$

Due to the log-normal distribution assumption of the prices, the expected prices are calculated from their expected logs and variance as follows (see Jaillet et al. (2004)):

$$E(p_{fu,RN,t}) = e^{E(X_{RN,t}) + \frac{1}{2} Var_0(X_{RN,t})} \qquad [3.8]$$

This model for the coal price is similar to the one factor model developed by Schwartz for the simulation of commodity prices. The one factor model is extended in the two factor approach by Gibson and Schwartz, which is based on two mean-reversion processes, one for the commodity spot prices and a second one for the convenience yield, regarding correlation between both parameters.

CO_2-certificate prices are also simulated with the aid of ARMA processes or mean-reversion processes, whereas risk-neutral processes are considered (see Wagner (2007)) if the simulated prices are used again in a real option model. As CO_2-certificates and coal are storable products (in contrast to electricity), no larger price jumps are expected in their price process. Therefore it is sufficient to apply a standard mean-reversion process without any jump component for CO_2-certificate prices. At last, it is worth mentioning that the correlation of electricity prices and CO_2-certificate prices is also considered in the CO_2-certificate price model by Muche (2007). Therefore the error term of the risk-neutral ARMA process of the CO_2-certificate prices is extended by the product of the correlation coefficient ρ_{ec} and the error term of the electricity prices:

$$\varepsilon_{CO_2,t} = \varepsilon_{e,t}\rho_{ec} + \varepsilon'_{CO_2,t}\sqrt{1-\rho_{ec}^2} \qquad [3.9]$$

Thereby $\varepsilon'_{CO_2,t}$ represents the original error random variable of the CO_2-certificate price process, $\varepsilon_{e,t}$ the error random variable of the electricity prices. However, only a few models simulate CO_2-certificate prices. The behaviour of this highly volatile market parameter should be further addressed in future research.

3.1.3. Other uncertain parameters

Other uncertain parameters which are considered in some electricity market models are especially inflow to hydro reservoirs and wind electricity production. A lot of stochastic models for energy currently deal with fluctuating feed-in of renewable energies. However, it is not attempted to cover fully the stochastic issues in wind and renewable energies, only some aspects are shortly mentioned in this section.

Some models integrate different uncertainties into their stochastic modeling approach (see Fleten et al. (2002)). They describe uncertain parameters, like inflow to hydropower plants or the backup power for load balance, with the help of ARIMA processes. As there is no deterministic part of the backup power process;

it is directly analysed by an ARIMA (1,0,1) process. But the inflow to hydropower plants has a seasonal component. Thus the seasonal value for each month X_m^{seas} is determined by the average inflow of the same named months m derived from historical series:

$$X_m^{Seas} = \frac{12}{T} \sum_{j=1}^{T/12} X_{m+12(j-1)} \quad m = 1,..,12 \qquad [3.10]$$

The stochastic residue process is defined by an ARIMA(2,0,2) process:

$$X_t^R = \sum_{i=1}^{2} \alpha_i X_{t-i}^R + \sum_{j=1}^{2} \beta_j \varepsilon_{t-j} + \varepsilon_t \qquad [3.11]$$

The error term ε_t in the ARIMA(2,0,2) process represents a white noise process, the simplest stochastic process, whose expected value equals zero and whose variance remains constant.

Another uncertain parameter which is often modelled in energy market models is the wind electricity generation depending on the forecasted wind speed. Thereby the Weibull distribution, whose probability density and cumulative probability functions are defined as follows, fits the wind speed very well:

$$f(x) = \alpha \beta x^{\beta-1} e^{-\alpha x^\beta}$$
$$F(x) = 1 - e^{-\alpha x^\beta} \qquad [3.12]$$

The parameter α of the Weibull distribution is called shape parameter, while β represents the scale parameter. Furthermore, ARMA models are again chosen to describe the stochastic process of the Weibull distributed wind speed (see Torres et al. (2005)). But before an ARMA model can be applied, generally the wind data series are transformed (e.g. Box-Cox-Transformation) and standardized because hourly wind data reveals cyclic behaviour. As the transformed and standardized data is not stationary, the ARMA process can be applied successfully. Other models use any unvaried stochastic process combined with power spectral density function (see Olsina et al. (2007)).

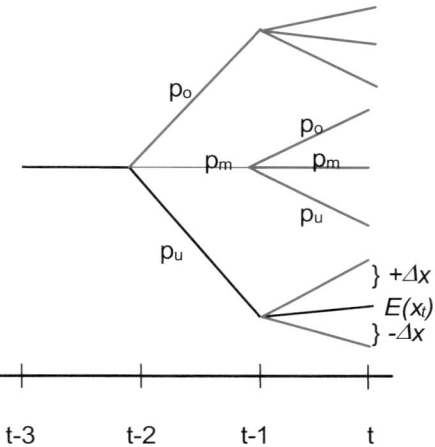

Figure 3.1.: Trinomial tree as an example of analytical scenario generation

3.2. Scenario generation and reduction

The different stochastic processes are used to simulate the uncertain parameters and to generate future data for them. The simulations of each uncertain parameter at a time can be combined to a scenario. The generation of a great number of scenarios is a method to capture the uncertainties in energy markets. Thereby two approaches of scenario generation have been successfully applied in energy market models: the analytic and the simulative scenario generation.

3.2.1. Analytical scenario generation

Analytical scenario generation is based on binomial or trinomial trees, which integrate higher and lower values in $t + 1$ than the values in t for the uncertain parameters (see Pilipovic (2007)). Figure 3.1 illustrates a trinomial tree for scenario generation.

The expected $E(x_t)$ value of the uncertain parameter follows a stochastic process, e.g. an ARMA process, but it can be extended by adding two more branches in each node (time step) to receive a trinomial tree. The value of the new leaves, belonging to the new branches, is calculated by adding or subtracting the same value Δx to the expected value. Δx is evaluated with the help of the variance of the stochastic process (see Eq. 3.13).

$$\Delta x = \frac{\sigma}{\sqrt{2 p_{u/d}}} \qquad [3.13]$$

Thereby it is important to determine the probabilities of each branch. In a trinomial tree, the probability of the upper and the lower branches $p_{u/d}$ can be chosen constant corresponding to one-sixth, while the probability of the middle branch p_m would in this case equal to two-thirds. The whole tree is built up repeating this procedure forwards for each time step and for all existing nodes. Alternatively the stochastic behaviour of uncertain parameters can be described via binomial trees (see Göbelt (2001)).

3.2.2. Simulative scenario generation and scenario reduction

However, the more common approach in energy markets is the simulative scenario generation. Therefore the uncertain parameters are simulated via the stochastic processes described above (see section 3.1). With the help of Monte-Carlo-Simulation, based on a great number of scenario simulations via the described stochastic processes, the uncertainties can be handled very well. Thereby the number of scenario simulations has to be so large that the "law of large numbers"' can be applied to receive reasonable data for the uncertain parameters. But if the generated scenarios should be used in a stochastic optimization model, the large number of scenarios has to be reduced to a level at which the solution of the optimization problem can be calculated within an acceptable time. The scenario reduction of a stochastic optimization problem is done with the help of different methodologies.

Recombining trees represent a feasible methodology to solve a stochastic optimization problem. The idea of recombining trees is the combination of different states $(s_1, s_2, s_3, ...)$ of a scenario tree with similar descendant subtrees to a single state s' at a time t. The probability of the appropriate branches of the former subtrees is cumulated and assigned to the new accordant subtree branches. Further,

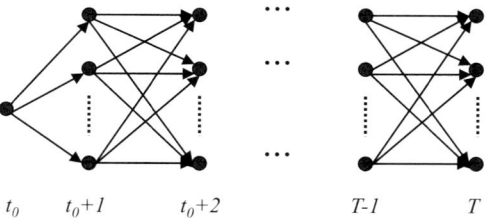

Figure 3.2.: Scenario lattice with different states

the former original states are summarized in a cluster of states, whose mean becomes the representative value for this state cluster at the appropriate time t. This procedure is repeated as long as the required number of states (or clusters) n_0 is reached in each time. The number of states does not need to be truly constant in each time step, but it simplifies the optimization problem to apply a constant number of states to many stochastic models based on recombining trees. Finally, the recombination procedure results in a scenario lattice with nodes representing the different clusters of each time and arrows illustrating the transition between clusters of time t and $t+1$ (see Figure 3.2).

Before a stochastic optimization problem based on such a lattice can be solved, the probabilities of each state transition have to be determined. This can be done via a Monte-Carlo simulation for the uncertain parameter, e.g. electricity price, whereas the whole price range is divided into intervals with equal range (see Tseng and Barz (2002)). These intervals represent the state clusters s of the scenario lattice. The probability $Pr_{s,t \to s',t+1}$ of a transition $s \in t$ to $s' \in t+1$ is defined as the ratio between the number of transitions from the state s to s' and the number of all transitions from s to all other states in $t+1$.

$$Pr_{s,t \to s',t+1} = \frac{card\left\{s | p_t \in [p_{s,t}^{min}, p_{s,t}^{max}] \wedge p_{t+1} \in [p_{s',t+1}^{min}, p_{s',t+1}^{max}]\right\}}{card\left\{s | p_t \in [p_{s,t}^{min}, p_{s,t}^{max}]\right\}} \qquad [3.14]$$

The transition probabilities and the means of the price intervals are used in the next step to solve the stochastic optimization problem. For example, a profit maximizing problem within a time period $[t_0, T]$, based on uncertain electricity prices $p_{s,t}^{El}$ and fuel prices $p_{s,t}^{FU}$ can be solved by maximizing the profit G_t in each time step t and stage s backwards from the leaves $(t = T)$ to the root $(t = t_0)$:

$$G_{t \to T,s}^*(X_{t,s}^{El}) = max\left(\left(p_{s,t}^{El} - p_{s,t}^{FU} \frac{1}{\mu^{FU}} \right) X_{t,s}^{El} - C_{s,t}^{Op}(X_{t,s}^{El}) - C_{s,t}^{St} \right.$$

$$\left. + \sum_{s'} Pr_{s,t \to s',t+1} \cdot G_{t+1 \to T,s'}^*(X_{t+1,s'}^{El}) \right)$$

[3.15]

This function (Eq. 3.15) maximizes the profit from electricity production and sales in t, which consists of the optimal profit in $t + 1$ and the revenues from electricity output $X_{s,t}^{El}$ reduced by the operational costs $C_{s,t}^{Op}$ and the plant start-up costs $C_{s,t}^{St}$ in t. A more detailed description of optimization models will be introduced below (see section 3.3).

Besides recombining trees, there are other approaches to reduce a large number of scenarios generated with the help of a stochastic process. The received scenarios are connected with a same root forming a scenario tree, whereas the root represents the initial value of the analyzed uncertain parameters. In the next step, this "fan" of scenarios has to be transformed into a real scenario tree. The reduction of the scenario fan can be done with combining similar ancestor branches instead of the descendant subtrees in each time step. Therefore the Kantorovic-Distance, applied often in power production and sale models, leads to a transport problem, whose solution delivers the pair of scenario branches and the nodes which should be composed to a single branch (see Dupacova et al. (2003)). However, minimizing the Euclidean distance between each pair of branches would also deliver the most similarities. After receiving the most similar two branches, one of them can be eliminated and its probability can be added to the other. This is possible, because the new scenario tree is a subtree of the former tree (see Schmoeller (2005)). But it is worth mentioning that the Euclidean distance is calculated for all uncertain parameters in a common approach, assuming that the scenario tree is representing the forecast development of all considered uncertainties jointly.

3.3. Optimization models applied to power production and investment planning

The reduced scenario tree or the scenario lattice, which are generated with the methods described in section3.2.2, form the base of a stochastic optimization model. In electricity markets, these optimization models concentrate on finding out the optimal investment decision or the optimal power production plan for a given time period. Some of these stochastic models even optimize whole energy systems in a long-term view (see Göbelt (2001)). Table 3.2 gives a short overview of some stochastic models developed for energy markets in recent years.

For each of the main application fields - investment decision (IDM), short/mid-term power production planning (SMPP) and long-term system optimization (LSO) - a different model is described in the following section to cover the main fields in energy markets for which stochastic optimization models are used.

3.3.1. Short- and mid-term power production planning and portfolio management

Portfolio management and production planning models optimize an objective function, which can describe the total costs or the profit of a whole energy system, particularly of an energy company. However, the profit maximizing approach fits the objectives of an operator of power plants better. As operators of power plants are private companies, they have to cover their costs as well gain profits on the short-term and long-term. Otherwise investors will be not willing to invest in these companies. In short-term power production models, the profit function G is defined as the difference between total expected revenues R from electricity or other energy sales and total expected costs C of generation. Some models also consider a correction term for stock changes ΔS if the company is also dealing with other energy carriers, such as heat or fuel (see Weber (2005)). G is maximized to find out the optimal solution for unit commitment and power production.

Table 3.2.: Overview of stochastic modeling approaches for energy markets

Model and Author	Model Type		Fundamental Model/ Application			Uncertain Parameter	Stochastic Process
	Finan.	Fund.	SMPP	LSO	IDM		
Tseng and Barz (2002)	⊠	⊠	⊠	☐	☐	Electricity and fuel prices	Mean reversion (MR)
Muche (2007)	⊠	⊠	☐	☐	⊠	Electricity price, coal price and CO_2 price	AR(1) process derived from MR
Weber (2005)	⊠	⊠	⊠	⊠	☐	Electricity price and fuel prices	Mean-reversion process
Göbelt (2001)	☐	⊠	☐	⊠	☐	Electricity price and fuel prices, energy demand	—
Fleten et al. (2002)	⊠	⊠	⊠	☐	☐	Electricity spot and contract prices, inflow into water reservoir	—
Schmoeller (2005)	⊠	⊠	⊠	☐	☐	Electricity and fuel prices, inflow into water reservoirs and reserve power	ARMA(p,q) process, ARIMA(0,1,0), VARIMA (0,2,0)
Swider (2006)	☐	⊠	☐	⊠	☐	Wind intermittency	—

Table 3.2.: Overview of stochastic modeling approaches for energy markets

Model and Author	Model Type		Fundamental Model/ Application			Uncertain Parameter	Stochastic Process
	Finan.	Fund.	SMPP	LSO	IDM		
Olsina et al. (2007)	⊠	⊠	⊠	☐	☐	Load demand, available capacity, wind speed	Gauss-Markov Process, two-state Markov mo., univariate stochastic process
Hundt et al. (2008)	⊠	⊠	☐	☐	⊠	Electricity prices, coal and gas prices	Mean-reversion process
Dupacova et al. (2003)	⊠	⊠	⊠	☐	☐	(Load) demand, inflow to hydro-reservoirs and prices	Cluster-analytic approaches
Felix and Weber (2007)	⊠	⊠	☐	☐	⊠	Gas prices	Mean reversion
Bowden and Payne (2008)	⊠	☐	☐	☐	☐	Electricity prices	ARIMA model, EGARCH model
Karakatsani and Bunn (2008)	⊠	☐	☐	☐	☐	Electricity prices	AR model, Linear Regression
Ladurantaye et al. (2009)	⊠	⊠	⊠	☐	☐	Electricity prices	Periodic AR(1) model

Table 3.2.: Overview of stochastic modeling approaches for energy markets

Model and Author	Model Type		Fundamental Model/Application			Uncertain Parameter	Stochastic Process
	Finan.	Fund.	SMPP	LSO	IDM		
Krey et al. (2007)	⊠	⊠	□	⊠	□	Fuel prices	Multivariate AR(1) model
Fleten and Kristoffersen (2008)	⊠	⊠	⊠	□	□	Water inflow, electricity prices	ARMA model
Yang et al. (2008)	⊠	⊠	□	□	⊠	Electricity price, fuel prices and carbon price	Geometric Brownian Motion
Kumbaroglu et al. (2008)	⊠	⊠	□	□	⊠	Electricity price, fuel prices	Geometric Brownian Motion
Blyth et al. (2007)	⊠	⊠	□	□	⊠	Carbon price	Geometric Brownian Motion
Kanudia and Loulou (1998)	□	⊠	□	⊠	□	CO_2-emissions, electricity and fuel supply, capacities	—

$$max\ G = R - C - \Delta S$$

$$R = \sum_{t=1}^{T} \sum_{s \in S_t} Pr_s \left(R_{t,s}^{EL} + R_{t,s}^{HT} + R_{t,s}^{FU} \right)$$

[3.16]

The total revenues of the power plant system consist of expected revenues of electricity sales $R_{t,s}^{EL}$ on the spot and OTC market, heat sales $R_{t,s}^{HT}$ on the OTC market and (re)sales of fuels $R_{t,s}^{FU}$ on the OTC market. The revenues are calculated for each scenario s and time step t. The sales can be calculated from the sold quantities multiplied with the time- and state-dependent prices of each commodity.

$$R_{t,s}^{EL} = \sum_{OTC} p_{OTC,t,s}^{EL} X_{OTC,t,s}^{EL} + p_{Spot,t,s}^{EL} X_{Spot,t,s}^{EL}$$

$$R_{t,s}^{HT} = \sum_{OTC} p_{OTC,t,s}^{HT} X_{OTC,t,s}^{HT}$$

[3.17]

$$R_{t,s}^{FU} = \sum_{f \in F} \sum_{OTC} p_{OTC,t,s}^{f} X_{OTC,t,s}^{f}$$

The total costs of the system or company are made up of power plant operating costs $C_{u,t,s}$ of each unit u and costs $C_{OTC,t,s}$ (for fuel, heat or electricity purchase) resulting from OTC contracts. Both cost components can be divided into variable costs and fixed costs. Thus, the total cost function is formulated as follows:

$$C = \sum_{t=1}^{T} \sum_{s \in S_t} \left(\sum_{OTC} \left(C_{OTC,t,s}^{fix} + C_{OTC,t,s}^{var} \right) + \sum_{u \in U} \left(C_{u,t,s}^{fix} + C_{u,t,s}^{var} \right) \right)$$

[3.18]

The variable operation costs $C_{u,t,s}^{var}$ consider continuous operation as well as start-up and shut-down costs of power generation, whereas binary variables determine the operation mode, the start-up or shut down action. The variable contract costs $C_{OTC,t,s}^{var}$ are determined by the mathematical product of the time-varying prices p_{OTC} and amounts Y_{OTC} for each purchase contract of electricity, heat and fuel.

$$C_{OTC,t,s}^{var} = p_{OTC,t,s}^{EL} Y_{OTC,t,s}^{EL} + p_{OTC,t,s}^{HT} Y_{OTC,t,s}^{HT} + p_{OTC,t,s}^{FU} Y_{OTC,t,s}^{FU}$$

[3.19]

The last component of the objective function, the stock change ΔS, corresponds to the fuel storage changes, which can be determined by the difference between the storage level for each fuel type f at the beginning $S_f(1)$ and at the end of the planning period $S_f(T)$ multiplied with the appropriate fuel prices:

$$\Delta S = \sum_{f \in F} p_{f,1} S_{f,1} - p_{f,T} S_{f,T} \qquad [3.20]$$

However, beside these more general models, which optimize trade portfolios combined with power generation planning, there are models which maximize the profit of only electricity generation. The generation costs are described as the plant operation costs above. Some models are based on linear cost functions for the variable operation costs, but some consider a more detailed cost structure. Troncoso et al. (2008) use a genetic algorithm to solve a non-linear model for the optimal short-term electricity production. Thereby the total cost of electricity production cost is minimized assuming a non-linear cost function. A quadratic cost function is also used instead of a linear function for the operation costs $C_{u,t,s}^{var}$ of each plant u at time t and state s by Tseng et al. (see Tseng and Barz (2002)), whereas the start-up costs $C_{u,t,s}^{SU}$ are no longer fixed ones, but they depend on the time $SD_{u,t,s}$ passed since the beginning of the last shut down:

$$C_{u,t,s}^{var}(X_{u,t,s}^{EL}) = p_{f,t,s} \left(a_0 + a_1 X_{u,t,s}^{EL} + a_2 X_{u,t,s}^{EL2} \right) \qquad [3.21]$$

$$C_{u,t,s}^{SU}(U_{u,t,s}) = \begin{cases} p_{f,t,s} b_1^u \left(1 - e^{SD_{u,t,s}} \right) + b_2^u & U_{u,t,s} = 1 \\ 0 & U_{u,t,s} = 0 \end{cases} \qquad [3.22]$$

The first summand of the first term for the start-up costs represents the fuel costs in the start-up time; the second one b_2^u covers other costs for start-up (e.g. labour). The binary variable $U_{u,t,s}$ indicates the shut down status of a plant at time t and state s (1 = plant is offline, 0 = plant is online).

Based on these cost functions, Tseng and Barz maximize the total profit function (Eq. 3.23).

$$G_{t_0 \to T}\left(U_{u,t,s}, X_{u,t,s}^{EL}\right) = \sum_{t=0}^{T} \sum_{s \in S_t} Pr_s \sum_{u \in U} \left(p_{t,s}^{EL} X_{u,t,s}^{EL} - p_{f,t,s}\left(a_0 + a_1 X_{u,t,s}^{EL} + a_2 X_{u,t,s}^{EL2}\right) \right.$$

$$\left. -C_{u,t,s}^{SU}(U_{u,t,s}) \right)$$

[3.23]

This profit function can also be formulated as a recursive term, in which the profit $G_{t \to T}$ between time t and T is calculated with the help of the expected profit $G_{t+1 \to T}$ between $t+1$ to T adding the expected profit attained at time step t. Therefore it is enough to maximize the profit in time step t and state s adding the expected profit $G*_{t+1 \to T}$:

$$G*_{s,t \to T}\left(U_{u,t,s}, X_{u,t,s}^{EL}\right) = max\left(\left(p_{t,s}^{EL} X_{u,t,s}^{EL} - C_{u,t,s}^{var}(X_{u,t,s}^{EL}) - C_{u,t,s}^{SU}(U_{u,t,s}) \right) + \right.$$

[3.24]

$$\left. \sum_{s \in S_t} Pr_{s,t \to s',t+1} G*_{s',t+1 \to T}\left(U_{u,t,s}, X_{u,t+1,s'}^{EL}\right) \right)$$

So the calculation has to be done backwards against the time axis. The recursive computation ends at the single root state at time t_0 resulting in the total profit maximum during the planning horizon t_0 to T.

At last, it is worth mentioning that these approaches for short- and mid-term power production planning can be extended to optimize an energy system in the long-term planning horizon.

3.3.2. Long-term system optimization

Long-term stochastic models can be solved - analogue to the others - with the help of single-stage or multi-stage modeling for the uncertain parameters. While single-stage models handle uncertainties at time t_0, multi-stage models handle uncertainties in each stage separately. Like the one developed by Göbelt (see Göbelt (2001)) and derived from the MOTAD[4] approach (see Tauer (1983)), single-stage

---

[4]MOTAD means "minimization of total absolute deviations". The approach was developed first by Hazel in 1971 to handle risks in agricultural economics and was extended by Tauer as Target MOTAD in 1983.

stochastic models use several input parameters adjusted via their standard deviations within the objective (profit) function. In energy modeling, these uncertain parameters are at the income side electricity prices p^{EL} and at the cost side fuel prices p^{FU} and CO_2-certificate prices p^{cert} for the production of one unit electricity X^{EL}. Besides, in these models the variable costs c_u^{var}, the fixed costs c_u^{fix} of all plants and also investment costs c_u^{inv} for new plant capacities Cap_u are also taken into account. Further, instead of using constant values for the stochastic parameters, as it is done in deterministic models, the standard deviation of each parameter is subtracted at the income side or added at the cost side of the profit function. But before subtracting or adding the standard deviation σ of each parameter, they are weighted with risk aversion coefficient γ. At last, it should be pointed out that uncertainties on the demand side are also modelled with the help of the standard deviation of the total demand D_t for time t. The standard deviation is weighted with a probability factor Pr_D representing the probability that this constraint should be fulfilled.

$$
\begin{aligned}
max \\
\sum_{t \in T}(1+r)^{-t}
\left(
\begin{array}{c}
\left((p_t^{EL} - \gamma\sigma_{EL}) X_t^{EL} \right. \\
-\sum_{u \in U}\left[\left((p_t^{FU} - \gamma\sigma_{FU})\eta_u + (p_t^{cert} + \gamma\sigma_{cert})carb_u + c_u^{var}\right)X_{u,t}^{EL} + c_{u,t}^{fix}\right] \\
\left. -\sum_{u_n \in U_n}\left(c_{u_n}^{inv} + c_{u_n}^{fix}\right)Cap_{u_n,t} \right)
\end{array}
\right)
\end{aligned}
$$

[3.25]

$$
\sum_{u \in U_t} X_{u,t}^{EL} \geq D_t + Pr_D\sigma_D
$$

$$
X_{u,t}^{EL} \leq Cap_u
$$

[3.26]

The advantages of single-stage modeling are the simple practicability and the low effort for additional data. The complexity of the model corresponds to that of the deterministic one, so that no extra computing time is necessary. The main disadvantage of single-stage stochastic modeling is that only the information about uncertain parameters is used, which exits at the beginning of the planning period because all decisions are made at the beginning.

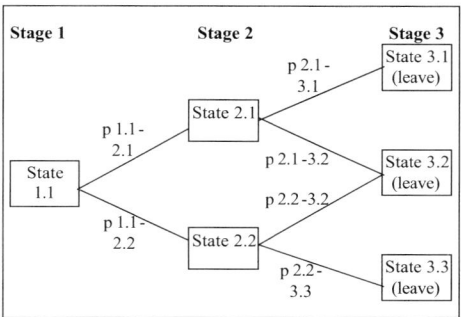

Figure 3.3.: Example of two-stage binomial decision tree

As multi-stage models can handle information that might appear later, they are a much tougher approach than the single-stage approach and therefore their use is more widespread. But the long computing time of this kind of models limits their use for long-term problems. In this case a deterministic approach can be seen as a multi-stage decision tree consisting of only one path with a probability of 100 %. So the complexity of a model based on a non-branched decision tree corresponds to the complexity of the deterministic model multiplied with the number of possible paths. This makes stochastic models with many stages and some thousand nodes in an appropriate computing time impossible. Therefore scenario reduction algorithms (see section 3.2) have to be applied before the optimization problem can be solved. The results of scenario reduction are recombining trees or usual decision trees (binomial, see Figure 3.3, trinomial trees, etc.).

Long-term system optimization models for energy markets usually consider a time horizon of more than 20 years. So they can be seen as the time-extended version of the profit maximizing approach for short- or mid-term power production planning models, if the analysed system is an energy company. In this case, it is suggested to use the profit maximizing approach in the long-term view. But if the analysed system is the whole energy system of a country or of a region, it is wise to choose the cost minimizing approach to maximize total welfare.

min

$$\sum_{t \in T} (1+r)^{-t} \sum_{s \in S_t} Pr_s \left(\sum_{u \in U} \begin{bmatrix} \left(\left(p_{t,s}^{FU} - \gamma\sigma_{FU} \right) \eta_u + \left(p_{t,s}^{cert} + \gamma\sigma_{cert} \right) carb_u + c_u^{var} \right) X_{u,t,s}^{EL} \\ + c_{u,t,s}^{fix} \\ + \sum_{u_n \in U_n} \left(c_{u_n}^{inv} + c_{u_n}^{fix} \right) Cap_{u_n,t,s} \end{bmatrix} \right)$$

[3.27]

$$\sum_{u \in U_t} \sum_{s \in S_t} Pr_s X_{u,t,s}^{EL} \geq D_t + Pr_D \sigma_D$$

[3.28]

$$X_{u,t,s}^{EL} \leq Cap_u$$

This simplified cost function considers the total costs of total electricity production, i.e. fuel costs, variable costs, fixed costs and investment costs regarding all available power plants u within the model horizon T. As emission trading has been established, the emission certificate costs are also taken into account in deterministic energy system models (see Barreto and Kypreos (2004) or Enzensberger (2003)), but have to be integrated into stochastic energy models too.

The main constraint ensures that the expected value of electricity production in each time *t* meets the demand. The second constraint ensures the availability of enough power plant capacity in each state s of each time step t. Further constraints can be added to this simplified multi-stage approach, if other market restrictions exist.

These kind of multi-stage models deliver a tough solution for long-term system optimization and therefore they are applied usually in uncertain electricity markets. They can also be applied to other energy markets adjusting the uncertain parameters and the cost structure of the analysed energy market.

3.3.3. Investment decision models

Investment decision models generally calculate the value of energy investments and deliver a strong decision base before starting huge and capital intensive investments in energy markets (power plants, gas storages, emission reduction technologies etc.). Traditional investment decision models use the net present value approach and other basic evaluation methods. However, some advanced methods, such as the real options approach, have been applied in some evaluation models for energy investments in recent years. The real options approach is used to calculate the value of an investment, whereby some flexible mechanisms are taken into account. Generally, an investor has the option to defer or to stop an investment at the beginning phase. And this option or flexibility has a value which should be regarded within the evaluation of the investment. Another option is the shut down of the power plant, if this is the core of an investment, and running the plant only if a positive marginal return is expected. Actually this "real option" is evaluated with the help of a stochastic model for the evaluation of a coal power plant, developed by Muche (see Muche (2007)).

In this real options model the electricity price, the coal price and the carbon price are modelled as stochastic parameters. They are simulated by mean reverting processes (see section 3.1). The price for electricity per unit (MWh) is modelled for every day t and is declared as pe,t, which is a stochastic element varying each day due to its set up at the day ahead market. Accordingly the price for CO_2-certificates is $p_{c,t}$ and has to be multiplied with a constant factor *carb*, which defines the amount of CO_2-certificates needed to produce one unit of electricity. This product equals to the costs of CO_2 emissions during the production of one unit of electricity. It is assumed that the plant is equipped with enough CO_2-certificates and the investors do not need to buy anymore, so the costs for CO_2-certificates have to be seen as opportunity costs, as they could be sold e.g. at the EEX exchange. Another important cost component is the fuel cost, here the coal price $p_{coal,t}$, which is multiplied with the constant heating value *coal* to evaluate the fuel costs for one MWh power production. Both the coal price and the CO_2-certificate price are stochastic parameters, which have to be estimated like the electricity prices, while the following cost components are considered as deterministic ones. The other variable operating costs are summarized in c_{var} (also a value for one MWh power output) and are considered as constant elements. Besides, the fixed costs c_{fix} per MWh and the non-cash item depreciation c_{dep} per MWh are also included in the model. As a simplification, the taxes are added via a tax rate s to the cash flow extended by the depreciations. Due to these definitions the cash flow per MWh at day t is calculated as follows:

$$z_t = p_{e,t} - p_{c,t}carb - p_{coal,t}coal - c_{var} - c_{fix}$$
$$- s\left(p_{e,t} - p_{c,t}carb - p_{coal,t}coal - c_{var} - c_{fix} - c_{dep}\right) \quad [3.29]$$
$$\Leftrightarrow z_t = (1-s)\left(p_{e,t} - p_{c,t}carb - p_{coal,t}coal - c_{var} - c_{fix}\right) + s \cdot c_{dep}$$

The definition of days as planning time periods makes the use of electricity, CO_2-certificate and coal prices in $t-1$ possible, which can be observed at the day ahead-market. That is why the marginal return $p_{e,t} - p_{c,t}carb - p_{coal,t}coal - c_{var}$ of production can be used for the real option approach to evaluate the investment in such a coal plant.

Depending on the optimal marginal return the operation of the power plant can be planned, whereas a plant operation in time period t only makes sense if the marginal return of this day t is positive. In this case the cash flow in t can be calculated as a call option warrant on the underlying "electricity prices":

$$z_t = max\left[p_{e,t} - p_{c,t}carb - p_{coal,t}coal - c_{var}, 0\right](1-s) - c_{fix}(1-s) + sc_{dep}$$
$$[3.30]$$

Thereby the term $max\left[p_{e,t} - p_{c,t}carb - p_{coal,t}coal - c_{var}, 0\right]$ of the cash flow equation comes up with the cash flow structure of a European Call on the underlying "electricity prices" with a striking price amounting to the sum of all variable costs.

Thus, the evaluation of the coal power plant can be done on the basis of these Call Options for each day within the useful life of the plant. The risk-adjusted total value of all these call options in t_0 corresponds to the value of the coal power plant in t_0.

After simulating the electricity, CO_2-certificate and coal prices using the approaches from section 3.1, Muche (2007) uses a real options approach for the evaluation of a coal plant. Eq. 3.30 estimates the daily cash flow of the plant considering the option to operate the plant in t only if the marginal return is positive. That means that the cash flow term illustrates a marginal return optimal plant operation. All daily expected cash flows z_t within the service life are adjusted by the risk-free interest, to calculate the net present value of the power plant (Eq. 3.31).

$$C_0 = -I_0 + \sum_{t=1}^{T} E_{RN,0}(z_t)e^{r_f t} \qquad [3.31]$$

Further it is worth mentioning that the risk neutral process of the electricity prices is to be used if the real option approach is applied as an evaluation method. Therefore the expected value of the cash flows is adjusted as $E_{RN,0}(zt)$ and it is determined after $N = 1000$ simulations as the mean value of all simulations. Based on the risk neutral expected value of all cash flows within the lifetime of the plant, the risk neutral net present value C_0 is calculated using the risk-free interest r_f and the initial investments I_0. If the risk-neutral NPV C_0 of a plant is positive, then the investment is executed; otherwise it should be cancelled analogue to the familiar NPV method.

In this section the evaluation of a coal plant is described via the real options approach. But by making some adjustments, the evaluation method can be applied also for other plant types, especially gas plants, and even for other investments in energy technologies, such as energy storage power plants.

3.4. Conclusions

Many models based on a deterministic approach can be found in energy modeling and they are suitable to cover several characteristics of today's markets. However, stochastic approaches are useful for the modeling of uncertain parameters, and in recent years several approaches have been developed for the application in energy markets. This chapter represented a survey of stochastic models focusing on electricity market prices, commodity prices and renewable power generation. The approaches about modeling renewable power generation are presented very briefly in this section, so that a separate overview about models dealing with fluctuating feed-in of renewable energies could be useful given in future work. Furthermore, this section introduces also some selected integrated approaches, which combine econometric models for the simulation of uncertainties with system optimization models. The reason for this combination can be seen in the fact that many risks in electricity markets are fundamentally related to the underlying cost structures. This involves the application of integrated methods which combine the advantages of standard methods in financial markets with fundamental energy market models.

At first, different econometric models, especially stochastic processes to simulate uncertain electricity and fuel prices, were described in this chapter. Some of these models consider deterministic trends and seasonality as well as stochastic components of the price processes. Others take price spikes, especially for electricity prices, into account. These approaches are used especially in energy trading companies to quantify price risks of trading position or of the power plant portfolio. Changing framework conditions such as the introduction of emission trading or the change in market design necessitates the development of new and adapted methods. Especially models dealing with uncertain CO_2 emission allowance prices are still relatively rare and further efforts should be made in this field[5]. The change in market design allowing negative electricity prices also necessitates some adaptations in energy models. The loss of an owner of long trading positions in electricity markets was up to now limited. With the introduction of negative prices, also owners of long trading positions are exposed to the risk of losses, which has to be taken into account in novel econometric models.

Econometric models are often used to simulate price paths, which serve as input for fundamental models. If the latter models are solved with these simulated price paths, distributed computing can play a crucial role, as the models with different input price paths can be solved in parallel. Standardized tools helping to distribute the generated models and aggregating procedures for the solutions are necessary for successful implementation in the energy industry. If the simulated price paths are instead considered in an integrated stochastic optimization approach, scenario reduction algorithms (see section 3.2) are a reasonable method for solving the models within an acceptable amount of time. However, scenario reduction algorithms are only applied for a small but growing number of stochastic models. Several approaches have been developed and advanced in recent years, but further research is still necessary in this field, especially when the stochastic models

---

[5]Fichtner (1999) describes models and strategies for energy suppliers focusing on the effect of carbon trading on energy prices.

are applied in the day-to-day business in energy trading. The reduced scenario trees or the scenario lattice forms the basis for the stochastic models. In electricity markets these models concentrate on determining the optimal investment decision or the optimal power production plan for a given period. Thereby the objective functions of these models include different simulated uncertain parameters and they are optimized based on scenario states representing different values of the uncertain parameters.

Beside system optimization models, which take the total energy system into account, models determining the value of a single power plant or the optimal short- and mid-term plant dispatch of one energy supplier can be distinguished. It is important to stress that if the evaluation of a plant is done via a real options approach, then the stochastic processes describing the uncertain parameters have to be adjusted by a term for the market price of risk. If several uncertain parameters, such as e.g. gas prices, electricity prices, wind power generation and hydro inflow, are considered in such a real option approach, the correlation between the different price paths and other uncertainties has a significant impact on the results. Thus, the correlation between different parameters has to be adequately considered.

In general, the overview of stochastic modeling approaches for liberalized electricity markets has shown that a combination of fundamental market models with financial modeling approaches provides an interesting and useful approach to derive electricity prices. The presented approaches can be used to derive both price forecasts and uncertainty ranges for the future development of prices. These can be used for the operational and strategic management of generation and trading portfolios as well as for assessing the risks associated with these portfolios. Further research in this field should aim at aggregating information e.g. with the help of reduced scenario trees and at developing efficient decomposition approaches, which allow dealing with a broad range of price and quantity uncertainty in reasonable computation time.

Interactions between energy prices and technology choice are analysed within the presented long-term optimization models. These models can be developed further by also incorporating the impact of fluctuating generation uncertainty as well as load uncertainty, e.g. due to new consumers such as electric vehicles, and their impact on optimal investments. In this regard additional investigations are necessary to answer the questions of long-term price equilibriums and the robustness of investment decisions under uncertainty. Furthermore, the questions of market design and market power are of importance, so that supply adequacy can be assured at the lowest possible costs.

4. Modeling electricity spot prices considering negative prices

Since the liberalization, the good electricity is no more sold by public companies with fixed tariffs, but more and more on energy exchanges, where prices are formed on day-ahead or intra-day spot markets. The prices on the spot markets vary in general for each hour of the day (see section 2.2). The load as one main driver of electricity prices shows some noticeable patterns, such as the peak at midday in summer days. This typical load pattern can also be recognized in hourly electricity prices. As electricity prices follow more or less typical patterns, these can be explained with deterministic functions.

Electricity spot prices are also influenced by uncertain parameters, such as power plant outages and fluctuant renewable electricity generation. The uncertainties are the drivers of the stochastic component of electricity prices. However, the stochastic components are characterized by specific properties of electrical energy, especially the non-storability[1]. Thus generation has to follow the more or less inelastic demand (load) and traders of electricity with physical delivering are forced to balance their accounts in every single hour independent of actual offers. This leads to extraordinary fluctuations in prices on the one hand and to a high correlation of the load and the electricity price curve on the other (see Weron (2006)). In times of peak load, prices can thus skyrocket especially if additionally unexpected capacity bottlenecks or breakdowns appear on the supply side (see Lucia and Schwartz (2002)).

Furthermore the electricity prices display typical daily movements that are influenced by calendar effects on the one hand, meaning that the daily movement shows a dependency on weekdays and weekends or holidays; and on the other hand the shape of the daily movement changes throughout the saisons of a year

---

[1]Electricity cannot be stored in large quantities and is thus often classified as non-storable.

(see Figure 2.3)[2]. While the midday peak is distinctive for the summer, an evening peak is added for the spring and autumn season. This evening peak will finally dominate the daily movement chart in the winter. Hence, for most of the electricity market worldwide it can be concluded that electricity prices are characterized by

- daily and weekly cycles and seasonality,

- high volatility,

- mean reversion and

- spikes or jumps (see Johnson and Barz (1999)).

The simulation of electricity prices should thus be based on an extended modeling approach considering both deterministic and stochastic components of the price process. Financial and time-series models are often chosen to simulate electricity prices in risk management and for a short-term planning interval.

In the following a combined approach is introduced, in which deterministic components, such as daily and weekly cycles and long-term trend, are modeled with the help of polynomial and trigonometric functions. Parameters of the functions are estimated from historical data derived from the European Energy Exchange (EEX). Afterwards different stochastic processes are applied for the stochastic component of the electricity price process: mean reversion process, (integrated) autoregressive moving average (ARMA or ARIMA) processes and GARCH processes. Therefore these four kinds of stochastic models are combined with the (same) deterministic model component. The different modeling approaches for the stochastic component are evaluated to contribute to a better understanding, which modeling approach is better suited to simulate electricity prices.

In addition to the modeling of the stochastic component a regime-switching approach will be presented which captures price jumps more adequately. Therefore, the presented approach differs between prices in a base regime and also in upper

---

[2]Both can mainly be traced back to the pattern of the load curve.

and lower jump regimes. Last but not least, a new approach, which enables the modeling of negative prices, will be presented. Since 2008 market design allows for negative prices at the European Energy Exchange, which also occurred for several hours in the last years.

The modeling of negative prices is discussed by de Jong in the case of the Dutch imbalance market Sewalt and de Jong (2007). A modeling approach considering negative prices has been introduced by Schneider (2012) applying an area sine hyperbolic transformation and afterwards fitting a deterministic component as well as a regime switching AR(1)-process. However, no financial and time series models for electricity prices exist, which consider the probability distribution of negative prices. In the following a new approach based on a Poisson process and on the empiric stochastic distribution of negative prices is presented to consider negative prices in electricity price modeling.

Furthermore different modeling approaches for electricity prices on the basis of financial and time-series models are applied on EEX spot prices and their results are compared to find the most appropriate approaches. But firstly, the historical process and the occurrence time of negative prices are analysed. Afterwards the whole modeling approach for electricity prices is introduced, focusing on the modeling of deterministic parts and different approached for the stochastic component of electricity prices as well as on negative prices. Then the simulation results of each model type and extension are evaluated and compared with each other. The evaluation contains the comparison of the price duration curves of each simulation with that of historical prices and of mean root square errors, to gain information on the quality of the different modeling approaches. The introduced models for electricity prices are critically reflected and the main characteristics are summarized at the end.

4.1. Negative electricity prices at the EEX

Since September 1st 2008, negative price bids have been allowed at the German power exchange EEX being the first energy exchange in Europe allowing negative prices. Negative electricity prices can occur due to special characteristics of

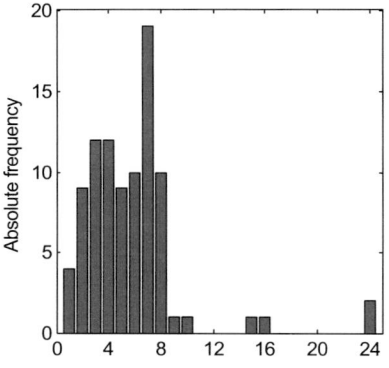 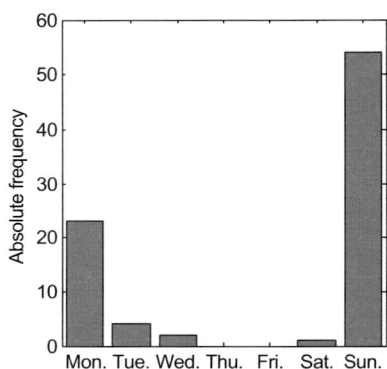

Figure 4.1.: Occurrence of negative prices between 2008-2010 for different hours of the day (left) and weekdays (right) (data source: EEX (2012))

the commodity electricity, such as limited load change flexibility, limited storage capacities and combined production of heat and power etc. (see Genoese et al. (2010)). From an economic perspective negative prices can be rational e.g. if the costs to shut down and ramp up a power plant unit exceed the loss for accepting negative prices. Negative prices also occur, if market actors have to fulfill other contracts, e.g. a heat delivery contract of a combined-heat and power plant (CHP), and therefore the power plant has to be run, although making losses due to negative power prices.

Historical spot market data EEX (2012) from the period of September 1st 2008 to November 2010 show a total amount of 86 hours with negative prices. Mostly, negative prices can be observed in the night and morning hours (23:00 to 08:00); there were only four hours with a negative price in the remaining time period (see Figure 4.1). The distribution of negative prices over the week has a maximum on Sundays (including public holidays) with the remaining hours being concentrated on Mondays (see Figure 4.1). Summarizing, negative prices so far have appeared during weekends and the off-peak period, which comprises the time between 20:00 and 08:00 o'clock at weekdays.

Figure 4.2 shows the absolute frequency of the prices in a histogram with clusters of 2 €/MWh. Two distinct peaks are shown in the distribution, also called

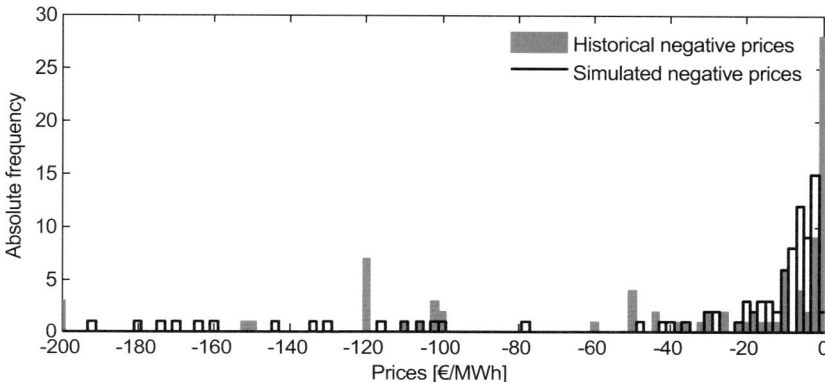

Figure 4.2.: Occurrence of negative prices 2008-2010 at different hours and weekdays (data source: EEX (2012))[4]

bimodal distribution. One peak is in the far minimum and is assumed to follow a lognormal distribution. The other part of the values is moderately negative and assumed to be an exponentially distribution. To analyse these distribution assumptions, two tests are performed. First, the left part of the distribution is tested using a X^2-test, then the right part of the observed distribution is tested using a KS-test[3]. For the X^2-test the logarithms of the values are taken to achieve a normal distribution which can easily be tested within the MATLAB environment. Both tests show that the distribution hypothesis cannot be neglected. The estimated distributions are shown in section 4.2.3.

---

[3]The distribution of the right part is tested with the KS-test instead of the X^2-test, as the latter test is not applicable for exponential distributions.

[4]Due to Figure 4.2, the simulated negative prices below -80€/MWh seem to be uniformly rather than normally distributed. This is caused by the small number N of realizations. However, a large number of realizations would illustrate that these negative prices are also normally distributed as the historical negative prices below -80€/MWh are. But for consistency reasons the number of simulated negative prices is chosen as the historical one.

4.2. Modeling approaches for electricity price simulation

Stochastic models for electricity prices, such as financial and econometric time-series models, will be analysed and compared with each other in this section. Thereby financial mathematical models, such as those invoking Geometric Brownian motion or the mean-reversion process, deal with the volatility of the electricity prices, and can be used especially for the evaluation of derivatives or real options in energy markets (Hirsch (2009), Gibson and Schwartz (1990)). The other theoretical model class, econometric time-series models, e.g. ARMA or GARCH models (Garcia et al. (2005)), focuses on patterns or autocorrelation within the historical price curve related to external impacts, such as electrical load, temperature, etc. The deterministic components of the price curve are analysed very well in time-series models, while the stochastic component is brought into focus in financial mathematical models[5]. These models are used to simulate hourly resolved electricity prices in general for a short-term planning period of maximum one year and their results are compared afterwards with real price curves (see Weron et al. (2004) or Swider and Weber (2007)). But as these models do not concentrate on the long-term price movements, which are analysed especially in fundamental models, a combined approach, in which both long and short-term movements of electricity prices can be simulated with fundamental models and stochastic processes, is proposed in the section "critical reflection and outlook".

Before financial and time-series models can be applied on stochastic price series, the historical data has to be adjusted. Therefore, in the first step the deterministic components are modeled and removed from historical price series. The deterministic components contain the long-term trend, the weekly and daily cycle and the annual seasonality. All of them are subtracted from the original electricity price series. The resulting stochastic residuals are then used to estimate the parameters of each stochastic process. With the help of the estimated parameters and the corresponding stochastic process the stochastic components for all hours of a year are generated. Furthermore, as jumps are one of the main charac-

---

[5]An overview of existing stochastic energy models including electricity price simulation is given in Möst and Keles (2010)

teristics of electricity prices, a regime-switching approach is applied to consider this characteristic within the simulation of the stochastic component. Afterwards all deterministic components are added again to the stochastic one to receive the simulated electricity prices. In addition to the comparison of different modeling approaches a novel model extension is presented, which is able to simulate negative electricity prices. Up to now, nearly all approaches have only been developed to simulate positive prices.

The whole electricity price model is implemented in the software-tool MAT-LAB and is illustrated in Figure 4.3.

4.2.1. Modeling approach for deterministic components

In a first step, prices are logarithmised and the price logs are passed to the illustrated simulation tool instead of the prices themselves (see Figure 4.3). The logarithms are used, as the lognormal distribution fits the empirical distribution and captures the left-skewness of the electricity prices (see Lucia and Schwartz (2002)). Besides, if electricity prices were assumed to be normally distributed, this would result in negative values nearly half of the time. To avoid this, simulation of the logarithms seems to be a reasonable solution. Since 2008, negative prices have also been allowed to occur at the EEX. This change in market design requires an adaptation of the presented modeling approach to capture negative prices also. Therefore the negative values are transformed to positive ones, so that the logarithmisation can be done for all values. After simulating and retransforming the price logs, some of the electricity prices are changed to negative values again representing the negative prices (see 4.2.3).

After the logaritmisation, the modeling approach is continued with the removal of the long-term trend from the original price logs. The daily and weekly cycles as well as the seasonal component are removed in the next steps receiving the stochastic residues, which are used for the parameter estimation of the stochastic processes (see 4.2.2). The trend is assumed to be a linear function, whose parameters X_0 and γ are estimated with least-square error estimation (see Eq. 4.1).

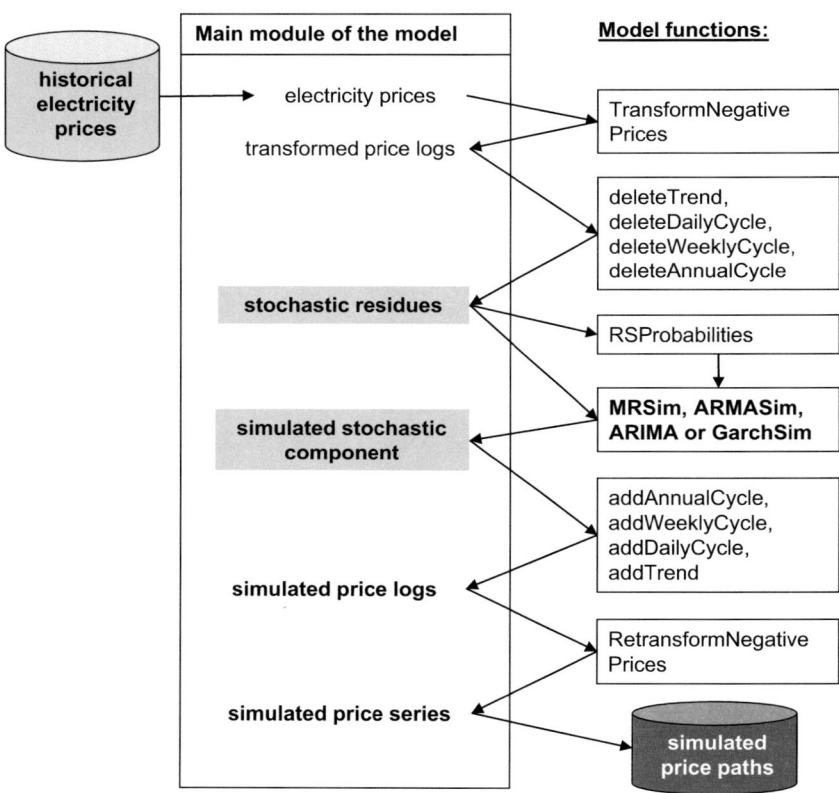

Figure 4.3.: Overview of the electricity price model

$$X_t^{Trend} = X_0 + \gamma \cdot t \qquad\qquad [4.1]$$

The trend curve is subtracted from the electricity price logs resulting in a de-trended series, which is passed to the next data preparation step: weekly cycles are removed from the price logs. The weekly cycle of the electricity prices is modeled via an adjusted absolute sinus-function (cp. Eq. 4.2), as its structure is fitting the weekly oscillation very well (for trigonometric functions applied for deterministic cycles see Thome (2005)).

$$X_t^{wc} = \alpha_{wc} + \beta_{wc} \left| sin\left(\frac{\pi \cdot t}{168} - \varphi_{wc}\right)\right| \qquad\qquad [4.2]$$

The parameters α and β of this function are estimated via linear regression using least square errors, based on detrended historical series of electricity price logarithms between 2002 and 2009. The phase shift parameter φ is determined as the deviation from the time point, in which the weekly cycle reaches its minimum in the historical series. To determine this time point the mean values of the electricity prices are calculated for each hour of the 168 hours of a week. This calculation delivers the seventh hour of sundays as the minimum value and as the absolute value of the sinus function is considered for the weekly cycle, the phase shift is set to "0" for this specific hour. If a simulation starts with another day and time then the phase shift can be determined as the deviation to the last Sunday's seventh hour. With the help of these parameter values the weekly season is calculated and removed from the detrended price logs[6].

In the next step, the daily cycle is defined as the hourly means for the 24 hours of the day and is removed. Thereby it is worth mentioning that different daily cycles are determined for each season (*seas* winter, spring, summer and autumn).

$$X_{i,seas}^{dc} = \frac{24}{T} \sum_{t=0}^{(T/24)-1} X_{i+24t,seas} \forall i \in \{1,2,..,24\} \vee \forall seas \qquad\qquad [4.3]$$

---

[6]The estimated values of the parameters depend strongly on the time-period of the data series used for the estimation. This is discussed for stochastic oil price models by Heidorn et al. (2009)

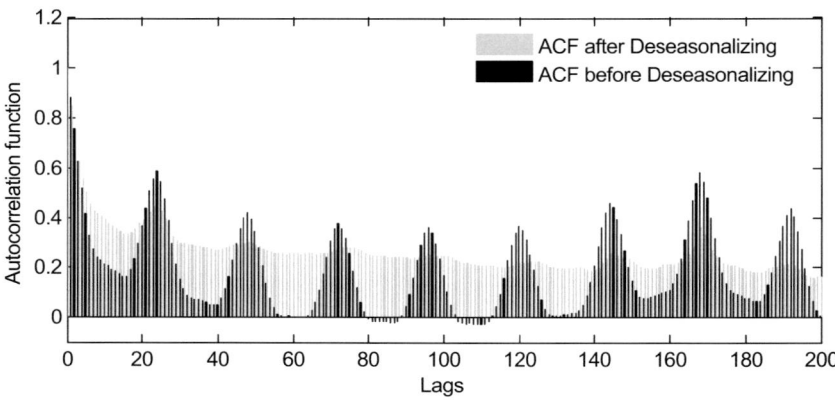

Figure 4.4.: Autocorrelation of hourly electricity price logs before and after deseasonalising for 200 Lags

The weekly and daily cycles are very important, as the autocorrelation function (ACF) (see Figure 4.4) for the price series shows a considerable autocorrelation[7] between the values of same hours of different days and between the same days of different weeks.

The last seasonal effect is the annual cycle which can be modeled via the trigonometric function of the basic oscillation presented by Seifert and Uhrig-Homburg (2007):

$$X_{d,h}^{ac} = \alpha_{d,h} + \beta_{d,h} cos\left(2\pi\frac{t-\tau}{8760}\right) + \gamma_{d,h} sin\left(2\pi\frac{t-\tau}{8760}\right) \qquad [4.4]$$

However, as the results of the trigonometric function above have not been satisfying, the mean values of each month are calculated and defined as the seasonal component instead of the basic oscillation. The monthly means are removed resulting in a deseasonalised series (Eq. 4.5)

---

[7]Autocorrelation is the correlation between the series (X_t) and the adjusted series (X_{t-q}), which is the same series moved by a lag of the length q (see Chatfield (2004))

$$X_t^S = X_t - \left(\sum_{d' \in \{wd,sd,wed\}} 1\left(d'|d' = d(t)\right) \sum_{h=1}^{24} X_h \cdot 1\left(h|h = t \bmod 24\right) \right.$$

$$\left. + \alpha_{wc} + \beta_{wc} \left| sin\left(\frac{\pi \cdot t}{168} - \varphi_{wc}\right) \right| + \sum_{m'=1}^{12} \bar{X}_{m'} 1\left(m'|m' = m(t)\right) \right) \qquad [4.5]$$

This deseasonalised series (X_t^S) is assumed to contain only stochastic elements, such as the volatility of the price logs and randomly occurring jumps or peaks, which can be simulated via different stochastic processes described in the following.

4.2.2. Modeling stochastic components with financial and time-series models

An important characteristic of electricity prices are spikes, also called peaks, and jump groups. Jump groups occur, as electricity prices jump into another price level, in the following called "jump regime", and remain there for some hours. Afterwards the prices jump back to the base price level, called "base regime". Therefore a regime-switching approach is implemented into the price model to simulate the transition of prices between the base and jump regime. The description of the regime-switching approach is described in 4.2.2.4, but at first the focus is set on the modeling of the base regime. The base regime, which most of the prices within a year can be allocated to, can be simulated via different stochastic processes, such as geometric Brownian motion or the best known mean-reverting process, the Ornstein-Uhlenbeck process. Due to these processes, which are derived from financial mathematics, the marginal change rate dX of the electricity prices are modelled instead of themselves (see Eq. 4.6). However, as electricity prices are formed in a discrete hourly resolved framework, these processes are mostly turned to discrete stochastic processes, as it is the case for time-series models, such as autoregressive moving average (ARMA) or generalized autoregressive conditional heteroscedasticity (GARCH) processes. In this analysis the mean-reversion process, the ARMA as well as integrated ARMA (ARIMA) processes and the GARCH process are implemented and evaluated to find the appropriate model, which can describe the electricity spot prices on the EEX best.

4.2.2.1. Mean reversion model

The mean-reversion process is one of the most applied stochastic processes for electricity prices. As logarithms of the electricity prices ($X_t = lnp_t$) are modeled to reach variance stabilisation, the mean-reversion process or the so-called Ornstein-Uhlenbeck process (see Uhlenbeck (1930)) can be formulated for the price changes with the following stochastic differential equation (SDE):

$$dX_t^S = \kappa(\mu - X_t^S)dt + \sigma \cdot dW_t \qquad [4.6]$$

The first term of the mean reversion process describes the so-called drift component $(\mu - X_t^S)$. The parameter κ determines the "reversion speed" of the stochastic component to their long-term mean μ. The economic interpretation of this mean-reversion component is that stochastic price fluctuations around the mean and price peaks are only temporarily, caused by e.g. power plant outages or capacity shortages. The second term, the stochastic component dW_t in fact, corresponds to the standard Brownian motion. The stochastic driver is the so-called Wiener Process $dW_t = \varepsilon_t dt^{1/2}$, whereby ε_t is a standard normally distributed random variable (see Hull (2005), Muche (2007) Weron et al. (2004)). The SDE is solved applying Ito's Lemma, receiving the following exact solution derived from Karatzas and Shreve (2000).

$$X_{t+1}^S = X_t^S \cdot e^{-\kappa\delta} + \mu(1 - e^{-\kappa\delta}) + \sigma\sqrt{\frac{1 - e^{-2\kappa\delta}}{2\kappa}} \cdot \varepsilon_t \ , \ \varepsilon_t \sim N(0,1) \qquad [4.7]$$

The substitutions $a = e^{-\kappa\delta}$, $b = \mu(1 - e^{-\kappa\delta})$ and $\sigma_\varepsilon = \sigma\sqrt{\frac{1-e^{-2\kappa\delta}}{2\kappa}}$ lead to the Eq. 4.8, whereas δ is the time difference between t and $t+1$, here i.e. one hour.

$$X_{t+1}^S = X_t^S \cdot a + b + \sigma_\varepsilon \cdot \varepsilon_t \ , \ \varepsilon_t \sim N(0,1) \qquad [4.8]$$

Using Maximum Likelihood (ML) estimates the parameters a, b, σ_ε can be calculated via the historical stochastic residues. Another approach for the parameter estimation is least-squares estimation. The resubstitution of the parameters a, b, σ_ε delivers the original parameters of the exact solution κ, μ and σ. With the help of the estimated parameters the exact solution of the SDE is applied to generate the stochastic component of a simulated price path.

4.2.2.2. ARMA and Integrated ARMA (ARIMA) models

The autoregressive moving average (ARMA) process describes another method to simulate the stochastic residues. The ARMA process enables the simulation of time dependences within a time-series. This process consists of two parts, the autoregressive and the moving average part. While the autoregressive component of an ARMA process considers the last p-prices for the calculation of the electricity price X_t^S in t, the moving average component takes the weighted mean of the last q error terms into account, i.e. the weighted moving average of the last q components of the white noise process (see Swider and Weber (2007)). Therefore an ARMA (p,q) process has the orders p and q representing the orders of each partial process. The calculation of the price in t depends at last on a new error term ε_t, which can be e.g. normally or Laplace distributed.

$$X_t^S = \sum_{i=1}^{p} \alpha_i X_{t-i}^S + \sum_{j=1}^{q} \beta_j \varepsilon_{t-j} + \varepsilon_t \qquad [4.9]$$

The parameters α_i describe the weight of the impact of X_{t-i}^S on the actual value X_t for all $i = 1, .., p$. The parameters β_j define the weights of the last q error terms (innovations) ε_{t-j} $(j = 1, .., q)$ within the moving average component. To apply the ARMA model, the historical stochastic residuals X_t^S of electricity prices have to be normally distributed. But the normal distribution hypothesis is rejected by the X^2- and the Kolmogorov-Smirnov test. Therefore the historical residuals have to be transformed to normally distributed residuals. The transformation can be carried out using the inverse of the cumulative distribution function (CDF) of the standard normal distribution $F^{-1,SN}(y)$ on the empiric CDF values $F^E(x)$. The resulting series are standard normally distributed. Calibrating an ARMA model with the standard normally distributed values and running simulations will generate again standard distributed stochastic components of electricity prices. To

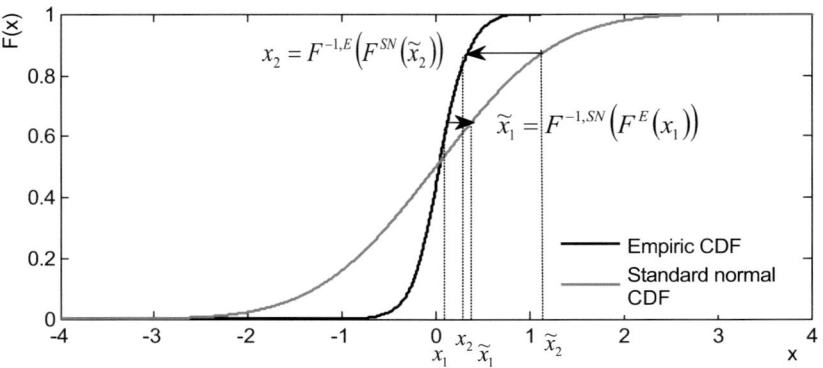

Figure 4.5.: Transformation of the historical stochastic residuals of electricity prices to standard normal distributed residuals

receive the original distribution of the stochastic component, the simulated normally distributed residuals need to be retransformed using the inverse of the CDF of the original empiric distribution $F^{-1,E}(x)$. Figure 4.5 illustrates the transformation and retransformation procedure.

Furthermore, the use of the ARMA process presumes that the stochastic residues are weak stationary and the error terms (innovations) are normally distributed. If these conditions are given in the stochastic residues, the approach of Box and Jenkins (Box et al. (2008)) can be applied to find out the specification of the ARMA model and to estimate its parameters[8]:

1. The specification of an ARMA model describes the orders p and q. Thereby as much as possible time dependences should be captured on the one hand, which can be achieved with high model orders; on the other hand the modeling of very small time dependences should be avoided to reduce the model order, as high model orders can lead to instability (see Schmoeller (2005)).

2. Then the parameters α_i and β_j as well as the variance of the white noise ε_t have to be estimated from the original stochastic residues. For that purpose

---

[8]In this analysis the ARMA specification and the parameter estimation are realised with the GARCH-Toolbox of MATLAB.

a starting solution is generated for an autoregressive process (AR) with a high order using least-square errors estimation. Afterwards the innovations of this AR process are regarded to be equal to that of the specific ARMA process. Using ML estimates the parameters of the original ARMA process can be estimated and used for the simulation of the stochastic component (Brockwell and Davis (2002), Schlittgen and Streitberg (2001)).

3. At last the model quality has to be checked, especially in regard to the model orders p and q. If the model quality is not satisfying, a new model order has to be chosen and the parameter estimation has to be started again.

As mentioned above ARMA models are based on at least weak-stationary time series. That means that the expected value of the stochastic process X_t is constant for all t and therefore independent from the time t. However, time series common in practice do not show this characteristic, their expected value and their variance can change over time. But as non stationary processes are more or less homogeneous, i.e. their behaviour in different periods is distinguished only by different, slowly changing levels or locally deviating trend slopes, time series that are not weak-stationary can be transferred into weak-stationary processes using linear filters. Filters are tools that help to eliminate or remove undesirable components from a time series. Filter processes that are focused on adjusting the trends of a time series, are called integrated ARMA processes or autoregressive integrated moving average (ARIMA) processes. Filters adjusting seasonal changes are called seasonal ARIMA processes (SARIMA(P,D,Q) process). A combination of both filter techniques is also possible (Stier (2001); Thome (2005)). The approach of Box und Jenkins tries to transfer time series with clear trends or cycles into stationary series using appropriate cycles. Of special interest are thereby difference filters and their powers, that are preferably but not exclusively used. A difference filter of first degree (or first order) is defined by

$$\Delta X_t^S = X_t^S - X_{t-1}^S \qquad [4.10]$$

Where necessary, difference filters can be used repeatedly (d-times), to obtain a weak stationary process. After applying the filter d-times, the time series are passed through to an ARMA process, that is why the process is called integrated ARMA process or ARIMA(p,d,q). As deterministic components are filtered within the ARIMA process, the model could be directly applied for the electricity price logs without removing the deterministic components, as it is described in 4.2.1. However, the detrended and the deseasonalised price-logs could still contain some deterministic parts. That is why both time-series, the price logs series and the detrended and deseasonalised series are examined by ARIMA processes separately (see 4.3), comparing the results afterwards.

4.2.2.3. GARCH process

Within the GARCH approach the assumption of homoscedasticity is dropped for a heteroscedastic variance. That means the variance is no more constant within all parts of the time series. Indeed time-series phases of lower and higher volatility alternate within electricity prices. In phases of higher volatility markets are often nervous and electricity prices remain longer within the jump-regime, implying a higher conditional probability for high price changes, when such price movements have already occurred within the recent past. With GARCH models such behaviour of electricity prices can be described mathematically. In the following the most common GARCH(p,q) process according to Engle and Bollerslev (Engle (1982), Bollerslev (1986)) is described, which possesses the following variance function (Eq. 4.11).

$$\sigma_t^2 = \omega + \sum_{i=1}^{p} \alpha_i \sigma_{t-i}^2 + \sum_{j=1}^{q} \beta_j \varepsilon_{t-j}^2 \qquad [4.11]$$

The time-variant variance σ_t^2 contains a constant component ω, an autoregressive part of the order p and a moving average part of the order q. Thereby it has to be ensured, that the variance at any time t is positive, that means that parameters $\omega, \alpha_i, \beta_j$ are positive or equal to zero at any time. These parameters can be also determined by maximizing the Log-Likelihood function (Börger (2004), Kreiss (2006) Swider and Weber (2007)). In practice GARCH(1,1) models are frequently used, so that the Eq. eq:GARCH1 can be reduced to:

$$\sigma_t^2 = \omega + \alpha\sigma_{t-1}^2 + \beta\varepsilon_{t-1}^2 \qquad [4.12]$$

The GARCH approach is then used to simulate the stochastic component, as the heteroscedastic variance is passed into an ARMA-process modeling the price logs X_t (see 4.2.2.2). Therefore GARCH processes can be seen as an extension of ARMA-processes with a time-variant variance for the normally distributed innovations ε_t. At last it is worth mentioning that GARCH processes can handle the heteroscedasticity caused by jumps. In this case a regime-switching approach would not be necessary anymore to manage the different volatilities of jumps groups and of the other prices. However, it has to be checked, if the applied GARCH process can capture the whole heteroscedastic behaviour of the electricity price or if including a regime-switching approach into the GARCH process delivers more appropriate results.

4.2.2.4. Regime-switching approach

As mentioned before, electricity prices stay mainly at base price level, called "base regime" and then jump into a higher price level; they stay there for some hours and according to their mean-reverting characteristic they jump back to the base price regime again (see Seifert and Uhrig-Homburg (2007)). For the case of price logs a further regime can be added, i.e. the "lower jump regime" [9].

To capture the different price regimes, a regime-switching approach with different models for base and jump regimes is introduced[10]. Thereby the base regime is modelled with the help of the stochastic processes described above. The jump regime is defined with an extended version of these stochastic processes simulating base price logs $X_t^{S,base}$. In this approach, the same ARMA model extended by a jump component is used for the jump regime. This maybe unusual and new in the case of regime switching models, but it is not totally new for electricity price

---

[9]The analysis showed that some of the price logs are below a preset confidence interval representing the base regime. Therefore the introduction of a lower jump regime is necessary.

[10]To avoid mismatching of high prices to the jump regime because of daily cycles or other seasonal effects, the models for base and jump regimes are developed for the stochastic component, which does not contain seasonal components (see 4.2.1).

modeling, as it is derived from the jump diffusion approach (see Weron et al. (2004)). The reason for using the same ARMA model for the jump regime is that the jumps are not completely removed from the historical residues in this model, but they are replaced by the mean of the residual series. This approach ensures that the residual series is not shortened by elimination of a significant number of jumps. So the replaced jumps are assumed as mean values for the estimation of the ARMA or mean reversion parameters. The added "jump height" to the base regime process corresponds to the deviation of the jump value from the mean. Thus, the normal distribution applied for the jump height is based on parameters, which are estimated from the historical deviations of the jump values from the mean of the residues. Therefore the simulated jumps are consistent with the historical and the approach is reasonable, as the mean and volatility of jumps are considered by the applied mean and variance parameter within the applied normal distribution and their occurrence time is considered by the regime switching probabilities described in the following. Finally, it is worth mentioning that the use of the extension of the same ARMA-model for the jump regime ensures the auto-correlation between prices in the base and in the jump regime. Using a normally distributed random variable with $\mu_{lnJ}^{+/-}$ and $\sigma_{lnJ}^{2+/-}$ for the jump height and adding it to $X_t^{S,base}$ in the case of the upper jump regime and subtracting in the case of the lower regime, the jump regime can be described as follows:

$$X_t^{S,jump+} = X_t^{S,base} + \varepsilon_{t,lnJ}^{+} \varepsilon_{t,lnJ}^{+} \sim N(\mu_{lnJ}^{+}, \sigma_{lnJ}^{2+})$$
$$X_t^{S,jump-} = X_t^{S,base} - \varepsilon_{t,lnJ}^{-} \varepsilon_{t,lnJ}^{-} \sim N(\mu_{lnJ}^{-}, \sigma_{lnJ}^{2-})$$

[4.13]

For example, if an ARMA process is used for the base regime, the upper jump regime is modelled as (the lower jump regime is analogue):

$$X_t^{S,jump+} = \sum_{i=1}^{p} \alpha_i X_{t-i}^{S} + \sum_{j=1}^{q} \beta_j \varepsilon_{t-j} + \varepsilon_t \sim N(\mu_\varepsilon, \sigma_\varepsilon^2) + \varepsilon_{t,lnJ}^{+} \sim N(\mu_{lnJ}^{+}, \sigma_{lnJ}^{2+})$$

[4.14]

To combine the different regimes to a common approach, transition probabilities between the regimes and probabilities of remaining in the same regime have to be calculated based on historical stochastic residues of electricity prices. Thereby it should be noted that the regime-switching model is separately applied for week-days and weekend days and the transition probabilities are determined for each case, as the number of jumps and the length of jump groups can conspicuously differ for the two day types. Furthermore, the weekdays are separated into winter and summer weekdays (the weekdays between October and March being declared here as "winter days", whereas the others are denoted as "summer days"), as the electricity prices for these day types also show a different "jump structure". A further differentiation is made between upward and downward jumps, as the above mentioned logarithmisation of electricity prices also causes a noticeable number of jumps downwards. Hence, downward jumps are not to be understood as price logs or residues with negative values, but as values which are below the level $\mu - 3\sigma$, while positive jumps are defined as values above the level $\mu + 3\sigma$. A last differentiation is done for the occurrence of upward and downward jumps within a day. In this approach it is assumed that upward jumps occur in peak period 08:00am to 08:00pm and downwards jumps vice versa. This limitation can be observed in the historical data and is therefore applied within the simulation. Transition probabilities for the three day types d as well as for upward and downward jumps are calculated by the following formula applied to the stochastic residues X_t^S.

Probability for remaining in the base regime:

$$P_{11} = \frac{card\left\{t \in [t_1, T] | X_t^S \in [\mu - 3\sigma, \mu + 3\sigma] \wedge X_{t+1}^S \in [\mu - 3\sigma, \mu + 3\sigma]\right\}}{card\left\{t \in [t_1, T] | X_t^S \in [\mu - 3\sigma, \mu + 3\sigma]\right\}}$$

[4.15]

Probability for moving from the base regime into the upper jump regime:

$$P_{12} = \frac{card\left\{t \in [t_1, T] | X_t^S \in [\mu - 3\sigma, \mu + 3\sigma] \wedge X_{t+1}^S \in (\mu + 3\sigma, ln3000]\right\}}{card\left\{t \in [t_1, T] | X_t^S \in [\mu - 3\sigma, \mu + 3\sigma]\right\}}$$

[4.16]

Probability for moving from the upper jump regime into the base regime:

$$P_{21} = \frac{card\left\{t \in [t_1, T] | X_t^S \in (\mu + 3\sigma, ln3000] \wedge X_{t+1}^S \in [\mu - 3\sigma, \mu + 3\sigma]\right\}}{card\left\{t \in [t_1, T] | X_t^S \in (\mu + 3\sigma, ln3000]\right\}}$$

[4.17]

Probability for remaining in the upper jump regime:

$$P_{22} = \frac{card\left\{t \in [t_1, T] | X_t^S \in (\mu + 3\sigma, ln3000] \wedge X_{t+1}^S \in (\mu + 3\sigma, ln3000]\right\}}{card\left\{t \in [t_1, T] | X_t^S \in (\mu + 3\sigma, ln3000]\right\}}$$

[4.18]

The upper interval limit $ln3000$ for upper jumps results from the fact that the highest permitted prices at the EPEX are equal to 3000 €/MWh. The probabilities for switching from the base regime to the lower jump regime and backwards (P_{13}, P_{31}, P_{33}) are calculated analogue to Eq. 4.15 - 4.18, whereas the corresponding interval for downward jumps is defined as $(-inf, \mu - 3\sigma]$. These probabilities are combined to a transition probabilities matrix T_d for the appropriate type day d, which has following structure:

$$T_d = \begin{bmatrix} P_{11} & P_{12} & P_{13} \\ P_{21} & P_{22} & 0 \\ P_{31} & 0 & P_{33} \end{bmatrix}$$

[4.19]

The 0 items in the matrix T_d indicates that there is no transition from the upper jump regime to the lower jump regime, as it is not plausible for electricity prices. These kinds of transitions cannot be observed from historical data.

Based on the different transition matrices the regime switching is simulated for each hour of the year, whereby a parameter *regime* is included in the model, marking whether the base or jump process is used for the simulation of the stochastic component of the latest price. Thereby the *regime* $= 0$, if the base process is used, and the *regime* $= 1$, if the upper jump process is applied. Furthermore a decision variable δ is added to the model to describe the regime switch itself in each hour h, whereby the value of δ is determined according to the algorithm shown in Figure 4.6, which incorporates positive jumps (or jump groups)[11].

The decision variable δ is passed afterwards to the simulation tool, which uses the base regime model or the jump regime model to simulate the stochastic component X_t^S depending on the value of δ. Eq. 4.20 shows the approach for modeling the stochastic component using the ARMA model.

---

[11]For the lower jump regime the algorithm is analogous, but the value of $\delta(h)$ is set as -1, if a negative jump occurs.

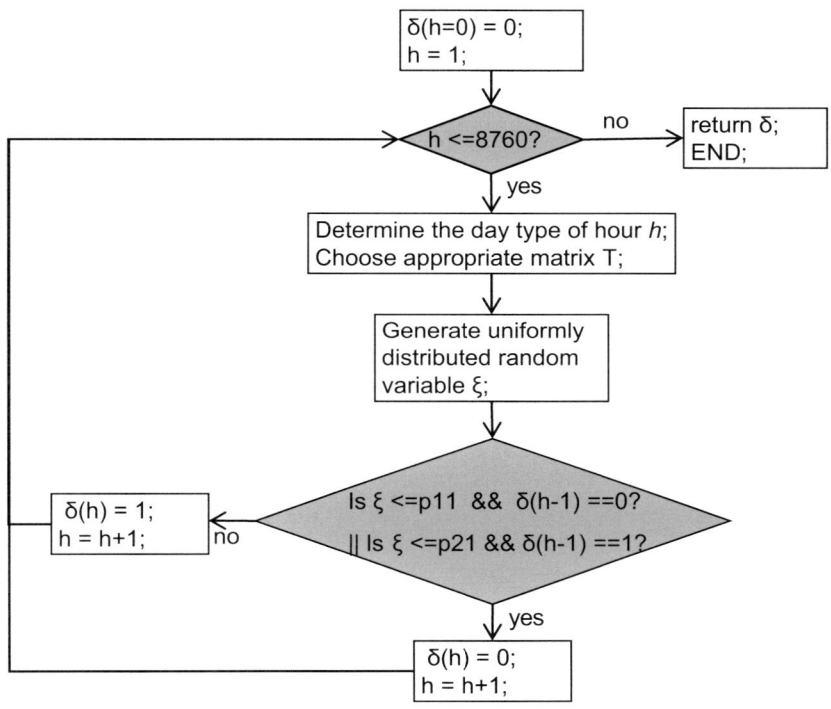

Figure 4.6.: The regime-switching algorithm for positive jumps

$$
X_t^{S,Sim} = \begin{cases} \sum_{i=1}^{p} \alpha_i X_{t-i}^{S,Sim} + \sum_{j=1}^{q} \beta_j \varepsilon_{t-j} + \varepsilon_t & \delta(t) = 0 \\ \sum_{i=1}^{p} \alpha_i X_{t-i}^{S,Sim} + \sum_{j=1}^{q} \beta_j \varepsilon_{t-j} + \varepsilon_t + \varepsilon_{lnJ,t}^{+} & \delta(t) = 1 \\ \sum_{i=1}^{p} \alpha_i X_{t-i}^{S,Sim} + \sum_{j=1}^{q} \beta_j \varepsilon_{t-j} + \varepsilon_t - \varepsilon_{lnJ,t}^{-} & \delta(t) = -1 \end{cases}
$$

[4.20]

$$
\varepsilon_t \sim N(\mu_{\varepsilon_t}, \sigma_{\varepsilon_t}^2)
$$
$$
\varepsilon_{logJ,t}^{+} \sim N(\mu_{lnJ}^{+}, \sigma_{lnJ}^{2+})
$$
$$
\varepsilon_{logJ,t}^{-} \sim N(\mu_{lnJ}^{-}, \sigma_{lnJ}^{2-})
$$

The simulation of electricity price paths for a year concludes with the addition of the deterministic components to the stochastic one and retransformation of the received price logs into the original price level. Afterwards, the deterministic components are added including the annual, daily and weekly cycle as well as a trend. Finally, the simulated price logs are retransformed receiving a simulated price path.

$$
\begin{aligned}
X_{t-i}^{Sim} = X_{t-i}^{S,Sim} + &\sum_{d' \in \{wd,sd,wed\}} 1\left(d'|d' = d(t)\right) \cdot \sum_{h}^{24} \bar{X}_h(h|h = t \bmod 24) \\
&+ \alpha_{wc} + \beta_{wc} \left| \sin\left(\frac{\pi \cdot t}{168} - \varphi_{wc}\right) \right| + \sum_{m'=1}^{12} 1\left(m'|m' = m(t)\right) \cdot \bar{X}_{m'}
\end{aligned}
\qquad [4.21]
$$

As the retransformed price logs only consist of positive prices, a method has to be carried out to incorporate also negative prices, whereby the structure of the negative prices should fit the historical one very well. In the following a method is introduced to generate negative prices based on the statistical structure of historical negative prices.

4.2.3. Modeling negative electricity prices

As it can be observed from the model overview (see Figure 4.3), negative electricity prices are at first transformed to positive ones. The logarithms of the positive values are then calculated. The price logarithms are in turn necessary, because modeling price logs delivers more robust results due to the mentioned variance stabilisation reason and the left-skewed characteristic of electricity prices.

The transformation procedure can be described as follows: All negative prices within the historical time-series are coded to 0.01 €/MWh, the smallest positive price value. Furthermore, the average relative frequency of negative prices is calculated for the years after 2008, in which negative prices were allowed. This average relative frequency is assumed as the future probability Pr_{neg} of negative prices. Besides, the transformation procedure delivers also a series with the original negative prices.

The probability Pr_{neg} and the distribution of the negative prices are required to transform some of the simulated downward jumps (see 4.2.2.4) into negative prices. The limitation of the retransformation to some of the downward jumps relies on the fact, that the initially transformed values are grouped to the class of downward jumps in the historical price log series.

The retransformation of a simulated downward jump to a negative price is done with the help of a uniformly distributed variable dq. If dq is smaller than or equal to the adjusted probability Pr'_{neg} of negative prices, a downward jump is replaced by a negative value, and no action is performed if dq is higher than Pr'_{neg}. Thereby the probability Pr'_{neg} is defined as the adjusted relative frequency of negative prices within the series of downward jumps (see Eq. 4.22).

$$Pr'_{neg} = Pr_{neg} \cdot \frac{card(P_t^{jumpdown})}{card(P_t)} \qquad [4.22]$$

In the case of a decision for a transformation, a negative price is generated as a bimodal distributed random variable. More precisely, here the bimodal distribution is defined as a combination of the lognormal and the exponential distributions. The analysis of the historical negative prices showed that the empirical distribution of negative prices smaller than "-80 €/MWh" can be described by the lognormal distribution. On the other hand, negative prices above -80 €/MWh follow the exponential distribution[12]. To decide which part of the bimodal distribution should be chosen, another uniformly distributed variable dn is introduced. The realisation of dn is then compared with the historical ratio r^{-80} - the ratio between the number of negative prices greater than -80 €/MWh and the total number of negative prices-, so that the appropriate distribution can be chosen (see Eq. 4.23).

$$P_t^{sim} = \begin{cases} P_{t,neg} \sim Exp(\mu_{1,neg}) & dq \leq Pr'_{neg} \wedge dn \leq r^{-80} \\ P_{t,neg} \sim N(\mu_{2,neg}, \sigma_{2,neg}^2) & dq \leq Pr'_{neg} \wedge dn > r^{-80} \\ P_t'^{sim} & else \end{cases} \qquad [4.23]$$

It can be observed that the negative prices are handled separately in this approach, because of the use of price logs instead of the prices themselves within

---

[12]No negative prices occurred in the interval [-100;-60] €/MWh in the last two years. The choice of -80 €/MWh as the switching price level from one part of the bimodal distribution to the other is motivated by the fact, that indeed any prices have not occurred in the interval mentioned above, but some could occur in future. To allow future prices within this interval, the upper border for the lower prices is not chosen as -100 €/MWh and the lower border for the higher negative prices is not chosen as -60 €/MWh. Instead, the middle of the interval [-100;-60] €/MWh is chosen.

the stochastic model for variance stabilization reasons. To keep the approach with logarithmisation, any kind of transformation of the negative ones to positives is necessary. The transformation method introduced above, which replaces negative prices by downwards jumps (initialized by 0.01 €/MWh) and retransforming some downward jumps at the end, is chosen, as this approach does not shifts the level of price logs to another one. The majority of the prices are not affected and their price logs remain unchanged. If another transformation is applied, in which all prices are shifted, so that no negative prices occur, then the price logs are at a different level. The volatility can differ very strongly after retransforming the simulated price logs to real prices by the exponential function. The transformation by shifting the prices would indeed take negative prices into account in a closed approach by keeping the modeling approach with price logs. Initial tests of the author showed that the volatility of simulation results, applying a closed approach, was totally deviated from the historical one after retransforming the simulated price logs. The approach with separate modeling of negative prices is therefore chosen in this analysis. However, it is worth mentioning that the introduced approach is one method to generate adequate negative prices. This method can further be developed in future work.

After the additional modeling of negative prices, several electricity price paths are generated with the entire modeling approach for electricity prices. The simulation results of the different stochastic models are compared in the following

4.3. Evaluation of the different stochastic models

The above described models are applied on the hourly electricity spot prices gained from the EEX for the years 2002 to 2009. Based on these historical prices, the models are calibrated estimating the parameters of deterministic as well as stochastic models. After calibrating the models, several simulations are carried out to evaluate the goodness of fit of each stochastic model for electricity price simulation.

Table 4.1.: Estimated model parameters based on historical price logs 2002-2009 (data source: EEX)[13]

	Stoch. Model	MR	ARMA (5,1)	ARIMA (1,1,1)	GARCH (1,1)	MR w/o RS	ARIMA w/o deseas
Estimated	μ	0.04	-0.001	-0.001	$--$	$-2e^{-4}$	-0.015
parameters	σ_ε	0.17	0.10	0.10	$--$	0.36	0.15
of	MR-κ	0.21	$--$	$--$	$--$	0.23	$--$
stochastic	α_i		1.652				
model			0.626				
			0.035				
			0.001				
		$--$	0.004	0.719	0.249	$--$	-0.638
	β_i	$--$	-0.932	-0.961	0.567	$--$	0.614
	GARCH-ω	$--$	$--$	$--$	0.013	$--$	$--$
Estimated	Trend:	X_0		3.07			3.07
parameters		Y		$1.16e^5$			$1.16e^5$
of deter-	Weekly	α		-0.45			
ministic	Cycle	β		0.71			$--$
components		ρ		0.77			

4.3.1. Estimated parameters and simulation results

The parameters of the different models are estimated using linear regression and maximum likelihood (ML) estimation. Thereby the parameters of the deterministic components are determined at first to calculate the deterministic components of the electricity prices, which are removed from the historical prices in the next step. The stochastic residues received are used for the estimation of the parameters of the stochastic models shown in Table 4.1.

From a graphical comparison of simulated and historical prices, it can be concluded that the simulated electricity price curves of all price models are similar to the observed price curves. Simulated electricity price curves possess also daily, weekly and annual cycles. This is of course caused by the initial removal and addition of these deterministic patterns. The other important properties, such as single peaks or jump groups, are also generated within the simulated price paths. Furthermore the mean-reverting property is captured very well not only by the mean reversion process, but also by the other models (see Figure 4.7).

However, some of the models simulate price curves, which are more fluctuant in the base regime than real prices. While the mean reversion process and especially the ARMA(5,1)- process capture the stochastic volatility quite well, the others show a higher volatility. As the GARCH-process delivers price paths which are significantly more volatile than historical ones, it is less suitable for the simulation of electricity prices, although it can handle the heteroscedasticity of the stochastic residues. Heteroscedasticity of time-series means that the series are not uniformly distributed. If for example the normal distribution is applied, the variance parameter should vary over the time (see section 4.2.2.3). The existence of the heteroscedastic characteristic is tested, considering homoscedasticity within the stochastic residues as null hypothesis, which is rejected for different significance levels ($\alpha = 0.01$ or 0.05) by the "archtest"-function, a test for homoscedasticity (for tests for homoscedasticity see Gourieroux (1997)). That means the stochastic residues still posses heteroscedastic behaviour. However, as the heteroscedasticity is strongly reduced by the regime-switching and the deseasonalising approaches, it could be disregarded, and satisfactory results can be also gained with the help of mean-reversion process or ARMA-processes.

---

[13]The stability of model parameters has been checked, by estimating the parameters for several years separately. The values of the estimated parameters do not change significantly over the time (see Table A.2 in the appendix). They change only in the second comma decimal and a few in the first comma decimal. Thus, it can be deduced that the parameters stay relatively stable applying different historical time periods for model calibrating.

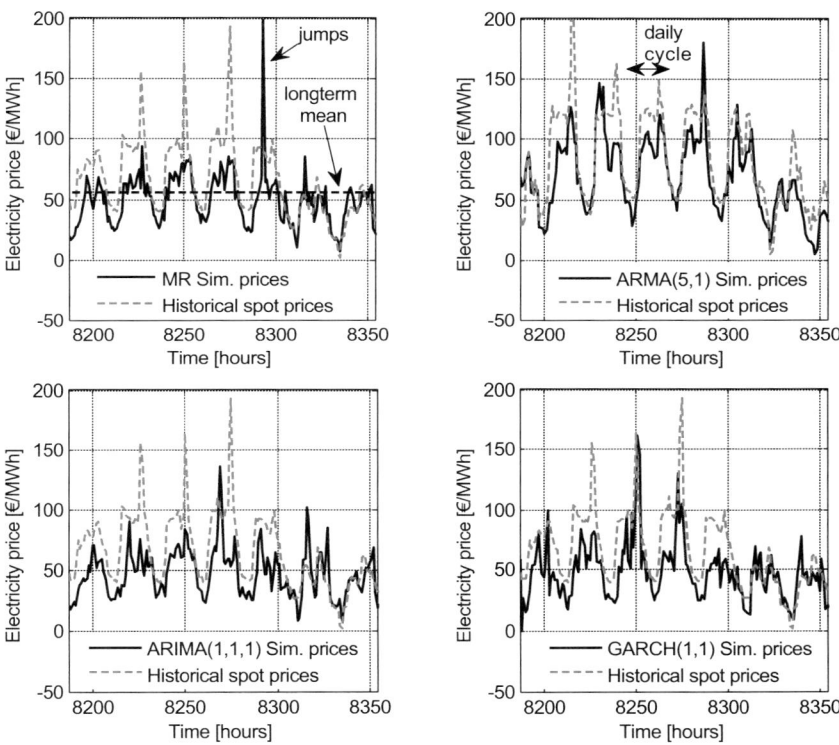

Figure 4.7.: Historical and simulated price curves of the different price models for a week

4.3.2. Importance of the regime-switching and deseasonalising approaches

The impact of the regime-switching and deseasonalising approach becomes clear, if the results of model versions including these approaches are compared with the model outputs without the approaches. In the latter case, the simulated price paths are only based on the stochastic processes, which do not appropriately capture the structure of electricity prices. The volatility of the simulated price paths is higher than the historical and the seasonal cycles are missing, if the separate modeling via de- and reseasonalizing is not applied. Besides, the analysis of price paths generated by models without the regime-switching approach makes clear that not

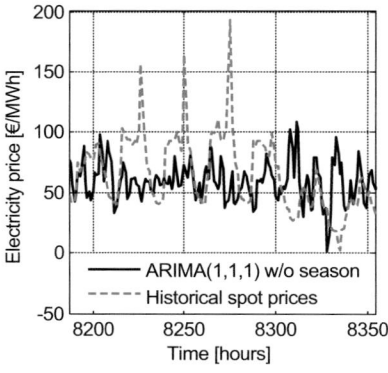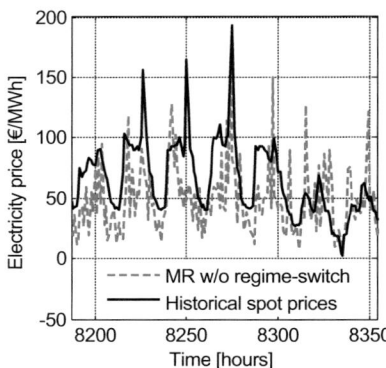

Figure 4.8.: Simulated price curves of ARIMA(1,1,1) model without deseasonalising and of a GARCH(1,1) process without regime switching

only the volatility of the price paths is not well-fitted, but also jumps are not adequately produced. The price paths are again more volatile than they are in reality and more jumps than in real price paths are generated (see Figure 4.8).

In addition to the graphical comparison of simulated and historical price paths, different quality factors, such as then root mean square error (RMSE), are calculated for the results of each model. But as the RMSE can vary strongly depending on the historical price level of the chosen reference year, the mean average percentage error (MAPE) is also taken into account to get further meaningful results. The MAPE represents the normalized deviation of simulated prices from historical ones in absolute numbers, whereas RMSE defines the Euclid distance between the simulated and historical prices (Eq. A.5 and A.4). Both quality factors are calculated for the sorted[14] simulated price paths and the sorted real prices, also called price duration curves (PDC). To achieve a more robust result, an expected value for both parameters is determined based on N = 30 simulations for each model. Besides these quality factors, the coefficient of determination R^2 is also calculated to examine the goodness of fit for the different models. Again an ex-

---

[14]The calculation with sorted prices results from the fact that the occurring time of jumps is stochastic and differs from the time of jumps within historical prices. The calculation with the original series would lead to falsified and non meaningful MRSEs.

pected value for R^2 is computed from 30 simulations. All results of the error terms are summarized in Table 4.2.

The expected RMSE is lowest for the mean-reversion and ARMA(5,1) models, if historical electricity prices between 2002 and 2009 are considered as historical data source and comparison period. But only if a single year is analysed, the ARIMA models deliver a smaller RMSE. The other error term and validation factors, such as MAPE or R^2, show that again the mean-reversion and the ARIMA models deliver well-fitting price paths and PDCs. The ARMA models also produce satisfactory results, although their error factors are calculated somewhat higher. Analysing the error terms of the fourth model group, i.e. the GARCH models, it can be stated that these models are less applicable for the simulation of the stochastic component of the prices, as the error terms are generally higher than the other model errors and R^2 of the GARCH models are significantly lower than those of the others. Besides, the standard deviation of the simulated price paths differs significantly from the historical one. A further analysis of the RMSE, MAPE and R^2 is done for the same models, but this time without the above described regime-switching approach. The calculated expected error terms RMSE and MAPE are higher by a multiple of the ones of model versions including the regime-switching approach. Besides, the mean and standard deviation of price paths differ very strongly from the historical values, if the regime-switching approach is disregarded. Therefore, it can be derived that this approach is essential for electricity price simulation, if this kind of models is applied. Finally, the quality factors are calculated for the ARIMA(1,1,1) model, whereby the price logs are not deseasonalised, i.e. the daily, weekly and annual cycles are not removed. As the ARIMA model includes a difference filter, the seasonal effects should be removed by this filter. However, the higher values for the error terms show that this is not the case (see Table 4.2). Therefore the deseasonalising makes sense, even if an ARIMA model is applied. But as mentioned above, the importance of

---

[15]In the table, the average results of 30 simulations instead of a large number of simulations are represented, as preliminary large number of simulations, i.e. several hundred runs showed that the results differ only in the second decimal position after the comma from the results of runs with 30 simulations. To save calculation time due to the large number of model variations, further runs have been limited to 30 simulations.

Table 4.2.: Expected MRSE, MAPE, R^2, mean and standard deviation for different stochastic models based on 30 simulations [15]

Stochastic Model	RMSE [€/MWh]		MAPE [%]		R2 [%]	
	2008	2002-09	2008	2002-09	2008	2002-09
Mean-Reversion (MR)	6.11	3.67	6.50	3.82	50.90	13.54
ARMA(1,1)	6.91	4.81	8.4	6.6	46.1	12.17
*(5,1)	7.07	4.84	8.5	6.7	45.6	12.42
ARIMA(1,1,1)	5.95	4.79	7.4	5.4	48.3	12.80
*(5,1,1)	5.87	4.81	7.3	5.4	50.0	12.66
GARCH(1,1)	11.67	6.01	9.23	6.3	33.1	8.55
*(5,5)	11.07	5.46	9.30	6.4	30.9	7.69
MR w/o RS	17.52	5.57	17.10	7.60	31.49	18.99
GARCH(1,1)w/o RS	102.00	54.07	24.40	14.10	3.90	1.14
ARIMA(1,1,1)w/o des.	15.08	11.27	18.10	17.93	0.12	1.03

Stochastic Model	mean μ			std σ		
	2008	2002-09	historical	2008	2002-09	historical
Mean-Reversion (MR)	67.65	39.03		34.61	29.21	
ARMA(1,1)	65.25	38.45		34.41	30.5	
*(5,1)	65.09	38.51	2008:	34.61	30.1	2008:
ARIMA(1,1,1)	64.93	37.96	65.75	34.01	29.5	28.66
*(5,1,1)	64.92	37.96		33.43	29.6	
GARCH(1,1)	68.32	36.09		45.36	36.8	
*(5,5)	68.46	39.91		50.41	40.0	
MR w/o RS	68.99	38.51	2002-09:	44.16	23.39	2002-09:
GARCH(1,1)w/o RS	76.46	43.37	39.99	135.81	101.81	31.10
ARIMA(1,1,1)w/o des.	57.21	34.72		18.00	29.63	

Table 4.3.: Out-of-sample error measures of the different stochastic models for the period 2006-
2009[16]

Stochastic Model	RMSE [€/MWh]	MAPE [%]	R2 [%]
Mean-Reversion (MR)	10.78	18.02	10.24
ARMA(1,1), *(5,1)	10.06; 9.95	18.30; 18.15	8.75; 9.00
ARIMA(1,1,1), *(5,1,1)	12.25; 12.34	21.03; 21.06	9.95; 10.03
GARCH(1,1), *(5,5)	8.65; 8.43	16.32; 16.02	6.58; 7.37
MR w/o RS	12.74	19.64	10.82
GARCH(1,1) w/o RS	23.53	16.10	2.01
ARIMA(1,1,1) w/o des.	17.03	26.51	0.01

the deseasonalising and regime-switching becomes very clear, if the price paths of the models without these approaches (Figure 4.8) are compared with the price paths in Figure 4.7.

After the in-sample analysis of the model errors, different out-of-sample simulations are carried out to determine the goodness-of-fit of the different approaches for out-of-sample studies. Therefore the first half of historical prices (2002-2005) is used to calibrate the models and afterwards simulations are run for the period 2006 to 2009. The simulated prices paths are compared with the historical prices of 2006 to 2009. The performance of each model is illustrated in Table 4.3.

Considering all three measures, the mean-reversion model and the ARMA models again deliver the best results. Therefore they seem to be more adequate for electricity price simulation. Finally, Table 4.3 shows that the results of the out-

[16]The out of-sample results are as expected worse than the in-sample analysis. However, due to the fact that no fundamental parameters, such as oil price or economic development, are considered in the modeling approaches, the achieved error measures are especially in the case of the mean-reversion and ARMA models still acceptable. These results can be improved introducing fundamental data via linear or multivariate regression to the time-series models. Another interesting approach would be to combine in future work the models discussed here with fundamental energy system models, such as MARKAL (Fishbone and Abilock (1981)), TIMES (Remme (2006)) or PERSEUS (Möst (2006)), to capture structural changes of the energy system and further economic parameters.

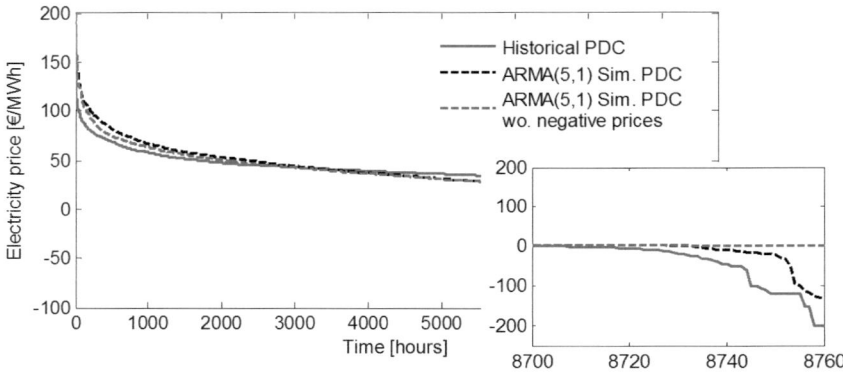

Figure 4.9.: Real and simulated price duration curves of price models with and without negative prices

of-sample analysis also get worse, if the deseasonalizing and regime-switching approaches are not applied. Thus, these two approaches are applied to the price simulations in the following sections, to capture appropriately the properties of electricity prices.

4.3.3. Model results with versus without negative prices

The simulation of price paths with negative prices improves the results of the price models. This issue becomes obvious, if the price duration curves (PDC) based on models with and without negative prices are analysed. Therefore the historical PDC of 2009 is compared with simulated ones for the same year. Thereby a PDC is simulated with the help of a model version considering negative prices, another based on a model excluding negative prices. Figure 4.9 illustrates that with the help of the approach described in 4.2.3 negative prices are well captured.

The improvement of the simulation becomes also evident, if the error measures of model simulations with and without negative prices are compared with each other. The RMSE and MAPE are significantly smaller for simulations based on the approach with negative prices than for that without. Only the expected mean and standard deviation become negligibly worse applying the ARMA(5,1)

Table 4.4.: Comparison of quality factors for models with and without the negative prices approach (based on 30 simulations for the year 2009)

	RMSE [€/MWh]			MAPE [%]			R2 [%]		
Stochastic Model	with NP	w/o NP	historical	with NP	w/o NP	historical			
Mean-Rever. MR	9.05	10.65	14.09	14.42	37.17	36.95			
ARMA (5,1)	8.87	10.63	14.52	15.01	31.63	32.22			

	mean μ			std σ		
Stochastic Model	with NP	w/o NP	historical	with NP	w/o NP	historical
Mean-Rever. MR	41.28	41.40	38.85	23.75	24.02	19.41
ARMA (5,1)	37.70	37.83		23.56	23.22	

model with negative price modeling. However, these factors are also improved, if the mean-reversion model is applied considering negative prices (see Table 4.4). Therefore it can be stated that all in all the consideration of negative prices within the modeling approach leads to not an immense but significant improvement of the price simulation.

4.4. Critical reflection of the electricity price models

The above described models simulate different electricity price characteristics, such as trend, seasonal cycles, jumps and stochastic volatility quite well. However, some of the models, such as the ARIMA(1,1,1) or GARCH(1,1)-processes, generate higher volatile price paths. Therefore, electricity prices should be initially transformed, so that ARIMA and GARCH processes can be appropriately applied. A possible transformation could be the repeated logarithmisation of the price logs, as this could lead to further variance stabilisation[17].

---

[17]The repeated logarithmisation of prices for variance stabilization reasons requires the repeated (re-) transformation of negative values to positive ones. However, in this case it has to be checked, if the new transformation leads to instability of the price process and if the occurring bias is acceptable or not.

Besides, the modeling approach for the deterministic components indeed considers a long-term trend, but this trend is estimated from historical series and does not contain distinctive structural changes, such as an extremely increasing share of renewable generation capacities. These structural changes can lead to another price level as the one estimated with the help of a historical trend curve. To capture changes of the power plant structure other models are necessary, especially fundamental models. Future work could therefore focus on a combination of fundamental and stochastic models to consider both, price levels caused by significant changes of the power plant mix and the above modelled short and mid-term characteristics of electricity prices.

Furthermore the deterministic components are fitted iteratively by different methods. The iterative process can lead to different results depending on the order of removal and addition of the different cycles. A simultaneously estimation of the coefficients of the different cycles in a closed approach using a large regression would avoid the question which order to choose. This approach was also tested by the author. However, the fitting results are less satisfying. The RMSE of this approach combined with the ARMA model is 6.37 €/MWh for a simulation for the period between 2002 and 2009, while the one of the iterative approach is only 4.84 €/MWh. Moreover the daily and weekly structure of the electricity spot prices is not captured adequately by the closed approach, as it is done by the iterative approach (see Figure A.2 in the appendix). For this reason and due to the fact that the different cycles have different period length, which are in the ideal case independent, the iterative approach has been applied in this study to model seasonal cycles.

Besides, further work has to be carried out to improve the simulation of negative electricity prices. Single negative prices can be generated with the help of the above described approach, but as negative prices occur consecutively for several hours and as they show autocorrelation for a lag of some hours, an extended approach with an autoregressive approach could fit the structure of negative prices better. The introduced approach can be also improved, if more historical data including negative prices are available after some years.

Moreover, the use of a bimodal distribution for the simulation of negative electricity prices raises the question, if there is a fundamental reason for the bimodal distribution and if it is likely that the future negative prices will be also bimodally distributed. It is hard to find a fundamental reason for the distribution of negative prices, as prices are formed in the spot market, where beside fundamental reasons psychological and strategic behaviour of market actors play an important role. Nevertheless, a reason for the two peaks of the negative price distribution could be the fact, that in the case of negative prices near 0 the energy suppliers are ready to pay a small "fee" for not shutting-down their middle-load plants (coal plants) for a single or a few hours to avoid start-up or ramp costs. However, if the wind penetration is very high and the load is very low, then the base-load power plants, such as lignite or nuclear plants, are concerned by shut-down. But the shut-down and start-up of these power plants for a couple of hours are much costlier. Especially for nuclear power plants, these opportunity costs are higher and quite uncertain as an authorisation from the state is necessary to restart. Thus, the utilities try to avoid a shut-down and are willing to pay a much higher "fee" (up to 120€/MWh and more) to get rid of the electricity, which they produce in surplus.

It is possible that the distribution of negative prices posses two peaks, one nearby 0€/MWh and one nearby 120€/MWh, due to these reasons. This is why a two-peaking (bimodal) distribution is likely in future. However, depending on future negative price observations, the distribution of negative prices might have to be adapted or could also be confirmed.

Thus, the method introduced above is an initial approach, which generates negative prices, whose absolute values and occurrence probabilities are similar to that of historical ones.

4.5. Conclusions

In this section different stochastic models are applied for the simulation of electricity prices, to evaluate and compare the different approaches. Therefore a model with two modules is introduced, the first for the deterministic parts of electricity prices, the second for the stochastic parts. The separate analysis of deterministic components and their removal from price logs is necessary to receive the stochastic part of electricity prices, for which the application of the considered stochastic process is reasonable. The removal of deterministic components from the historical prices and their addition to the simulated stochastic component is an adequate method, even if the ARIMA process is used to model the electricity prices. The analysis pointed out that a difference filter used within the ARIMA process can not remove and add deterministic elements sufficiently. Therefore a separate handling of the deterministic elements is more effective. Another remarkable outcome of the analysis is the importance of a regime-switching approach for the adequate simulation of price jumps. The stochastic processes are not able to simulate price peaks or jump groups by themselves. Even the GARCH process, the only method that can handle heteroscedasticity, cannot incorporate jumps with the height that is usually observed in historical electricity prices. However, the introduced regime-switching approach generates jumps, whose structure is fitting the historical ones very well.

Furthermore, the evaluation of the different stochastic models showed that the mean reversion and the ARMA(5,1) processes are fitting the daily and weekly movements and especially the stochastic volatility very well, while the other models, especially GARCH processes, generate volatile price paths higher than the historical ones. Furthermore the expected RMSE and MAPE are significantly lower applying mean-reversion and AR(i)MA models instead of GARCH processes, which is another sign for a good fit of the structure of historical electricity prices by the former models. Finally, it could be determined that the novel approach for negative prices could successfully incorporate these prices and that it leads to a significant improvement of the error measures RMSE and MAPE. A further improvement of electricity price modeling could be achieved, if the impact of renewable power generation on electricity prices is determined and appropriately modeled. This impact is caused by the so-called merit order effect of renewable power feed-in (see section 5.1), which is quantified and added to the electricity price models in the following.

5. Modeling wind power feed-in and its impacts on electricity spot prices

The influence of electricity from renewable energy sources on spot market prices is gaining in importance with increasing shares of renewable energy feed-in (see Ryu et al. (2010)). The electricity feed-in from renewable resources reduces the remaining system load, which has to be satisfied by conventional power capacities. As the renewable feed-in shifts market prices along the merit-order curve of power plants, this effect is often called the merit-order-effect of renewable energies (see Sensfuss et al. (2008), Menanteau et al. (2003)). The following figures for the German electricity system illustrate the impact of renewable feed-in especially based on wind energy: wind energy capacities in Germany amounted to approx. 26 GW in 2010 which corresponded to more than 30 % of the maximum load in that year[1]. This means that in times with a strong wind at least 30 % of the maximum load are served by wind power, which replaces the adaequate amount of conventional capacities. Thus, it is obvious that the feed-in from wind energy has an significant impact on spot market prices.

As the feed-in from wind energy is increasingly important for electricity price modeling, also financial and time-series models have to integrate this new uncertain parameter in their modeling approach. Up to now, there exists hardly any financial or time-series modeling approach which explicitly models wind power feed-in and which incorporates this uncertainty of wind power feed-in into an electricity price model. Therefore this chapter presents an analysis of the wind power feed-in (in Germany) and proposes a modeling approach for wind power feed-in. At last it presents an integrated approach for the simulation of electricity spot prices under consideration of wind power feed-in within a time-series modeling approach.

---

[1]For the load data see BDEW (2013) or the websites of the German TSOs

This chapter is structured as follows: The next section gives an overview about the uncertainty in wind power generation and quantifies its impact on the electricity spot prices that is related to the merit-order effect of wind energy. Section 5.2.2 focuses on the simulation of wind power feed-in (WPF) based on the hourly utilization of the overall wind power capacity installed in Germany. Thereby the focus will be set on the removal of deterministic patterns, such as seasonality, and on the modeling of stochastic properties of the hourly capacity utilization series. The autoregressive behaviour of the stochastic part of the capacity utilization will be captured by an recursive method simulating the change rate of the next capacity utilization level by its preceding values. After generating the stochastic component, the time-series will be reseasonalised to receive final capacity utilization series representing the hourly WPF of a year.

The hourly WPF series will be used in section 5.2.3, to extend the simulation of electricity prices considering the short-term impact of WPF. Thereby, an already existing electricity model will be shortly described, before the focus is set on model extensions integrating the impacts of WPF. The description of the extended electricity price model will be followed by the summary of the main results in the conclusions section, presenting also further work that can be carried out in that area.

5.1. Impacts of wind power feed-in on electricity prices

The effect of wind power feed-in on electricity prices has been analyzed in various papers (see Ray et al. (2010)). In general it can be distinguished between model based analysis (see Sensfuss et al. (2008), Weigt (2009), Delarue et al. (2009), Bode and Groscurth (2006), de Miera et al. (2008)) and statistical analysis. Main goal of the statistical approaches is to quantify the price spread of market prices with a high and a low wind feed in (see Jonsson et al. (2010), Neubarth et al. (2006)).

The price reducing impact is also called merit-order effect (see Figure 5.1) and can be explained with the right shift of the supply curve when wind power with low variable costs is integrated into the supply curve. Assuming an inelastic demand, electricity price as intersection between supply and demand will thus decrease. The height of the merit-order effect depends apart from the feed-in of wind power mainly on the two factors demand height and gradient of the supply curve. The gradient of the supply curve depends mainly on the technologies, efficiencies, fuel price spreads and the CO_2 price.

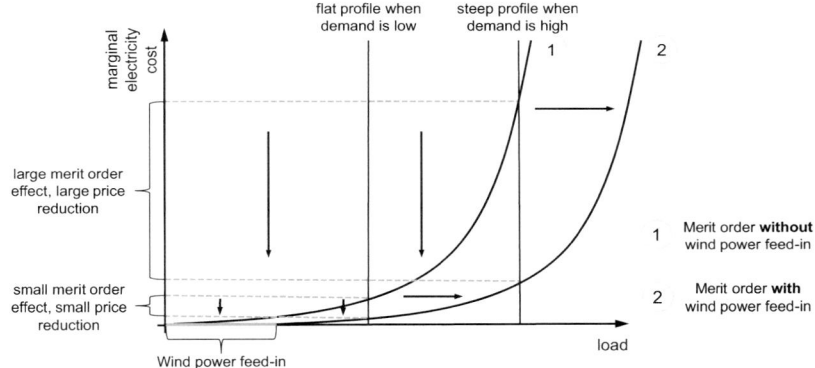

Figure 5.1.: Right shift of the merit order and the supply curve particularly due to wind power feed-in

The merit-order effect can be quantified using the historical market prices from the European Power Exchange (EPEX). A linear regression of market prices depending on wind power feed-in shows that the electricity price decreases on average by 1.47 € for every additional GW of wind power[2]. However, this average effect can not explain extreme price events (i.e. negative prices of -500 €/MWh). Thus, the correlation of electricity price and wind power feed-in might depend on the point of time and is presumably nonlinear.

In the following, the price reduction effect of wind power feed-in will be analysed depending on the demand situation. In advance, the time series of the prices

---
[2]Own calculation based on electricity spot prices from the EEX and wind power feed-in data (see BDEW (2013)) for the years 2006 to 2009

is deseasonalized to expose the correlation between wind power feed-in and prices. The deseasonalization is performed for yearly, weakly, and daily cycles (see section 4.2.1).

For every hour of the period 2006-2009, a triple of electricity price, wind power feed-in and demand (load) is formed and sorted ascendingly by the load. Thereby 2 GW clusters based on the load are formed for the data triples.

With a linear regression, the correlation of electricity price P_t^L and wind power feed-in W_t^L is determined for every load interval L.

$$P_t^L = \alpha_L \cdot W_t^L + \beta_L \qquad [5.1]$$

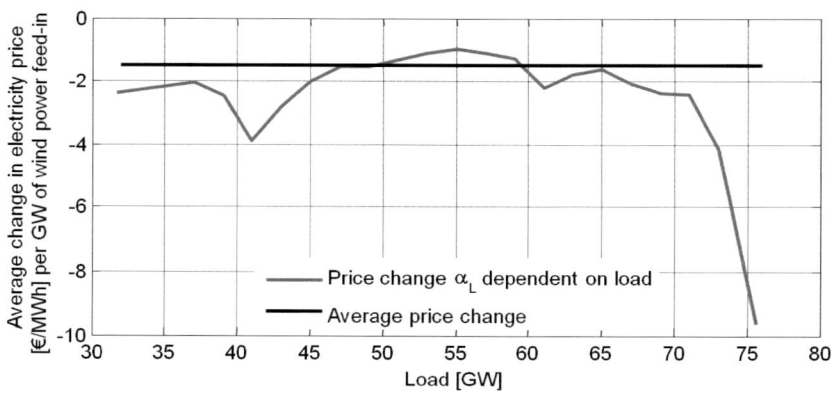

Figure 5.2.: Average change of the deseasonalized electricity price per GW wind power depending on load interval

Figure 5.2 shows the parameters α_L (determined with Eq. 5.1). The values are negative showing that the feed-in of wind power leads to lower electricity prices. It also shows that the price reducing effect highly depends on the load situation and can be significantly higher than the average reduction of 1.47 €/MWh per GW wind power, which is also shown in Figure 5.2.

In the following, the price reduction is compared to the merit-order curve. Figure 5.3 shows the price reduction (absolute value) together with the merit-order curve of the German electricity market. There are some characteristics in the price reduction curve that can also be observed in the merit-order curve. The similarities even increase if the price reduction curve depending on the load is shifted to the left by the average wind power feed-in. This can be interpreted as a price reduction curve of WPF depending on the residual demand.

There are four significant changes in the curve. These changes can be also found in the merit-order curve. In area I (see Figure 5.3) a local peak of the price reduction per GW feed-in can be observed. The comparable step in the merit-order curve represents the change from lignite to coal fired power plants. Thus the price reduction effect increases when lignite power plants are the price setting units instead of coal fired power plants, as the shutdown of lignite power plants are more costlier than coal power plants. Hence, power plant operators are accepting also very low prices to avoid the shutdown and restart of a lignite power plant. A similar step can be observed in area III. Here the corresponding switch in the merit-order is from gas to coal fired power plants. In this case it is more expensive to shutdown a coal power plant than a combined cycle power plant.

Another strong increase of the price reduction effect can be observed in area IV. Here peak load power plants (oil or gas fired) have to be used. These are the most expensive power plants because of their low efficiency and the high fuel price. If the use of these power plants is avoided, the price reduction is very high. On the other side, the flat areas (II and right of III) of the price reduction curve represent quite a low price reduction. The merit-order curve shows the corresponding parts with a low slope.

The price reducing effect in area I is much higher than in area III. This areas represent the power plant switch from lignite to coal (area I) and coal to combined cycle power plants (area III). As the spread of the variable costs is not in the same ratio as the price reduction effect, there are other reasons for the higher reduction in area I. In this area the occurrence of negative prices is high, because shut-down and ramp-up costs are tried to be avoided and reserve requirements may cause further restriction on the operation of power plants. Furthermore, combined heat and power plants have to be kept online to fulfill contracts on heat delivery and this can lead to excess supply and thus to negative prices.

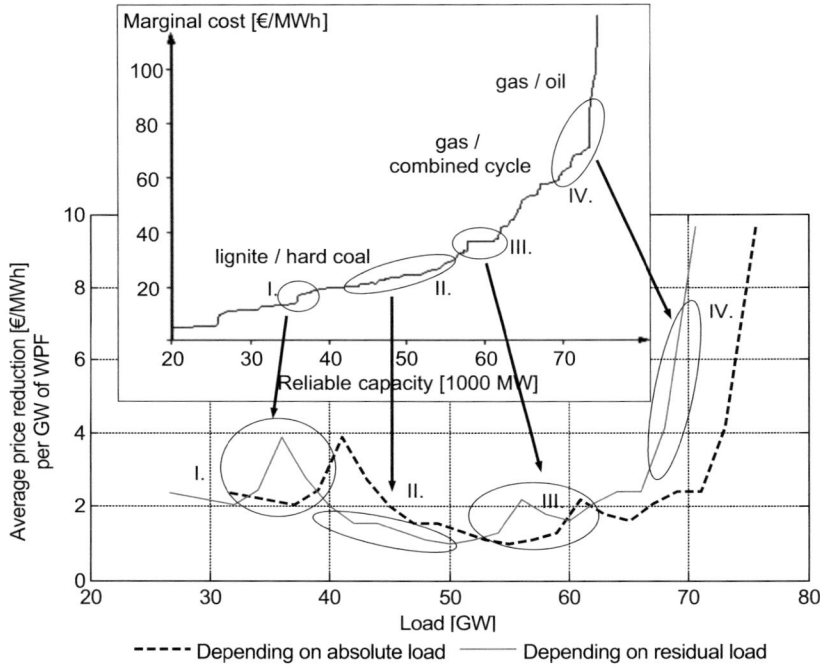

Figure 5.3.: Price reduction per GW wind power feed-in depending on the load level and the German merit order curve (source: Erdmann (2008) and own calculation)

5.2. Integrated approach for modeling wind power feed-in and electricity prices

As electricity prices are strongly influenced by the amount of wind power feed-in to the grid, a combined approach of a wind power feed-in (WPF) and electricity spot price model has been developed. Thereby the relationship between WPF and prices, especially the price reduction effect of WPF on electricity prices (see section 5.1), is taken into account. In the combined modeling approach, historical electricity price and WPF series are used to calibrate the model components, which in turn are applied to generate simulated price and WPF series. The simulation of prices and WPF allows the evaluation of power plant technologies, such as wind parks, under uncertainty, as a big number of simulation runs can be carried out to describe and handle the uncertainty. For the evaluation it is important that both, the WPF series and electricity prices, are adequately simulated. The advantage of the combined modeling approach is that it not only provides both series, but it also captures the correlation between them. Therefore the following combined modeling approach is introduced.

5.2.1. Overview of the modeling approach

The whole modeling approach consists of two main models. In the first model WPF series are simulated for a whole year with an hourly resolution. In the second model electricity spot prices are modeled using the simulated WPF series to determine the price reduction effect of WPF via a linear regression approach.

The WPF model component is based on a stochastic process with an autoregressive component. However, since historical WPF series show significant seasonal patterns throughout the year and also within a day, in the first step they have to be removed from the historical data[3]. This procedure avoids overlapping by deterministic seasonal patterns during the analysis and simulation of the stochastic component of WPF. The historical WPF series without the seasonal pattern are then used to calibrate a stochastic process, which is applied to simulate the stochastic component of WPF series. In the last step, the seasonal patterns are again added to the stochastic component resulting in final WPF series.

Afterwards the simulated WPF series are processed to the electricity price module, which also consists of two components, one for the simulation of the deterministic elements of electricity prices (trend, daily, weekly and annual cycle) and the other for the stochastic residuals. But before the electricity price module is

---

[3]Deseasonalization methods for time-series are precisely described in Kreiss (2006)

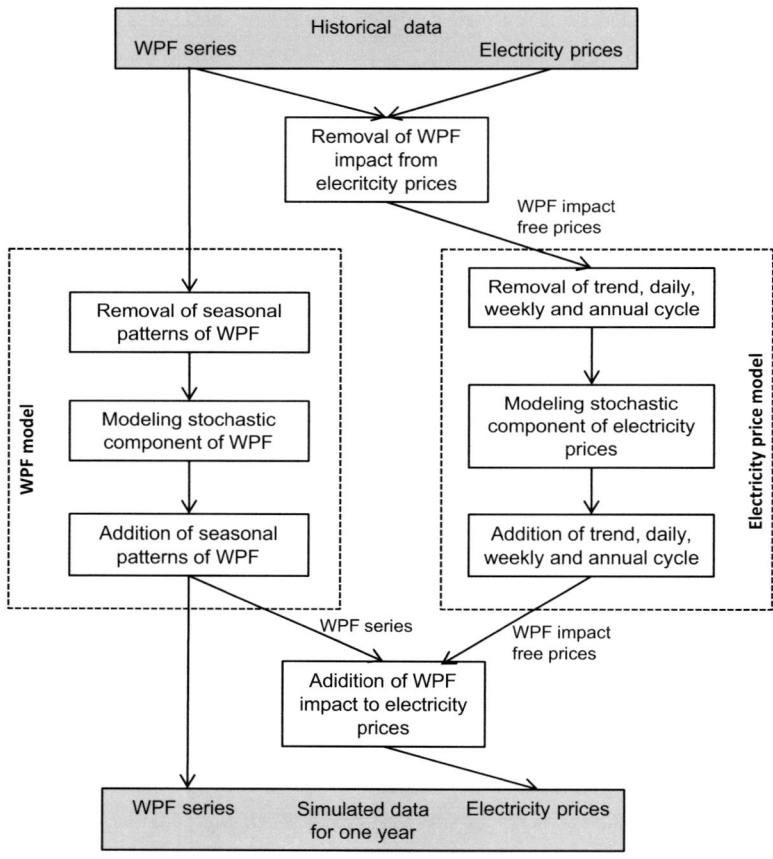

Figure 5.4.: Overview of the WPF simulation model

applied, it has to be calibrated. Therefore the historical electricity prices are integrated to the model. However, the historical electricity prices contain beside the deterministic components a further explanatory component, the price reduction effect of WPF. That is why, this effect is removed from the prices at first and the "WPF-impact-free" prices are then passed to the electricity price module. In the electricity price module, the deterministic components of prices are removed; the stochastic residuals are used for the calibration of the stochastic component via an autoregressive time-series model (see Box et al. (2008)) and then simulated time series are extended by adding the deterministic components. The resulting series describe simulated electricity prices without any price reduction effect of WPF. Thus, the WPF series simulated with the first module are now used to determine the price reduction effect, which is determined via linear regression of electricity prices on WPF. The addition of the WPF price reduction effect to the electricity price series leads to completes electricity spot price simulation (see Figure 5.4).

5.2.2. Wind power feed-in model

In the following the first module of the combined approach, the WPF model, is described, which simulates the progress of the wind power feed-in (WPF) throughout a year. The WPF model focuses on the simulation of daily and seasonal patterns as well as on the stochastic component of WPF. Within the model the historical WPF series for whole Germany are directly used to describe the characteristics of WPF and to calibrate the model.

Existing studies about simulating wind power feed-in and models established therein mostly depend on an indirect approach, as not wind power feed-in but wind speed series are simulated based on historical data (see e.g. Safari (2011), Torres et al. (2005) or Kamal and Jafri (1997)). The simulated wind speed series afterwards are transformed into WPF series. Generally, these studies consider solely regional limited areas, since representative wind speed data for large territories is hardly to find, due to wind speed's high dependencies on local effects. Papaefthymiou and Kloeckl (2008) modify the wind speed approach, as they propose to transform wind speed into WPF data at first and to model WPF afterwards.

Using a Markov chain Monte Carlo method for modeling WPF, their approach implicates a significant simplification of a stochastic model represented in a reduced number of states and a higher level of accuracy.

According to Suomalainen et al. (2012) auto-regressive models as preferred by Billington et al. (1995) and Markov models mentioned above do not take into account the high variability and correlation of wind power evident in daily, seasonal, or annual seasonalities. That is why they identify in a first step seasonality, average wind speeds, and day types. Afterwards these characteristics of wind speed are simulated with the help of AR-models and probability distribution matrices. Kennedy and Rogers (2009) also apply seasonality adjusted wind power simulation. However, these approaches also model wind speed at first and then transform the output into WPF series.

Now it is worth mentioning that the model presented in this approach is no longer based on wind speed data, but simulates WPF directly using historical WPF data. The indirect modeling via wind speeds is not chosen in this approach, as a representative wind speed for whole Germany cannot be found and separate modeling of wind speeds for each wind power site is nearly impossible due to the large number of wind power plants spread throughout Germany. Besides, historical data is only available for the total wind power feed-in, but not for wind speeds at each wind power site. Thus, a direct modeling approach for the total wind power generation in Germany is developed.

Furthermore, the developed WPF model does not only simulate the amount of wind energy feed-in, but also the percentage utilization level of the overall generation capacity installed in Germany. More precisely, the average capacity utilization is firstly modeled and then multiplied by the total installed capacity of the analysed year resulting in a simulated WPF series for that year. With the help of this method the future expansion of the overall capacity can be considered.

The underlying modeling approach for the simulation of the capacity utilization is based on a recursive determination of its hourly values. Therefore every capacity utilization value W_t is determined by its predecessor W_{t-1} and the actual change rate ΔW_t in t, which itself is dependent on the previous capacity utilization values W_{t-q}. This autoregressive procedure was chosen in order to meet the special behaviour of the capacity utilization level, as the historical values posses a significant autocorrelation.[4]

The modeling approach based on the autoregressive approach is introduced in the following, but at first the description of the seasonal patterns are presented. The seasonal patterns have to be simulated at first and then removed from the historical WPF series, so that the autoregressive model can be applied for the stochastic residuals, i.e. the deseasonalised series.

5.2.2.1. Modeling seasonality of wind power feed-in

The analysis of the observed wind power feed-in data revealed significant seasonal patterns. In the winter for example, the utilization of the installed capacity is significantly higher than in the summer. This results from the geographical position of Germany and corresponding weather changes: in Europe west winds are much stronger in the winter than in the summer (see Raczkowsky (2008)).

Figure 5.5 depicts the development of the annual seasonality showing the average monthly 0.9 and 0.1 quantiles of the observed capacity utilization. The average 0.1 as well as 0.9 quantiles are larger in winter than in summer months, whereby the variation of the latter is significantly stronger. The stronger variation of the 0.9 quantile is caused on the one hand by generally higher wind speeds in the winter and by more frequent and stronger peaks of WPF due to a larger number of storms on the other hand.

Beside the annual seasonality, the time series of capacity utilization are also influenced by a strong daily cycle. The cause of this cycle is mainly the solar radiation changing throughout the day, which causes partly extreme temperature differences within the atmosphere resulting in the movement of large air masses. At coastal areas air masses over land heat up faster than over see, which leads to strong winds breezing from the see landwards. This effect becomes even stronger in the afternoon hours and as a large share of the German wind power plants is located in coastal regions (see Schaal and Kolshorn (2005)), the average WPF is

---

[4]The historical WPF series and the capacity utilization levels respectively originate from the network operators and are published for each hour of the years 2006 to 2009 by BDEW (2013).

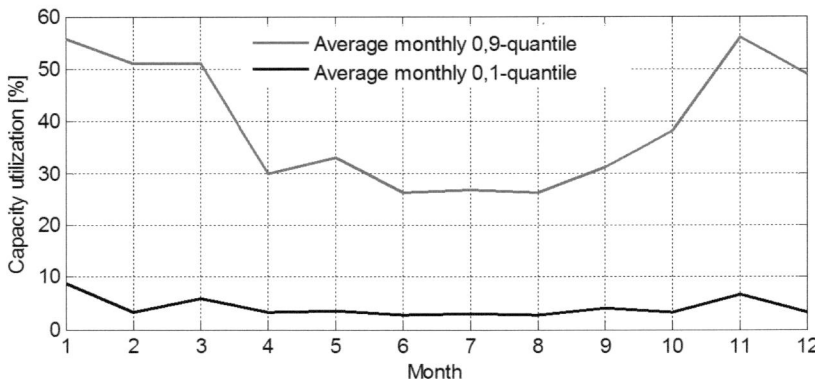

Figure 5.5.: Monthly 10% and 90% quantiles of the capacity utilization (based on WPF data between 2006 and 2009)

higher in the afternoon (see Figure 5.6). Furthermore it is noticeable that the minimum of average capacity utilization is in the early morning. This can explained by the change of the wind direction from off-shore to on-shore between 8 pm and 10 pm.

Hence, these seasonal patterns need to be formally modeled and removed from the time series in order to avoid bias within the analysis and simulation. The deseasonalized series can be used to calibrate a stochastic model, which in turn can be applied to simulate the stochastic part of capacity utilization and WPF series respectively.

a) Modeling annual seasonality

As already shown in Figure 5.5 the capacity utilization levels show a strong seasonal variation throughout the year. The causes for the variation of the 0.1 and 0.9 quantiles are explained above and will not be examined anymore. Therefore the focus is set on the mathematical description of the cycles and their removal procedure in the following.

The mathematical components describing the seasonal cycle, i.e. the 0.1 and 0.9 quantiles, are separately calculated for each month m and year a of the time

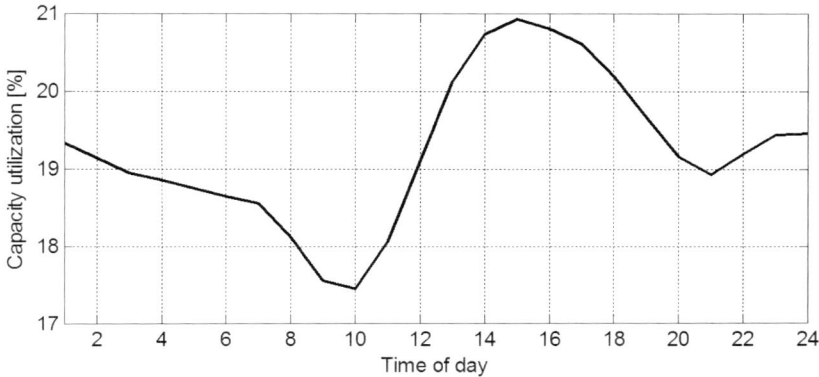

Figure 5.6.: Hourly means of the capacity utilization (based on WPF data between 2006 and 2009)

period, historical WPF data are available for. The differentiation of the seasonal cycle for each year is done, as the amplitude of the annual seasonality is of different strength in different years and thus each year needs to be separately deseasonalized. The elimination of one single season for all years would otherwise result in strong distortion. For that reason, at first the monthly 0.9 and 0.1 quantiles, $_{0.9}q_{m,a}$ and $_{0.1}q_{m,a}$, are determined from the observed capacity utilization W_t for each year a. From the monthly values the average annual 0.9 and 0.1 quantiles $_{0.9}q_a^*$ and $_{0.1}q_a^*$ are calculated for each year. In the next step the original capacity utilization data is modified, so that they do not follow the monthly quantiles but the average annual one representing the average trend for the specific year. To achieve that, the utilization levels W_t have to be moved by a summand $r_{m,a}$ and stretched by a factor $s_{m,a}$. Thereby $r_{m,a}$ and $s_{m,a}$ are determined in that way, that the adjusted monthly quantiles are equal to the annual quantiles. And as the operations, moving by $r_{m,a}$ and stretching by $s_{m,a}$, influence the original data, they have to be performed simultaneously. Consequently the moving and stretching factors

need to be correlated, so that they are not distorted by another. The following
linear equation system and its solution delivers the needed parameters:

$$0.9q_{m,a} \cdot s_{m,a} + r_{m,a} = 0.9q_a^*$$

$$0.1q_{m,a} \cdot s_{m,a} + r_{m,a} = 0.1q_a^*$$

$$m = 1, ..., 12$$

$$a = 1, ..., 4$$

[5.2]

$$\Rightarrow s_{m,a} = \frac{0.9q_a^* - 0.1\, q_a^*}{0.9q_{m,a} - 0.1\, q_{m,a}}$$

[5.3]

$$\Rightarrow r_{m,a} = -0.1q_{m,a} \cdot s_{m,a} + 0.1\, q_a^*$$

[5.4]

Finally each value of the original utilization time series W_t is multiplied with
the stretch factor $s_{m,a}$ of the corresponding month m of the respective year a and
adjusted by the according value $r_{m,a}$. The result is a first deseasonalized time
series $W_t^{deseas,year}$ without annual seasonalities.

$$W_{t,m,a}^{deseas,year} = s_{m,a} \cdot W_{t,m,a} + r_{m,a}$$

$$t = 1, ..., N$$

[5.5]

b) Modeling daily cycles

To balance the daily seasonality of the capacity utilization, a similar method as
before in the annual deseasonalization is applied. Firstly, the average value $\bar{W}_h$
of the deseasonalized utilization $W_t^{deaseas,year}$ is determined for each hour of the
day throughout the complete horizon of the available data. Afterwards the hourly
means $\bar{W}_h$ are subtracted from the corresponding values of the capacity utilization
$W_t^{deaseas,year}$ and the average capacity utilization $\bar{W}$ of the complete time series is
added (see formula 5). This implies a movement of all values to the mean of the
complete capacity utilization depending on the hour of the day.

$$W_t^{deseas} = W_t^{deseas,year} - \sum_{h=1}^{24} \bar{W}_h \cdot 1(h|h = t \bmod 24) + \bar{W}$$

$$t = 1, ..., N$$

[5.6]

The resulting time series W_t^{deseas} contains neither an annual nor a daily seasonality and is therefore suitable as a basis for the stochastic simulation. In the following section a novel approach is introduced to simulate the stochastic component, whereby the simulation is based on the learnings from the statistical analysis of the deseasonalized series.

5.2.2.2. Stochastic component of capacity utilization

In this section the simulation of the stochastic component W_t^S of the capacity utilization and WPF respectively will be carried out with an extended autoregressive model (see Eq. 5.7). Thereby the focus will be set on the modeling of the change rate ΔW_t^S as a stochastic random variable depending on the average value of the q preceding capacity utilizations $\bar{W}_{t,q}^S$.

$$W_t^S = W_{t-1}^S + \Delta W_t^S \ , \ \Delta W_t^S \sim L(\mu(\bar{W}_{t,q}^S), b(\bar{W}_{t,q}^S)) \qquad [5.7]$$

As the change rates ΔW_t^S play a key role within the simulation of the stochastic component of WPF, at first the stochastic distribution of ΔW_t^S the and its parameters has to be determined.

a) Distribution of the change rates and parameter estimation

The change rates ΔW_t^S of the stochastic component of the historical capacity utilizations seem to be Laplace distributed [5], as the density function of the Laplace distribution fits the histogram of the change rates quite well (see Figure 5.7). The Laplace distribution[6], also called double exponential distribution, assumes a symmetric curve for the distribution of the change rates around the mean value, which is equal to the modal value in this case. The symmetry in the histogram can be also verified by the very low value for the skewness ($S = -0.039$).

Based on Laplace distributed random values, the change rate and capacity utilization value could be simulated for each hour within the simulation time horizon.

---

[5]The null hypothesis of the two sample Kolmogorov-Smirnov test, which compares the distributions of the historical change rates and a series generated with Laplace distribution, is not rejected at a significance value of 1%. The null hypothesis indicates that both series posses the same stochastic distribution.

[6]for density and distribution function see Eq. A.2 in the appendix

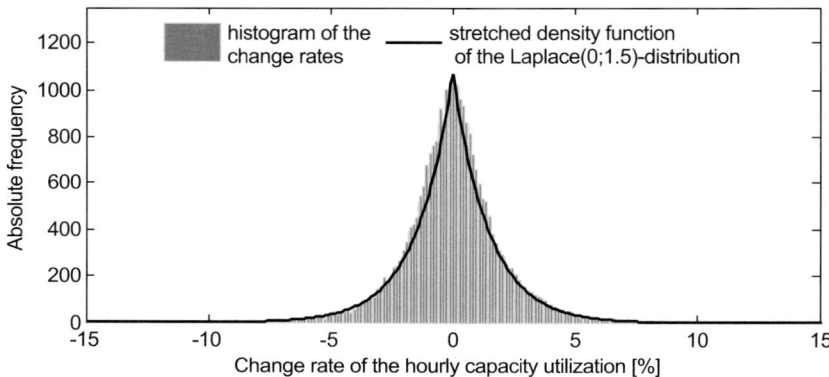

Figure 5.7.: Distribution of the hourly change rates of historical capacity utilizations

However, a more detailed analysis showed that the distribution of the change rates varies for different actual capacity utilization levels L_t^q, which is hereby defined as the mean value of the last q capacity utilization values:

$$L_t^q = \bar{W}_{t,q}^S = \frac{1}{q} \sum_{i=1}^{q} W_{t-i} \qquad [5.8]$$

The variation of the change rate for different capacity utilization levels L_t^q is caused by the approximately S-shape growths of the capacity utilization curve. The decline of the capacity utilization is a recursive S-curve noticeable again in the historical data. This S-shape growth or decline of capacity utilization can be explained by the fact, that the WPF is correlated with the cubic value of the wind speed (Jarass et al. (2009)). This correlation causes a polynomial growth for the WPF forming the first part of the S-curve. However, as the WPF is limited by the installed wind power capacity in the regions, where the actual wind is occurring, the growth is more and more dampened by the capacity bound. This effect forms the second half of the approximated S-curve (see Figure A.3 in the appendix).

As the growth and decline of the capacity utilization posses a S-shape structure, the change rates are unequally distributed and have to be separately modeled depending on the actual utilization level L_t^q. Therefore the overall Laplace distribution approach is replaced by an interval based one, whereby different Laplace distribution parameters are applied depending on the actual utilization level L_t^q.

However, the development of an approach, that is based on L_t^q, requires the appropriate number q of preceding utilization values, which influence the actual change rate ΔW_t. Thus, q corresponds to the optimal number of correlated values $W_{t-i}^S (i = 1,..,q)$ with the change rates ΔW_t^S. To determine the optimal lag for this correlation, several L_t^q series for different q are generated based on the historical capacity utilizations. It could be afterwards proved that the highest correlation - in absolute values - between the series of L_t^q and the change rates ΔW_t exist for $q = 11$ (see Figure A.4 in the appendix). Thus, the actual ΔW_t will be modeled based on the mean values series of capacity utilization L_t^{11} realized in the last eleven hours.

To capture the unequal distribution of the change rates ΔW_t, the historical utilization levels L_t^{11} are sorted in an ascending order and separated in i intervals. The corresponding ΔW_t are also classified into i intervals. This approach delivers two series for each class i, one for ΔW_t^i and the other for $L_t^{11,i}$. For each of the intervals the probability distribution parameters of ΔW_t^i are estimated separately via Maximum-Likelihood estimation [7]. Thereby it is worth mentioning that the Laplace distribution, which describes the change rates, is handled as a double exponential distribution. Each of the exponential distributions (for density function see Eq. A.3 in the appendix) represent one part of the Laplace distribution, the one smaller than the modal value m^i and the other greater than m^i. To apply the exponential distribution for both types, positive and negative change rates ΔW_t^i, a last modification has to be done: The modal value m^i has to be moved to zero, so that the adjusted $\Delta \tilde{W}_t^i$ are distributed around 0.

$$\Delta \tilde{W}_t^i = \Delta W_t^i - m^i \qquad [5.9]$$

---

[7]The classification in intervals and the application of different distributions for each class causes a heteroscedasticity in the simulated capacity utilization series as it can be observed in the historical series. Therefore the applied approach can be seen as a kind of ARCH model (see Engle (1982) or Bollerslev (1986))

Thus, the positive $\Delta \tilde{W}_t^i$ can be simulated via the first exponential distribution, the negative $\Delta \tilde{W}_t^i$ via the other.[8] The related distribution parameters $\mu^{i,+}$ and $\mu^{i,-}$ are estimated for each class i based on the corresponding classified data $\Delta \tilde{W}_t^i$. Figure 5.8 illustrates again the procedure of parameter estimation.

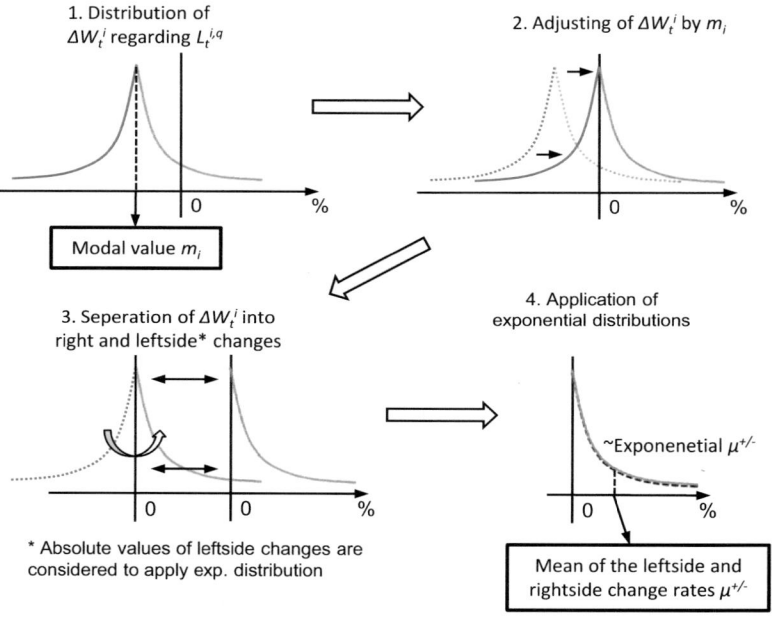

Figure 5.8.: Estimation procedure for the distribution parameters of change rates for interval i

A linear regression is applied for each of the estimated parameters m^i, $\mu^{i,+}$ and $\mu^{i,-}$ and the according utilization levels $L_t^{11,i}$, resulting in linear or polynomial function $f(L_t^{11})$ describing the parameter value dependent on L_t^{11} (see Eq. 5.10). This functional description for the parameters avoids a separate registry of the

---

[8]More precisely, the absolute value of the negative $\Delta \tilde{W}_t^i$ can be simulated with the help of the second exponential distribution, as this distribution describes only positive values.

parameters of each interval in a table and recalling them from this table during the simulation.

$$\mu_t^+, \mu_t^-, m_t = f(L_t^{11}) = a_0 + \sum_{j=1}^n a_j \cdot L_t^{11,j} \qquad [5.10]$$

b) Simulation of the change rates and of the stochastic component of WPF

Based on the functions described above the parameters m_t, μ_t^+ and μ_t^- are newly calculated subject to the actual capacity utilization level $L_t^{11,Sim}$ at each time step t during the simulation. μ_t^+ and μ_t^- respectively are used to generate a exponential distributed random variable, which is adjusted by the modal value m_t, representing a new change rate ΔW_t^{Sim}.

$$\Delta W_t^{Sim} = \begin{cases} \varepsilon_t + m_t & \varepsilon_t \sim Exp(\mu_t^+) \text{ ,if } z_t = 1 \\ -\varepsilon_t + m_t & \varepsilon_t \sim Exp(\mu_t^-) \text{ ,if } z_t = 0 \end{cases} \qquad [5.11]$$

As it noticeable from Eq. 5.11, a binary variable z_t is introduced, which determines the mathematical sign of the ΔW_t^{Sim}, i.e. it denotes whether a positive or negative ΔW_t^{Sim} should be generated by applying the right side or left side exponential distribution with the according μ_t^+ and μ_t^- respectively. The binary variable z_t is generated based on a uniformly distributed variable u_t, which is compared with the probability of a positive change rate following n positive preceding change rates, if the last n simulated change rates ΔW_{t-j}^{Sim} ($j = 1, ..., n$) are positive. If the last m simulated change rates ΔW_{t-k}^{Sim} ($k = 1, ..., m$) are negative, then u_t is compared with the probability of a positive ΔW_t following m negative change rates (see 5.12[9]). The probabilities for each case are defined as the according relative frequency within the historical data.

$$z_t = \begin{cases} 1 & u_t < P(\Delta W_t \geq 0 | \Delta W_{t-j} \geq 0) \mid u_t < P(\Delta W_t \geq 0 | \Delta W_{t-k} < 0) \\ 0 & \text{else} \end{cases} \qquad [5.12]$$

$$j = 1, ..., n \ k = 1, ..., m$$

---

[9]The introduced probabilities $P(\Delta W_t \geq 0 | \Delta W_{t-j} \geq 0)$ and $P(\Delta W_t \geq 0 | \Delta W_{t-k} < 0)$ are calculated based on the historical change rates of the capacity utilization values between 2006 and 2009.

The Eq. 5.7 - 5.12 can be now applied to simulate the capacity utilization values W_t^{Sim} for one year (8760 hours). However, the initial utilization level $L_1^{11,Sim}$ and the starting capacity utilization value W_0^{Sim} has to be previously defined. Therefore the mean value of the last eleven historical W_{T-i} ($i = 0, ..., 10$) is determined as the initial capacity utilization level $L_1^{11,Sim}$, which is required to simulate the first change rate ΔW_1^{Sim}. Besides, the mean value of the overall historical capacity utilizations $\bar{W}_t$ is chosen as W_0^{Sim}. After this last preparations the autoregressive model (Eq. 5.13) is applied delivering a capacity utilization series ($W_t^{S,Sim}$) without seasonal pattern.

$$W_t^S = W_{t-1}^S + \Delta W_t^S \ , \ \Delta W_t^S \sim L(\mu(L_{t,11}^S), b(L_{t,11}^S)) \qquad [5.13]$$

The addition of the seasonal patterns - reversing Eq. 5.5 and Eq. 5.6 - leads to a complete capacity utilization series W_t^{Sim} for one year. A final operation, i.e. the multiplication of the simulated series of capacity utilization with the overall installed wind power capacity of a specific year, results in a WPF series for the respective year. Figure 5.9 gives an overview of the whole WPF module.

5.2.3. Simulation of electricity spot prices under consideration of wind power feed-in

After simulating the wind power feed-in for an exemplary year based on the actual installed capacity in Germany, the impacts of WPF on the electricity spot prices are modeled in the following. Therefore the regime-switching model based on the ARMA(5,1)-process introduced in chapter 4 is extended to capture the WPF impacts on the electricity prices, i.e. the price reduction effect (see section 5.1) of WPF.

The electricity spot price models described in chapter 4 consider only the historical behaviour of electricity prices. Since the extension of renewable energy capacities, especially that of wind power capacities, the impact of renewable power feed-in on electricity prices has become more and more important. This impact is also caused by the market design of the EEX spot market, which preferably considers renewable energy feed-in at the supply side.

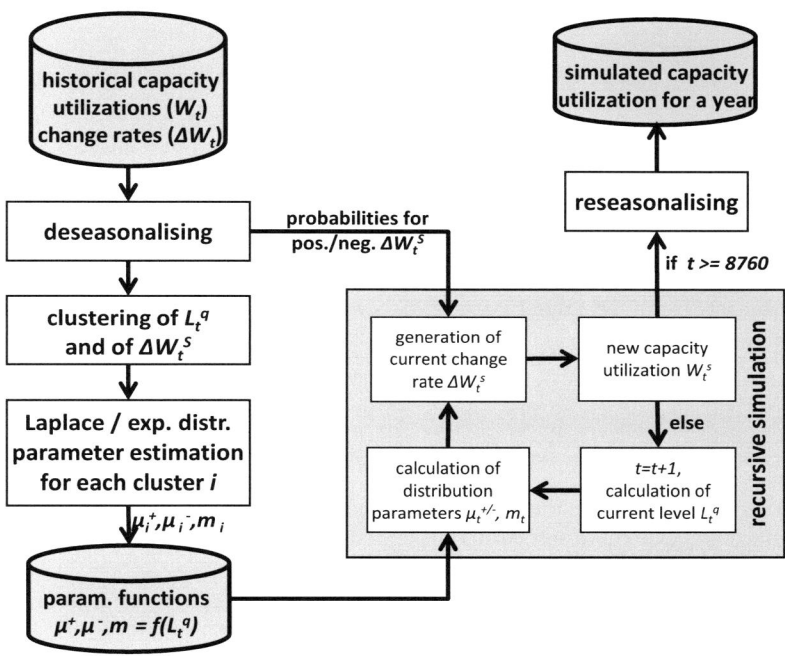

Figure 5.9.: Overview of the WPF simulation model

The feed-in of renewable power leads to a electricity price reduction effect varying for different load levels. The extended price model is designed in a way that it can capture this load-dependent effect. The shown load dependency is indirectly incorporated into the model, by separately carrying out a linear regression for each hour of the day based on the according data for electricity prices and WPF. This is an approximate solution to bring the load dependency into the model without explicitly integrating load data, as the variation of the load is reflected by the time within the day and by the development of the electricity prices throughout the day. Thus, a further modeling approach, that is used to simulate the electricity load, is not needed. This approach also avoids further modeling errors, which would occur, if the load as another factor is also simulated and incorporated to the model.

Executing a linear regression for each hour, based on the corresponding WPF and electricity price data, the price reduction rate for each hour is determined, as the gradient of the linear regression line. Thereby it is worth mentioning that the linear regression between WPF and electricity prices series is not only hourly differentiated, but it is also distinguished for different day types (summer, fall, winter, spring weekdays and weekend days). Thus, for each hour h of each type day d a separate price reduction rate $\Delta P_{WPF}^{h,d}$ is determined equal to the appropriate gradient of the linear regression rate. The determined price reduction rates are illustrated in Figure A.5 in the appendix. The total price reduction of WPF in a certain hour is then calculated as the product of $\Delta P_{WPF}^{h,d}$ and the actual WPF $W^{h,d}$.

The basic electricity price model is extended (see Figure 5.10) in a way that

- the total price reduction of WPF in each time step is removed from the historical price series,

- the adjusted prices are passed to the basic model to calibrate the basic regime-switching model,

- price series are simulated with the basic model

- and the price reduction effect is again added to the basic model outcome to receive the final simulated prices.

More precisely, the subtraction of the negative price reduction values of WPF from the historical price series in the first step (see Equation 5.14) is in fact an addition of the absolute value of the price reduction, as the determined price reduction rates, i.e. the gradients of the linear regression lines, and thus the total price reductions are negative. Hence, removing the price reduction values of WPF leads to an upwards shift of the electricity price series (see Figure A.6 in the appendix).

$$P_t' = P_t - \sum_{d'} 1(d'|d' = d(P_t)) \cdot \sum_{h'}^{24} 1(h'|h' = t \bmod 24) \cdot \Delta P_{WPF}^{h,d} \cdot W_t \qquad [5.14]$$

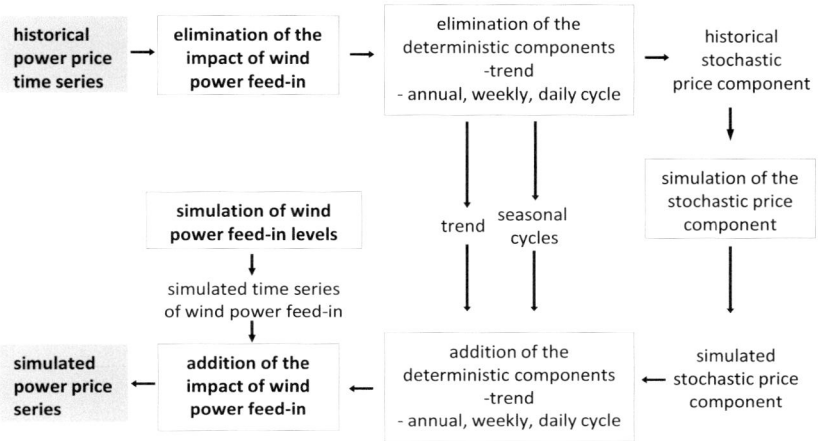

Figure 5.10.: Overview of the extended electricity spot price model

The adjusted price series P_t' are used for the modeling of the deterministic and stochastic components due to the approach described in section 4.2. After simulating the electricity prices $P_t'^{Sim}$, which contain only the deterministic and stochastic component, but not the price reduction effect of WPF, this effect is again added to the simulated price series. Therefore, a WPF series W_t^{Sim} is generated with the WPF model described in section 5.2.2. The WPF series is then used to calculate the corresponding price reduction values, which in turn are again added to the simulated price components (see Eq. 5.15). The addition of the negative price reduction values actually corresponds to a price shift downwards depending on the height of the WPF value W_t^{Sim}.

$$P_t^{Sim} = e^{X_t^{s,Sim} + X_t^{det,Sim}} + \sum_{d'} 1(d'|d' = d(P_t)) \cdot \sum_{h'}^{24} 1(h'|h' = t mod 24) \cdot \Delta P_{WPF}^{h,d} \cdot W_t^{Sim}$$

[5.15]

Based on these extended approach, electricity spot prices are simulated, which now contain the impacts of WPF. These price simulations will be compared with the basic model results in the following.

5.3. Wind and electricity price simulation results

Based on the combined modeling approach described above, 100 simulation runs are carried out delivering WPF series and electricity prices. The WPF series are generated via multiplying the capacity utilization series by the installed capacity of the analysed year. For future years, the expected installed capacity has to be estimated, so that WPF series for these years can be generated.

Besides, different electricity price series are produced with the two electricity model versions. As already mentioned, the basic model version does not consider a separate modeling approach for the WPF impacts on the electricity prices, the extended does. Therefore it is important to find out, if the extended modeling approach leads to an improvement of the electricity price simulation or not. However, an important outcome is that the price series based on the extended price series contain the relationship between the WPF series and electricity prices. So, if both series, electricity price and WPF series, are needed for further analysis, these price series are the appropriate ones.

5.3.1. Results of the WPF simulation

Several capacity utilization and WPF series are simulated, after calculating seasonality parameters and estimating stochastic model parameters with least squares method. The determined parameter values are summarized in Table 5.1 and Table A.3 in the appendix. An overall capacity of 26 GW[10] is applied to calculate the absolute WPF in each hour of the modeling time horizon, i.e. one year.

The results show that the simulated series posses the same patterns and structure as the historical ones. Figure 5.11 shows that the historical and simulated WPF curve posses similar upwards and downwards fluctuations. More precisely, the length of upwards and downwards motions corresponds to a few hours (mostly <15 hours). Another similarity is the short duration of WPF peaks occurring also for only a few hours.

---

[10]This value corresponds to the installed wind power capacity in Germany at the end of 2010 (see BMU (2011))

Table 5.1.: Estimated parameters of the regression functions for m, μ^+, μ^-

	a_0	a_1	a_2
m	-0.02356	0.0011	—
μ^+	-0.0507	0.0541	0.0084
μ^-	0.0425	0.0039	—

Besides, it can be observed from Figure 5.11 that the duration curves of simulated capacity utilization matches very well the historical one. The root mean square error (RMSE), which is calculated on the basis of these duration curves, is equal to 2.06 %. That means that the single values of the duration curves averagely differ by 2.06 %. Considering the average capacity utilization level of wind power plants for Germany, i.e. 19.2 %, the error of 2.06 % for capacity utilization correpond to a percentage root mean square error (pRMSE) of 10.73 %. The low values for the absolute and the percentage RMSE indicate an acceptable goodness of fit. Therefore the introduced modeling approach represents an appropriate method to simulate capacity utilization series and respectively wind power feed-in paths for onshore wind power plants in Germany.

5.3.2. Results of the electricity price simulation with and w/o wind power impacts

Several electricity price simulations based on the basic and extended electricity price models are carried out, using different data series for model calibration. Thereby the models are at first calibrated using the data of a single year, e.g. 2008 or 2009, then applying the data of the whole period, price and WPF data are available for. In Germany, the data for electricity spot prices are available since 2002, i.e. since the foundation of the European Energy Exchange (EEX). However, WPF data are published since 2006 by the German transmission system

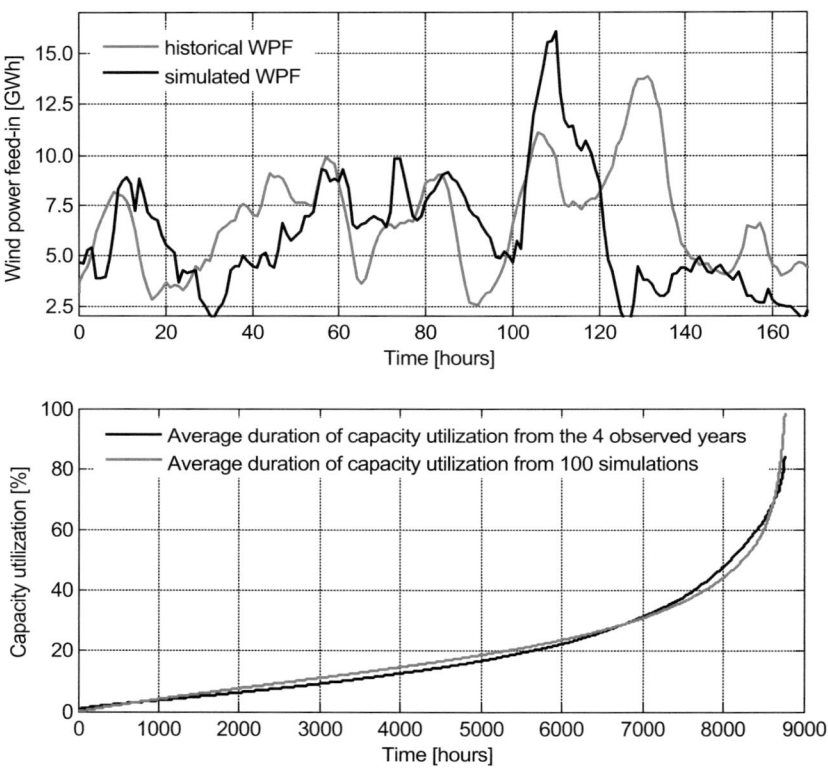

Figure 5.11.: Comparison of simulated and historical wind power feed-in (top) and duration curves of capacity utilization (bottom)

operators (TSOs). Therefore, the multi-annual modeling is limited to the period 2006 to 2009. Based on the data for these periods, available at EEX (2007) and BDEW (2013), the model parameters are separately determined (see Table 5.2).

Based on these estimated parameters, electricity price simulations are carried out. The graphical analysis of the simulations shows that the price paths, generated with both models, differ only slightly from each other. The deterministic components, such as daily and weekly cycles, are adequately captured by both models. The stochastic volatility is also well described by both models, as shown

Table 5.2.: Estimated model parameters

Period		2009		2006 - 2009	
Component		Basic	Extended	Basic	Extended
Trend	X_0	3.64	3.76	3.71	3.87
	γ	$-3.53e-05$	$-1.51e-05$	$-1.85e-06$	$-9.57e-09$
Weekly	α	-0.4730	-0.2708	-0.4858	-0.3840
Cycle	β	0.7420	0.4248	0.7628	0.6029
	ρ	-1.6643	-1.6643	-3.0107	-3.0107
AR-	α_i	1.686	1.610	1.640	1.611
param.		-0.676	-0.579	-0.598	-0.590
		-0.022	-0.045	-0.050	-0.025
		-0.065	0.000	-0.021	0.006
		0.063	0.009	0.022	-0.010
MA-p.	β_i	-0.932	-0.954	-0.927	-0.925
Normal	μ_{ε_t}	$3.78e-05$	$-1.09e-04$	$-1.96e-05$	$-1.12e-05$
distrib.	σ_{ε_t}	0.210	0.149	0.167	0.126

in the graphical illustration of the simulated and historical prices for a week (see Figure 5.12).

However, the effect of WPF on the prices and therefore the advances of the extended modeling approach become clearer, if the WPF paths and the price reduction paths of WPF are analysed (see Figure 5.13). The electricity prices are averagely reduced by some 5.90 €/MWh by an average WPF of about 4670 MW. But the price reduction reaches maximum values about 130 €/MWh at hours with high WPF.

Furthermore, the detailed analysis of error measures highlights the advances of the extended modeling approach. Again based on data for a single year on the one hand and for the whole period on the other, error measures, such as root mean square error (RMSE) and mean average percentage error (MAPE), are determined. The differences in the RMSEs, applying the data of the whole period, i.e. 2006 to

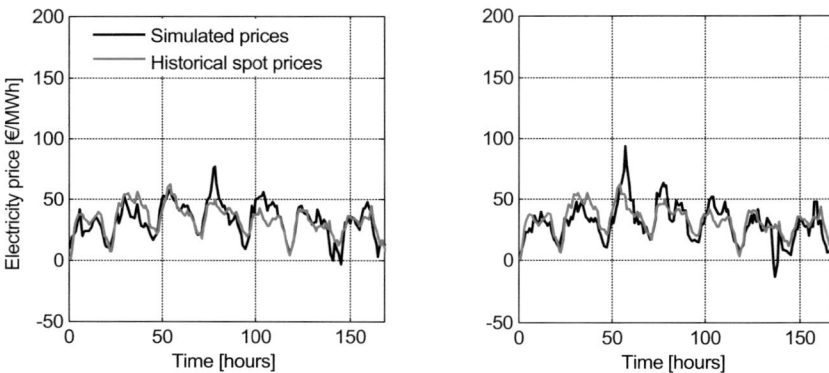

Figure 5.12.: Price simulation for a week based on 2009 data, considering WPF (left), without WPF impacts (right)

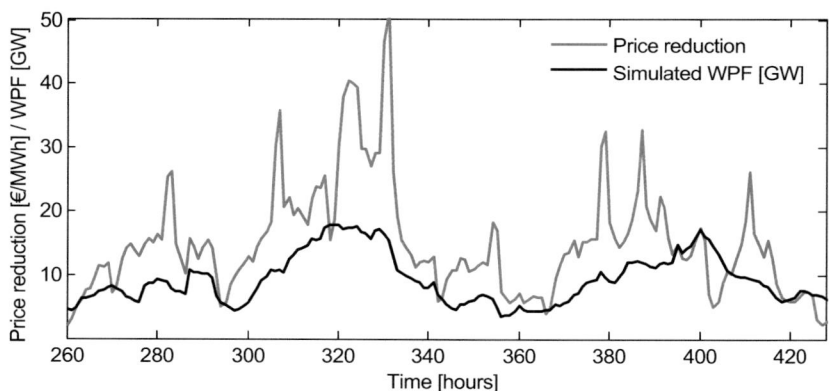

Figure 5.13.: Simulated WPF and absolute price reduction series

square error (RMSE) and mean average percentage error (MAPE), are determined. The differences in the RMSEs, applying the data of the whole period, i.e. 2006 to 2009, are less significant. The error terms are only slightly better for the extended case than for the basic case. However, if the MAPE is examined then the improvement by the extended modeling approach becomes more obvious, whereas the R^2 remains nearly unchanged.

Applying the 2009 data in both approaches, a significantly lower RMSE is determined for the price simulations via the extended model compared to the ones via the basic model. The MAPE corresponding to the extended approach with WPF is also noticeably lower than the one of the basic model, whereas a higher R^2 expectedly results from the extended model (see Table 5.3).

Table 5.3.: Calculated error measures and other parameters of the simulated prices

Period		2009		2006-2009	
Error measure		Basic	Extended	Basic	Extended
RMSE	€/MWh	7.58	5.54	5.36	4.93
MAPE	%	13.54	6.47	8.30	6.69
R^2	%	34.29	36.50	11.94	11.72
σ	€/MWh	22.09	19.51	29.38	27.52
kurtosis		15.72	71.40	418.99	546.82
μ	€/MWh	36.41	37.88	44.40	45.25
skewness		1.46	1.35	8.68	10.59

Summarily it can be stated that the extended modeling approach, considering the WPF impacts on electricity prices, leads to notably improvements of the electricity spot price simulation. It is also worth mentioning that the dependencies between WPF and electricity spot prices are captured by this approach and the simulated series of WPF and prices contain the correlation between each other. This is advantageous in particular, if assets, such as wind farms, are evaluated based on WPF series and on market prices instead of feed-in tariffs. Furthermore, the simulation of WPF and electricity prices can help to design and to optimize the operation of energy storage technologies. However, these evaluations and analyses are not in the scope of this study, but they can be addressed by future research.

5.4. Conclusions and future research

Wind power generation and feed-in have a significant impact on power prices. Especially in hours with high electricity demand (load) a high WPF leads to an immense price reduction, as the fed-in wind power avoids the dispatch of power plants with high variable costs, such as gas turbines. Therefore, an appropriate modeling approach for the simulation of the WPF is introduced based on an autoregressive method. It is worth mentioning that in this part of the thesis a direct modeling approach is chosen instead of the modeling of wind speeds and the calculation of WPF from the simulated wind speed series, a method, which can be often found in literature (see Safari (2011) and Gökcek et al. (2007)).

The introduced autoregressive method considers the WPF of the last eleven hours to determine the actual WPF incorporating a Laplace distributed term describing the change rate of the WPF. However, this method could be improved in future work considering not only the preceding capacity utilization and WPF values respectively for the calculation of the actual WPF value, but also the preceding change rates. This can be done by applying an autoregressive moving average (ARMA) model. The improvement potential with an ARMA approach for the simulation of WPF series may be limited, as the change rates of WPF are already extensively modeled. This can be checked in further work applying an ARMA approach for the simulation of WPF series. Anyway, the autoregressive approach developed in this study simulates appropriate WPF series, whose RMSE in percentage equals to only 10.73 % comparing the simulated series with the historical WPF series between 2006 and 2009.

Furthermore, it should be mentioned that the load-dependency of WPF impacts on electricity prices is only indirectly captured by calculating the WPF impacts, i.e. the price reduction, depending on the actual time of day (hour). Thereby it is assumed that the load varies over the day and its progress over the day is constant for each analysed day type. That is why the time of the day is used to diversify the price reduction, applying a separate linear regression of WPF series and electricity prices for each hour of the day. This approach could be specified, if the load series are directly incorporated into the modeling approach and the linear regression is carried out depending on load intervals and the related WPF series and electricity prices. However, this specification can be addressed in future research considering that a further uncertain variable, i.e. the load, has to be also modeled via an appropriate approach.

Finally, it is worth mentioning that the main outcome of this part is that the electricity price modeling can be significantly improved, if the price reduction effect of WPF is considered in the so-called extended electricity spot price model. The simulated price series posses significantly lower errors, especially a lower RMSE and MAPE, if the extended price model is applied. Besides, the combined approach of WPF and electricity price modeling captures the correlation between both parameters, which means that the simulated electricity price paths contains the impacts of the simulated WPF series. This issue is outstandingly important, if both series are used in a further evaluation approach. If e.g. a mark-to-market evaluation of wind power plants or integrated power plants, consiting of an energy storage and wind power plant, is to be carried out, then the simulated series for WPF and electricity prices are very reasonable, as the interdependencies between both series are considered in the modeling approach.

In the following chapter, the simulated wind power feed-in and electricity price series will be applied for the investment evalution of energy storages and integrated power plants under uncertainty.

6. Evaluation of energy storage and wind portfolios under uncertainty

Gas or hydropower plants can easily balance fluctuant feed-in of wind or PV electricity into the grid. Besides, emerging technologies like hydrogen storage (Ball and Wietschel (2009)) or new large-scale batteries can contribute to balance supply and demand, but they are still economically not viable. The gap between volatile electricity generation from renewable resources and load can also be bridged with the help of other bulk energy storage technologies, such as pumped storage hydropower (PSHP) or compressed-air energy storage (CAES) plants. At times of high wind power production and lower demand, for example, the surplus of electricity may be converted into pumped water or compressed air and stored in a upper reservoir and cavern respectively, from which the water or compressed air can be released again and used for electricity production at times of peak load and lower wind electricity production. PSHP and CAES plants can therefore contribute to the successful integration of large amounts of volatile wind-based electrical production capacity into the energy system (Arsie et al. (2007)). Therefore, the economic feasibility of both storage types is evaluated in the following.

6.1. Evaluation of bulk energy storage plants considering electricity price uncertainty

Several studies have been carried out to evaluate PSHP or CAES plants, operating in liberalized markets. However, most of the energy storage studies consider PSHP plants (Lu et al. (2004)) or battery storage systems (Kazempour et al. (2009)). While Lu et al. (2004) describe an optimal dispatch strategy for a PSHP plant based on deterministic weekly spot prices, Kazempour et al. (2009) optimize the bids of different storage technologies, such as batteries and PSHPs, on different energy markets including the day-ahead spot market, non-spinning and spinning reserve market. They use weekly deterministic prices to determine the optimal dispatch strategy of energy storages.

Beside the numerous studies about PSHP and other conventional energy storages, there are a meanwhile some studies which focus on CAES plants (see Greenblatt et al. (2007), Swider and Weber (2007), Lund et al. (2009), Drury et al. (2011) etc.). Greenblatt et al. (2007) describe how a "wind + CAES" system can operate as a base load power plant and compare the economic value of this system with "wind + gas turbine" systems, which can also provide base load. The economic analysis is based on the total cost of each system, so that the study does not include the market view and market prices for electricity. Swider and Weber (2007) analyze the role of CAES plants in an electricity system with significant wind power generation. They apply a bottom-up stochastic electricity system optimization model, in which new investments and technologies are added to the system minimizing the system total cost. The approach of Lund et al. (2009) optimizes the dispatch of the storage based on a profit maximizing approach, but deterministic prices only of the year 2003 from the Western Denmark system are applied in the modeling approach. Besides, auxiliary services, like providing reserve power, are not considered in their profit maximizing approach. In contrast, Drury et al. (2011) take the earnings on the reserve power market into account, but again they use deterministic historical prices of the years 2007 to 2009 from the NYISO market to determine the plant value.

As there is no study evaluating PSHP and CAES plants under uncertain electricity prices and renewable energy generation - according to the knowledge of the author -, this study focuses on the evaluation of energy storage investments under these uncertain parameters. To carry out the evaluation under uncertainty, a stochastic dynamic programming (SDP) model has been developed (see section 6.1.2.5). The SDP model optimizes the dispatch of PSHP and CAES plants, whereby the real option to delay the dispatch is also considered. The economical evaluation of both plant types based on the SDP model are compared with each other and also with the results of other storage dispatch strategies, such as a "simple strategy under uncertainty" and a Monte-Carlo simulation of plant dispatch under perfect price foresight assumption (see section 6.1.2).

But before the dispatch strategies for energy storage power plants are described in detail, the analysed plant types, i.e. PSHP and CAES plants, are shortly introduced in the following.

6.1.1. Large scale power storage plants

Bulk energy storages play an important role to balance the discrepancy between the electrical load and power production. On the one side they help to store the energy for several hours in times of electricity overproduction and to deliver the energy again to the system in times when electricity is most needed, e.g. if the electrical load is peaking. On the other side bulk storages help to provide reserve power to keep the transmission system stable (see Black and Strbac (2007)). Especially, PSHP and CAES plants can act in the minute and secondary reserve power market and deliver electricity within a few minutes according to the design of these markets.

6.1.1.1. Pumped storage hydropower plants

PSHP plants are large-scale energy storage facilities, which transform electrical energy into potential energy and enable the storage of large amounts of energy. First PSHP plants were developed at the end of the 19th century following the general development of hydropower. Today this plant type is the most applied technology for the transformation and storage of electrical energy (see Gieseke et al. (2005) and Sterner et al. (2010)). PSHP plants are operated in two modes: the first is the "pump operation" mode, in which electricity is used to pump water from a lower reservoir into a higher one. In the so called "reservoir operation" mode, the water is released back to the lower basin running a turbine and generator to produce again electricity.

More detailed, the water, which is needed for the operation of PSHP plants, is available in the lower reservoir, which can be an artificial or natural lake or a river. The lower and the upper reservoirs are connected with a penstock, which passes

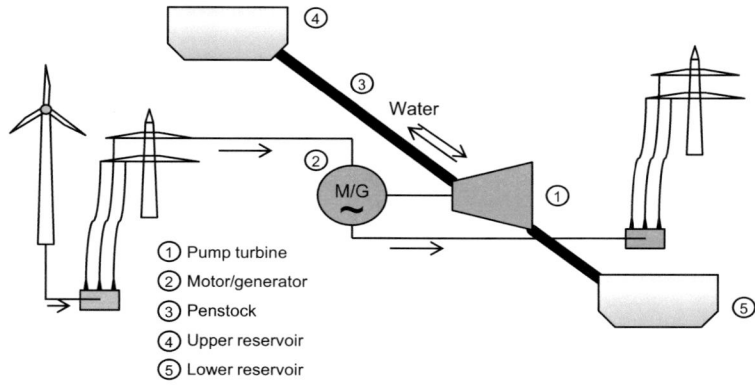

Figure 6.1.: Design of an PSHP plant (source: own illustration)

the power house at the lower reservoir. The power house contains the technical devices, which are needed to generate power or to transform electricity into potential energy, i.e. pump, turbine and generator/motor (see Figure 6.1). In many newer PSHP power plants the pump and turbine make up a single device, which can execute both operations. The application of the so-called pump-turbines reduces the amount of investment, as a smaller number of devices is installed at the plant. Furthermore, in larger PSHP plants there is a group of pump-turbines instead of a single one, so that in some plants the capacity is increased to more than 1000 MW (e.g. Goldisthal PSHP plant).

Some economical issues have to be considered operating PSHP power plants. The total efficiency of such power plants reaches values of at most about 80 % due to losses during the pump or turbine operation (the PSHP plants installed in Germany possess a technical efficiency between 60 % and 80 %, see DENA (2010)). The energy losses of pump and turbine operation have to be balanced by the price spread between the prices during both operations. An economical operation is only reasonable if the "efficiency adjusted" price spread is positive. Beside the efficiency of PSHP plants, the storage capacity plays a key role for an economical operation. Technically, the storage capacity is determined by the volume of the upper reservoir and the head of water. To optimize the total costs of a PSHP plants, a larger storage capacity is desirable, but higher construction costs have to be also added into the calculation. Therefore, storage volume and costs have to be balanced in a sensitive manner. The average storage capacity of the PSHP plants operated in Germany corresponds to about 6.1 full load hours of the installed turbine capacity (see Sterner et al. (2010)).

PSHP plants are used to achieve some techno-economic targets. The main goal of PSHP operation is to transform off-peak energy to peak load electricity. Originally energy was bought and stored during off-peak time, when baseload power plants produced electricity in surplus, and the stored energy was transformed to electricity and sold at peak load hours, when electricity supply was scarce and thus prices were quite high. However, since the share of fluctuant renewable energies increased, electricity surpluses are no more limited to off-peak hours, so that PSHP plants are nowadays also used to balance fluctuant electricity generation from renewable energy sources. Beside these reasons for PSHP plant commitment, these plants are also used to deliver some basic ancillary services, such as delivering secondary or minute reserve power (see Gieseke et al. (2005)). Besides, PSHP plants are also used for black starts after a power failure in the grid or in its sections (see OakRidge (2010)). Hence, PSHP plants play an important role for a smooth running of the electricity system.

6.1.1.2. Compressed air energy storage power plants

Compressed air energy storage (CAES) can store energy in the form of compressed air in large caverns. Although the concept of this technology exists since the 1970ies, there are only two operating CAES power plants in the world (Huntorf constructed in 1978, McIntosh in 1991). However, several power plant projects of this type are nowadays discussed worldwide (see BINE (2007), van der Linden (2006)), as energy storage becomes more and more important due to the strong extension of fluctuant electricity generation.

CAES power plants are operated in two modes: compressor operation and turbine operation mode. During the compressor operation ambient air is drawn in and compressed into a storage, which is generally a subsurface cavern. However, there are also plans for artificial storages above the ground (see Schoenung and Burns (1996) or Baker (2008)). But as this type of storage is costlier, the favored option will remain natural caverns. Furthermore, the storages have to possess large volumes, as the energy intensity of the compressed air is quite low. Hence, large geologic formations serve as appropriate storage chambers (see EPRI-DOE (2003)).

During the turbine operation, the compressed air is released and heated up, before it is fed to a turbine to generate again electricity. The heating of the released air is necessary, as gases cool down, if they are expanded in a turbine. For an efficient turbine operation it is essential that the air possess ambient temperature after its expansion at the turbine. The heating up of the compressed air can be carried out burning natural gas at the turbine or the heat can come from a heat storage, which could be filled with the heat resulting from the earlier compression process. If gas is burned with compressed air at the turbine and thus external heat is added to the system, the process is called diabatic and the corresponding plants diabatic CAES (see Figure 6.2 and EPRI-DOE (2003)). If no external heat is added to the system (plant), the process and the CAES are called adiabatic (see Zunft et al. (2006)).

Diabatic CAES do not use the heat which originates from the compression process. This heat is released to the environment with the help of heat exchangers. The heat release leads to important energy and efficiency losses. Energy losses can occur also during a possible cooling down of compressed air in the storage. To heat up the compressed air, it is mixed with natural gas in the turbine and the gas mix is burned in the turbine generating electricity. This type of turbine operation corresponds to that of a regular gas turbine operation. Both existing CAES types are based on this technology.

The total efficiency of a diabatic CAES power plant cannot be easily determined, as the total plant operation uses partly off-peak electricity and partly natural gas for generating electricity in peak load times. Actually, these plants reach a roundtrip efficiency above 50%, if they are operated at their optimum workload. Compared to a usual gas turbine, the CAES turbine operation itself is more effi-

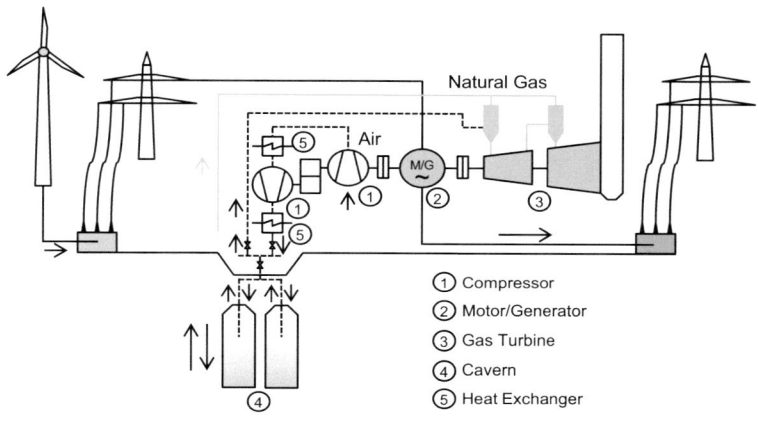

Figure 6.2.: The structure of a CAES power plant (source: own illustration)

cient. The required gas amount for generating a kWh electricity is reduced from 3 kWh gas to approximately 1.5 kWh (see Gatzen (2008)). A CAES power plant is also very efficient, if the turbine is run at partial load, as the amount of compressed air used for turbine operation can be exactly regulated. This is due to the fact that the required compressed air comes from the storage and not from pre-operated compressors (see EPRI-DOE (2003)). The availability of a storage enables the operation of the compressor at its optimum workload, although the turbine is run at partial load.

In an adiabatic CAES power plant the heat, which comes from the air compression process, is transferred to a heat medium with the help of heat exchangers. This heat is again used for the heating of the compressed air, before it is lead in to the turbine. Depending on the size of the heat storage, the additional burning of natural gas can be reduced or completely replaced. The use of the compression heat increases the efficiency of the total plant to values above 65 % (see EPRI-DOE (2003)). Therefore, this technology is in the focus of research and development departments of major companies. A first pilot plant is planned to be constructed in Strassfurt (Germany) by RWE (see ADELE project, RWE (2013)).

Similar to PSHP plants, CAES power plants are also used for the short-term storage of electricity and its supply at peak load times. They balance the load between off-peak and peak times. They can be also used for short-term load balancing, as they can deliver positive or negative reserve power. The black start capability is a further ancillary service that can be provided by CAES power plants. It is expected that CAES power plants will also contribute to the smooth feed-in of fluctuant renewable electricity generation in the near future. Therefore, the focus will be set in their techno-economical evaluation in the following.

6.1.2. Models and strategies for dispatching energy storage power plants under uncertainty

Different methods and strategies can be applied to optimise the dispatch of energy storages and to evaluate PSHP and diabatic CAES based on the return of these optimal dispatch strategies. As many of the existing approaches incorporate deterministic input parameters known a priori, in this part of the thesis methodologies are developed that can capture uncertain parameters. Uncertainties considered within the different approaches are electricity spot prices and wind power generation. All evaluation approaches focus on the assessment of energy stroage investments based on optimum annual returns. Optimum annual returns are calculated based on hourly cash flows, which are generated applying different strategies for storage dispatch. For each strategy a different modeling approach is introduced, whereby the same input data is applied in all models. Figure 6.3 gives a general overview about the structure, input data and output of the models.

The different models for each dispatch strategy use electricity spot prices, that are simulated with the electricity models described in chapter 4. Further economic parameters, such as CO_2-certificate prices, gas prices or variable and fix costs, and technical parameters (efficiency, turbine and pump capacity, storage volume etc.) are also incorporated into the models. Besides, bids on two markets (day-ahead spot and minute reserve power market) are considered to increase the annual return. The results of the models contain the optimal annual return, the amount of bids on both markets and technical parameters, such as full load hours of turbine

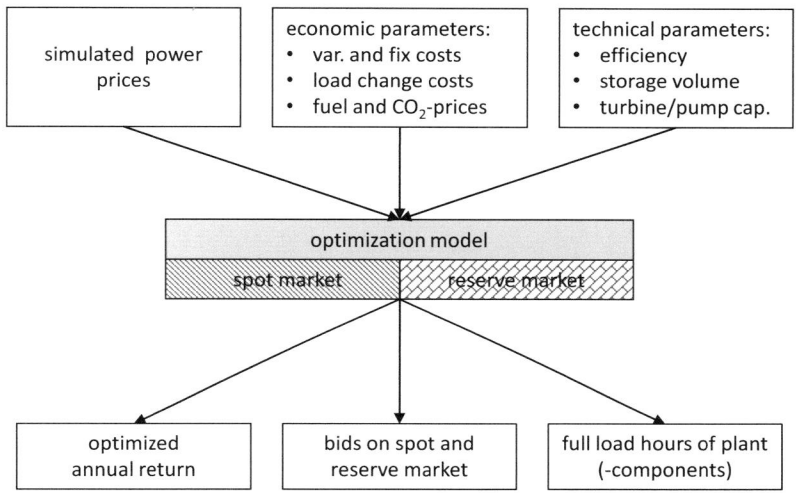

Figure 6.3.: Overview of model input/output and structure

and pump or compressor. However, these results can strongly vary depending on the dispatch strategy and the appropriate model (see section 6.1.3).

Four dispatch strategies and models have been developed: In the first strategy, the prices are assumed to be known apriori and an overall optimization with perfect price foresight is carried out for given yearly price paths. More precisely, a Monte-Carlo simulation, maximizing the annual return for 1000 different price paths, is applied to get an expected value for the optimal annual return. The second strategy is called "simple strategy under uncertainty", whereby the spread between peak and off-peak prices is compared and if this spread is positive within a single day, the energy storage is charged and discharged producing electricity in the peak hours of the day. The daily returns for each price scenario are cumulated via a stochastic recombining tree to determine the annual return.

The third strategy is again based on an optimization approach, which is maximizing the cash flows day-by-day, which in turn are added up to the annual return based on the same stochastic tree for uncertain price development. The fourth and main strategy applies a stochastic dynamic programming (SDP) approach with the help of the same recombining tree and optimizes jointly the daily cash flows and expected returns of future days. These four strategies will be precisely described in the following.

6.1.2.1. First strategy: perfect foresight optimization with Monte-Carlo simulation

Within the Monte-Carlo simulation[1], the annual return R is separately maximized for each run of an optimization problem, which calculates the optimal dispatch of a PSHP or a CAES power plant in each hour h of the year considering of several constraints, e.g. storage level constraint. In total 1000 runs of the optimization model are carried out forming the Monte-Carlo simulation. A higher number of runs (e.g. 10000) is also possible, but it would lead to very long calculation times without significantly improving the results.

The different runs of the Monte Carlo simulation[2] are performed based on different annual price paths, which themselves are realizations of the electricity spot price model (see section 4.2). This means, within a model run the annual return of the energy storage plant is optimized assuming a perfect foresight of electricity prices. That is why the result of the Monte-Carlo simulation for the annual return can be seen as an upper limit and the net present value calculated from these annual returns represents a maximum value.

Having a closer look at the optimization model, which is used in the Monte-Carlo simulation, it can be noted that the annual return R forms the objective function, which describes the sum of contribution margins in all of the 8760 hours of the year. The contribution margins themselves are calculated based on the bidding strategy of the operator on spot and reserve power markets. This means that the operator of such a plant has the possibility to generate income either on the spot market by selling electricity or on the reserve power market by offering the turbine capacity of the storage plant. More precisely, the turbine capacity can be

---

[1]Monte-Carlo techniques are also applied to electricity markets by Amelin (2004) dicussing which electricity market models are suited for Monte-Carlo simulation. Khalid and Langhe (2010) also apply Monte-Carlo techniques to carry out energy demand forecasts.

[2]For the definition and procedure of a Monte Carlo simulation see also Binder and Heermann (2010).

offered in the minute reserve power market[3]. This is due to the fact that PSHP and CAES plants fulfill the requirements of the minute reserve market[4], as they need a start-up time of only some seconds or a few minutes respectively (see Stoddard (1996)).

The amount of electricity sold in hour h on the spot market is defined as X_h^{spot} and the power sold on the reserve market as $X_{ts}^{reserve}$[5]. X_h^{spot} is priced with the electricity price p_h^{EL} received from the electricity price simulation. The amount of power sold in the reserve power market $X_{ts}^{reserve}$ has to be provided for a time slice (ts) of four hours. As the reserve power market has a different time solution, the hours of a year have to be matched with $4h$-time slices ts. Four subsequent hours starting with hour h_1 are matched to the same time slice ts_1 and the next four hours to the next time slice ts_2 and so on. At the end, 2190 time slices are received for 8760 hours of a year[6]. Due to this so-called slice-map, six time slices are modeled for each day. This procedure enables the formulation of a single optimization problem for both, reserve power and spot electricity.

The reserve power $X_{ts}^{reserve}$ of time slice ts is charged with the minimum prices $p_{ts}^{reserve}$ observed on the minumum reserve power market. Minimum prices are chosen, to guarantee that the power offered on this market is completely sold. This approach also maximizes the annual return of the energy storage plants for the worst case on the reserve market. Alternatively, for a less risk-averse investor this assumption can be changed by using average or even maximum historical reserve power prices. However, the analysis is continued for the risk-averse investor in the following applying minimum prices as reserve power prices. This approach captures the guaranteed income on the reserve power market.

A further assumption is that no costs for turbine operation occur if the turbine capacity is sold on the reserve power market. This is due to simplification reasons,

---

[3]In this thesis only the minute reserve market is considered for the evaluation of both energy storage types. However, in the case of PSHP plants the secondary reserve power market can play also a role, which can be adressed by future reasearch.

[4]The technical constraint of this market requires that reserve energy has to be delivered after 15 minutes if it is requested (see section 2.1.2).

[5]For bidding strategies on the spot market based on uncertain prices (see also Conejo et al. (2003)).

[6]For simplification reasons, leap years are not considered.

as it is assumed that the reserve power $X_{ts}^{reserve}$ has to be kept ready, but is not delivered[7]. Therefore, no electricity has to be produced and thus no gas, CO_2-certificates or compressed air and water from the reservoir respectively are used in this mode. The energy only has to be kept in the cavern storage / reservoir to guarantee the capacity within the time during which the sold reserve power must remain available. This is one of the main constraints of the optimization problem discussed in the following.

$$max\ R(S_h, X_h^{spot}, X_h^{comp}, X_{ts}^{reserve}) = \sum_{h=1}^{8760} \left[\begin{array}{c} \left(\begin{array}{c} p_h^{EL} - p_h^{FU} \cdot \frac{1}{\mu^{FU}} \\ -p_h^{CER} \cdot \frac{1}{\mu^{FU}} \cdot EF^{FU} - c_{var}^{turb} \end{array} \right) \cdot X_h^{spot} \\ -(p_h^{EL} + c_{var}^{comp}) \cdot X_h^{comp} \\ -c^{turb,LC} \cdot X_h^{turb,LC} \\ -c^{comp,LC} \cdot X_h^{comp,LC} \end{array} \right]$$

$$+ \sum_{ts=1}^{2190} p_{ts}^{reserve} \cdot X_{ts}^{reserve}$$

$$[6.1]$$

Major cost components within the objective function (Eq. 6.1) are expenses for the amount of electricity X_h^{comp}, which the compressor or the pump needs to charge the storage with compressed air and water respectively. Further cost components are - in the case of the diabatic CAES plant - gas costs and CO_2-certificate costs. These costs depend on the amount of electricity produced and sold on the spot market. The gas amount used for electricity production is equal to the produced electricity sold on the spot market X_h^{spot} multiplied by the "fuel factor" $1/\mu^{FU}$. The fuel factor defines the amount of gas needed to produce 1 MWh electricity in the diabatic CAES plant. The gas volume used in each hour h is valued using appropriate gas prices of the year 2011. The CO_2-emissions are calculated as

---

[7]This simplification is reasoned by the fact, that the reserve power is evaluated by minimum reserve power prices, assuming that the offers for reserve energy prices can be kept very high to avoid the delivery of energy. In reality, minute reserve energy is delivered, if the difference between load and electricity feed-in to the grid cannot be balanced with primary and secondary reserve energy.

the product of the fuel consumption and the emission factor EF_{FU}, which is here assumed to be $0.2\,t/MWh$ for gas (own calculation based on the data from Wagner (2007)). The CO_2-emissions are also priced with historical prices p_d^{CER} of the year 2011. However, in the case of a PSHP plant no gas and CO_2-emissions will occur, so that the objective function can be formulated as follows:

$$max\,R(S_h, X_h^{spot}, X_h^{pump}, X_{ts}^{reserve}) = \sum_{h=1}^{8760} \left[\begin{array}{c} \left(p_h^{EL} - c_{var}^{turb}\right) \cdot X_h^{spot} \\ -\left(p_h^{EL} + c_{var}^{pump}\right) \cdot X_h^{pump} \\ -c^{turb,LC} \cdot X_h^{turb,LC} \\ -c^{comp,LC} \cdot X_h^{pump,LC} \end{array} \right] \qquad [6.2]$$

$$+ \sum_{ts=1}^{2190} p_{ts}^{reserve} \cdot X_{ts}^{reserve}$$

The objective function above has to be solved under the so-called "storage constraint". The turbine can be run and electricity or power capacity can be sold in hour h or time slice ts to that amount to which the storage level S_h makes it possible. The storage level is measured by the electricity output, which can be produced with the compressed air in the cavern (in units of MWh_{el}). S_h is increased by the electricity amount used for the compressor or pump power X_h^{comp} multiplied by the "compressed air factor (CAF)" and pump efficiency μ_{pump} respectively. These factors define how much electricity can be produced with $1MWh_{el}$ stored energy. For example, the CAF of the diabatic CAES plant analysed here equals to the quotient $1/0.66$. This in turn indicates that $0.66MWh_{el}$ compressed air is needed for one MWh_{el} turbine output. Accordingly if the pump efficiency μ_{pump} of the PSHP plant corresponds to e.g. 0.8, this suggests that $1/0.8MWh_{el}$ electricity is needed for one MWh_{el} turbine output. The turbine output, which correponds to the power sold on the spot market X_h^{spot}, contrarily reduces the storage level S_h. Eq. 6.3 defines this relationship:

$$S_h = S_{h-1} + X_h^{comp} \cdot CAF - X_h^{spot} \quad \forall h = 2..8760$$
$$S_h = S_{h-1} + X_h^{pump} \cdot \mu_{pump} - X_h^{spot} \quad \forall h = 2..8760$$
$$[6.3]$$

A further constraint regarding the storage level describes the relationship between the sold reserve power $X_{ts}^{reserve}$ and the storage level S_h itself (6.4).

$$X_{ts}^{reserve} \leq \min_{h \in ts} \left[\frac{1}{4} S_h \right] \quad \forall ts \in TS \qquad [6.4]$$

Eq. 6.4 also shows that the sold reserve power $X_{ts}^{reserve}$ is lower or equal to a quarter of the storage level. This is caused by the fact that bids on the minute reserve power market have to last for four hours in the German energy market. This indicates that the storage level has to guarantee the offered reserve power for these four hours (see Bundesnetzagentur (2011a)). A reserve market bid for a time slice ts is then limited by the minimum quarter of the storage levels within the hours of this time slice.

Another constraint limits the offered power amount on both markets, as the sold reserve power $X_{ts}^{reserve}$ and the power sold on the spot market X_h^{spot} cannot in sum exceed the maximum turbine capacity X_{max}^{turb}:

$$X_h^{spot} + X_{ts}^{reserve} \leq X_{max}^{turb} \quad \forall h \in ts \wedge \forall ts \in TS \qquad [6.5]$$

Furthermore the offers in the different markets also have a minimum limit. They have to be above the minimum turbine capacity X_{min}^{turb} or equal to zero. The amount of electricity bought to run the compressor or pump has also to be above their minimum capacity X_{min}^{comp}. These constraints result from the technical feature of the power storage components, as they cannot be run under their minimum capacity:

$$X_{min}^{turb} \leq X_h^{spot}, X_{rs}^{reserve} \quad \vee \quad X_h^{spot}, X_{ts}^{reserve} = 0 \quad \forall h = 1..8760, ts \in TS \qquad [6.6]$$

$$X_{min}^{comp} \leq X_h^{comp} \leq X_{max}^{comp} \quad \vee \quad X_h^{comp} = 0 \quad \forall h = 1..8760 \qquad [6.7]$$

The last constraints ensure that the load variation $X_h^{turb,LC}$ and $X_h^{comp,LC}$ within an hour corresponds to the difference between power output before and after the load variation. This constraint holds for both the compressor/pump and the turbine. As the turbine output is sold on the spot market, the load variation equals to the difference between the sold electricity ΔX_h^{spot} in hours h and $h-1$ (see 6.8).

$$X_h^{turb,LC} = \left| X_h^{spot} - X_{h-1}^{spot} \right| \; , \; X_h^{comp,LC} = \left| X_h^{comp} - X_{h-1}^{comp} \right| \quad \forall h = 2..8760 \quad [6.8]$$

Finally, it is worth mentioning that, applying a Monte-Carlo simulation with 1000 scenarios in the software environment GAMS, the calculation time of the perfect foresight model is about 8 hours on an PC with Intel Core Duo CPU 2.4 GHz and 4 GB RAM.

6.1.2.2. Scenario tree for strategies under uncertainty

The method described in section 6.1.2.1 assumes a perfect price foresight of electricity spot prices, which is not given in real markets. Therefore, other methods and strategies that capture this price uncertainty will be developed in the following and compared with the best case approach, the perfect price foresight. However, to apply the new methods, at first a stochastic tree describing the price development has to be generated. The 1000 price paths applied in the Monte-Carlo simulation are "reduced" to a recombining stochastic tree following the approach described by Weber (2005):

The first step of the tree generation is that each of the 1000 price paths is divided into 365 price sections, which represent prices for the 24 hours of each day d. The seperated price paths are moved to a three-dimensional price matrix. Its first dimension stands for the 1000 price paths, the second for the 365 days, the third for the 24 hours in each price section. The price matrix is used to reduce the price scenarios s and to generate a scenario tree applying the k-means algorithm (see MacQueen (1967)). The resulting tree describes either ten or thirty price clusters ps for each day d, whereby each price cluster is represented by its centroid[8] of the cluster (see Figure 6.4).

Beside the price clusters and their centroids, transition probabilities between price clusters ps on day d and ps' on day $d+1$ are necessary to generate the recombining tree. These transition probabilities are calculated based on the number

---

[8]The centroid is defined as the price section (24 hours-price path) that has the smallest distance sum from the other price sections, which are grouped into the same cluster.

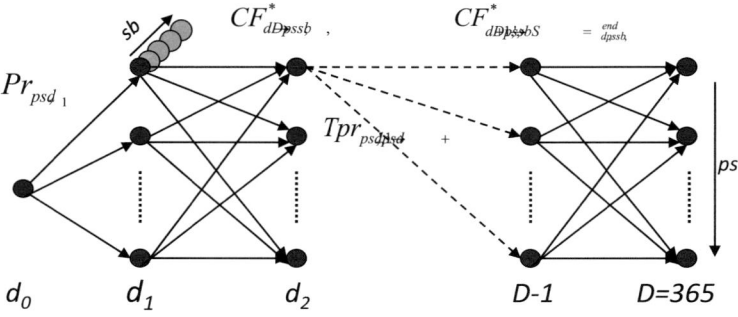

Figure 6.4.: Recombining tree for the price development

of transitions between price scenarios clustered in ps and price scenarios clustered in ps'. The number of these transitions is divided by the total number of transitions from ps to all clusters on day $d+1$ to receive the transition probability $Tpr_{d,ps\rightarrow d+1,ps'}$.

$$Tpr_{d,ps\rightarrow d+1,ps'} = \frac{card\left\{s|\forall s_d \in ps_d \wedge s_{d+1} \in ps'_{d+1}\right\}}{card\left\{s|\forall s_d \in ps_d\right\}} \qquad [6.9]$$

The transitions to the price clusters on the first day d_1 correspond to the probabilities of occurrence of the first day clusters. They are calculated as the ratio between scenarios matched to the price clusters and the total number of price scenarios of d_1.

$$Pr_{d_1,ps} = \frac{card\left\{s|\forall s_d \in ps_{d_1}\right\}}{card\left\{s\right\}} \qquad [6.10]$$

Based on these probabilities and the price cluster centroids ps, which represent the prices for 24 hours of day d, the power plant is dispatched applying the following models and strategies respectively.

6.1.2.3. Second strategy: simple model under uncertainty

A simple strategy can be a heuristic approach that focuses on electricity prices in peak hours p^p and offpeak p^{op} hours[9]. If the spread between peak prices p^p and offpeak prices p^{op} is positive, then the operator of an energy storage will be willing to exploit this timely arbitrage opportunity. He will therefore charge the storage at off-peak hours and discharge it and run the turbine at peak hours.

A simple strategy under uncertainty could work then in a way that the operator compares the highest price of peak time h_1^p with the lowest price at off peak-time h_1^{op} in each day d and corresponding price scenario ps. Based on these prices the spread between charging and discharging the storage is calculated. If the price spread is positive, these hours are added to a list K representing the positive spreads. Then the next hours h_2^p and h_2^{op} are analysed and if the spread is again positive, they are also added to the list K. This procedure is repeated k-times resulting in a list K, in which the last positive spread can be found between the prices of the hours h_k^p and h_k^{op}.

Based on the positive spread list K, the operator purchases electricity from the spot market and runs the energy storage plant in the pump mode with full load X_{max}^{pump} beginning in the hour h_1^{op} until h_k^{op}. If the difference between storage capacity S^{max} and the storage level $S_{h_j^{op}}$ is smaller than X_{max}^{pump} times η^{tot} than the pump output is adjusted to this difference. It is important to stress that the storage level S_h is again noted as the amount of output power producable with the stored energy amount.

$$X_{h_j^{op}}^{pump} = \begin{cases} X_{max}^{pump} & if\ S^{max} - S_{h_j^{op}} \geq \eta^{tot} X_{max}^{pump} \\ (S^{max} - S_{h_j^{op}})/\eta^{tot} & if\ 0 \leq S^{max} - S_{h_j^{op}} \leq \eta^{tot} X_{max}^{pump} \quad \forall h_j^{op} = h_1^{op}..h_k^{op} \\ 0 & else \end{cases}$$

$$[6.11]$$

The term $(S^{max} - S_{h_j^{op}})/\eta^{tot}$ has to be changed into $(S^{max} - S_{h_j^{op}}) \cdot CAF$, where CAF is again the "compressed air factor" described in section 6.1.2.1, if the com-

---

[9]Due to the electricity market design of the European Energy Exchange (EEX), peak hours are defined as the time between 8:00 and 20:00, while the offpeak time is contrarily the time between 20:00 and 08:00.

pressor output of the CAES plant $X_{h_j^{op}}^{comp}$ is calculated. The change of the storage level according to this operation of the pump and compressor respectively corresponds to:

$$S_{h_j^{op}} = S_{h_j^{op}-1} + \eta^{tot} \cdot X_{h_j^{op}}^{pump} \quad \forall h_j^{op} = h_1^{op}..h_k^{op}$$
$$S_{h_j^{op}} = S_{h_j^{op}-1} + CAF \cdot X_{h_j^{op}}^{comp} \quad \forall h_j^{op} = h_1^{op}..h_k^{op} \qquad [6.12]$$

In the peak hours h_1^p to h_k^p the plant is operated in the full load turbine mode X_{max}^{turb} as long as the storage is not empty. If the storage level $S_{h_j^p}$ is smaller than the maximum output capacity of the turbine, then the turbine output level $X_{h_j^p}^{turb}$ is reduced to this level $S_{h_j^p}$. A simplification within this strategy is that all the content of the storage has to be emptied until the end of the day. Thus, the turbine is operated until $S_{h_j^p}$ equals to "0".

$$X_{h_j^p}^{turb} = \begin{cases} X_{max}^{turb} & if \ S_{h_j^p} \geq X_{max}^{turb} \\ S_{h_j^p} & if \ 0 \leq S_{h_j^p} \leq X_{max}^{turb} \\ 0 & else \end{cases} \qquad [6.13]$$

The produced electricity is sold again on the spot market earning a positive daily return or contribution margin $CM_{d,ps}$. In the case of a PSHP plant, the dailiy return $CM_{d,ps}$ can be calculated as follows:

$$CM_{d,ps} = \sum_{j=1}^{k_{d,ps}} \left(p^{EL}(h_j^p) X_{h_j^p}^{turb} - p^{EL}(h_j^{op}) X_{h_j^{op}}^{pump} \right) \qquad [6.14]$$

The daily return of a CAES power plant is calculated by subtracting further cost components from the term in Eq. 6.14. Notably, the costs for gas and CO_2-certificates, which are necessary if electricity is produced, have to be regarded in the daily return calculation. The extended calculation is then formulated in Eq. 6.15.

$$CM_{d,ps} = \sum_{j=1}^{k_{d,ps}} \left[\begin{pmatrix} p^{EL}(h_j^p) - p_h^{FU} \cdot \frac{1}{\mu^{FU}} \\ -p_h^{CER} \cdot \frac{1}{\mu^{FU}} \cdot EF^{FU} - c_{var}^{turb} \end{pmatrix} \cdot X_{h_j^p}^{turb} \\ -(p^{EL}(h_j^{op}) + c_{var}^{comp}) \cdot X_{h_j^{op}}^{comp} \right] \qquad [6.15]$$

Based on the daily return for each day d and price scenario ps the annual return R can be determined. The daily returns are summed up considering the transition probabilities from price scenarios ps at day d to price scenarios ps' on day $d+1$. For example, the daily returns $CM_{d+1 \to D, ps'}$ from day $d+1$ to D are weighted with the appropriate transition probability $Tpr_{d,ps \to d+1,ps'}$ and added to the daily return $CM_{d,ps}$ of day d, resulting in the overall return $CM_{d \to D, ps}$ from d to D.

$$CM_{d \to D, ps} = CM_{d,ps} + \sum_{ps'} Tpr_{d,ps \to d+1,ps'} \cdot CM_{d+1 \to D, ps'} \quad \forall d = 1..364 \quad [6.16]$$

The backwards calculation of the $CF_{d \to D, ps}$ from D to d_1 delivers the annual return for different ps_{d_1}. The $CF_{d_1 \to D, ps}$ are weighted with the occurrence probability of each ps_{d_1}, resulting in the expected value of the annual return R.

$$R = \sum_{ps} Pr_{d_1, ps} \cdot CM_{d_1 \to D, ps} \qquad [6.17]$$

The simple strategy is implemented in the MATLAB software environment. The calculation time equals to only a few seconds on the same PC mentioned in section 6.1.2.1.

6.1.2.4. Third strategy: day-by-day optimization

The day-by-day optimization differs from the "simple strategy under uncertainty" in a way that the daily commitment of the storage components is optimized. Thereby, the daily returns $CM_{d,ps}$ are maximized running a mixed-integer linear program (MILP). The objective function of the MILP again represents the contribution margin, but contrarily to the prefect foresight model (section 6.1.2.1) only the one of the next 24 hours. The extended daily return $CM_{d,ps,sb}$ is calculated for each price cluster ps and for different starting storage levels sb at day d. The optimization is then carried out for the distinguished variables, storage volume $S_{d,ps,sb,h}$, spot market bid $X_{d,ps,sb,h}^{spot}$ and reserve market bids $X_{d,ps,sb,ts}^{reserve,pos}$ and $X_{d,ps,sb,ts}^{reserve,neg}$ as well as compressor or pump output $X_{d,ps,sb,h}^{comp/pump}$ for each hour h of day d, price cluster (scenario) ps and starting the storage level sb. The income and cost components are the same as in the perfect price foresight approach. However, this time they are separately calculated for each price scenario ps and starting level

sb on each day d. The objective function of the dispatch problem of a CAES can be formulated as follows[10]:

$$max\ CM_{d,ps,sb}(X^{spot}_{d,ps,sb,h}, \ldots) = \sum_{h=1}^{24} \begin{bmatrix} \left(\begin{array}{c} p^{EL}_{d,ps,h} - p^{FU}_d \cdot \frac{1}{\mu^{FU}} \\ -p^{CER}_d \cdot \frac{1}{\mu^{FU}} \cdot EF^{FU} - c^{turb}_{var} \end{array} \right) \cdot X^{spot}_{d,ps,sb,h} \\ -\left(p^{EL}_{d,ps,h} + c^{comp}_{var} \right) \cdot X^{comp}_{d,ps,sb,h} \\ -c^{turb,LC} \cdot X^{turb,LC}_{d,ps,sb,h} \\ -c^{comp,LC} \cdot X^{comp,LC}_{d,ps,sb,h} \end{bmatrix}$$

$$+ \sum_{ts=1}^{6} \left(p^{reserve,pos}_{d,ts} \cdot X^{reserve,pos}_{d,ps,sb,ts} + p^{reserve,neg}_{d,ts} \cdot X^{reserve,neg}_{d,ps,sb,ts} \right)$$

[6.18]

The solution to this optimization problem has to be subject to the same restrictions as in the perfect price foresight approach, but again further distinguished for the price scenarios ps and starting levels sb. The formulation of the model restrictions is illustrated for the CAES model in Eq. 6.19, but it can be anlogously formulated for the PSHP plant.

$$S_{d,ps,sb,h} = S_{d,ps,sb,h-1} + X^{comp}_{d,ps,sb,h} \cdot CAF - X^{spot}_{d,ps,sb,h} \quad \forall h = 2..24$$

$$X^{reserve,pos}_{d,ps,sb,ts} \leq \min_{h \in ts} \left[\frac{1}{4} S_{d,ps,sb,h} \right] \quad \forall ts \in TS$$

$$X^{reserve,neg}_{d,ps,sb,ts} \leq \min_{h \in ts} \left[\frac{1}{4} \left(S^{max} - S_{d,ps,sb,h} \right) \right] \quad \forall ts \in TS$$

$$X^{spot}_{d,ps,sb,h} + X^{reserve,pos}_{d,ps,sb,ts} \leq X^{turb}_{max} \quad \forall h \in ts \wedge \forall ts \in TS$$

$$X^{comp}_{d,ps,sb,h} + X^{reserve,neg}_{d,ps,sb,ts} \leq X^{comp}_{max} \quad \forall h \in ts \wedge \forall ts \in TS$$

$$S^{min} \leq S_{d,ps,sb,h} \leq S^{max} \quad \forall h = 1..24$$

[6.19]

The first restriction again describes the relationship between storage level $S_{d,ps,sb,h}$ and turbine $X^{spot}_{d,ps,sb,h}$ as well as compressor output $X^{comp}_{d,ps,sb,h}$. The next restrictions

---

[10]In the case of a PSHP plant, the objective function can be formulated analogue to Eq. 6.2

limit the bids on positive and negative reserve market. Again only a quarter of the minimum storage level of the four hours of time slice ts can be offered in the positive and a quarter of the difference $S^{max} - S_{d,ps,sb,h}$ on the negative minute reserve market. The other restrictions regarding reserve market and spot market bids are set up to keep the capacity limits of turbine and compressor. All bids on the different markets have generally to be made subject to capacity limits.

The starting storage level sb is introduced, to ensure that the end storage level $S_{d,ps,sb,h24}$ of day d and the starting storage level of following day $d+1$ are equal[11]. This constraint has to be considered for the addition of the daily contribution margins to determine the annual return. The optimal daily contribution margins are summed up considering again the transition probabilities from price scenarios ps at day d to price scenarios ps' at day $d+1$. For example, the optimal $CM^*_{d+1 \rightarrow D,ps'sb'}$ from day $d+1$ to D, which are weighted with the appropriate transition probability $Tpr_{d,ps \rightarrow d+1,ps'}$, are added to that of day d, leading to the overall contribution margin $CM^*_{d \rightarrow D,ps,sb}$ from d to D.

$$CM_{d \rightarrow D,ps,sb} = CM^*_{d,ps,sb} + \sum_{ps'} Tpr_{d,ps \rightarrow d+1,ps'} \cdot CM^*_{d+1 \rightarrow D,ps',sb'}$$

$$\forall ps, ps' \in PS \in PS, d = 1..364, sb = 0..4 \qquad [6.20]$$

The summary of the single optimizations to an overall optimization problem based on the recombining tree (see Figure 6.4) determines the structure of the annual return in the "day-by-day optimization strategy". It is important that those $CM^*_{d+1 \rightarrow D,ps,sb}$ are chosen for the addition (Eq. 6.20), which fulfill the so-called "time-coupled constraint". This constraint is a formalization of the restriction already mentioned and guarantees that the end storage level at day d and starting storage level at $d+1$ are equal.

$$S_{d,ps,sb,h24} = S^{end}_{d,ps,sb} = sb_{d+1,ps'} \cdot S^{max} \quad \forall ps, ps' \in PS \in PS, d = 1..364, sb = 0..4$$

$$[6.21]$$

---

[11]The optimization results for each day will suggest an empty storage at the end of the day. However, if negative prices occur in the last hours of a day, the results will indicate the charging of the storage. In this case the storage will not be empty at the end of a day.

Furthermore, the number of possible starting states $sb_{d,ps}$ are limited, so that the optimization problem can be solved in an acceptable computing time. Five beginning storage states are defined, i.e. $sb = 0, 1, 2, 3, 4$. The number of elements in sb is caused by the chosen storage size, which exactly corresponds to four times of the turbine output. The five beginning storage states indicate, whether the storage is empty (sb_0), quarter full (sb_1), half full (sb_2), three quarters full (sb_3) or completely filled (sb_4) at the beginning of a day. As the number of starting states sb is limited to five storage states, the time-coupled constraint is formulated by adding a set of five binary variables b_{sb} to the optimization problem (Eq. 6.18 - Eq. 6.21). Hence, the time-coupled constraint of the SDP problem can be formulated as follows:

$$S_{d,ps,sb}^{end} = \sum_{sb'} b_{sb'} \cdot sb' \cdot S^{max} \quad \wedge \sum_{sb'} b_{sb'} = 1 \quad \forall ps, ps' \in PS, \forall d = 1..364 \quad [6.22]$$

Under the consideration of this time-coupled constraint, the backward computation of the contribution margins $CM_{d \rightarrow D,ps,sb}^{*}$ from day $D(= 365)$ to first day d_1 leads to the total annual return R. As the five beginning storage states sb_{d_1} are also applied to the first day, the optimal annual return for each ps of day d_1 is finally chosen as the one $CM_{d_1 \rightarrow D,ps,sb}^{*}$, whose beginning state corresponds to the pre-defined final state of the storage S_D^{end} at the end of the model horizon.

$$R = \sum_{ps} \sum_{sb} \left(Pr_{d_1,ps} CM_{d_1 \rightarrow D,ps,sb}^{*} \mid sb \cdot S^{max} = S_D^{end} \right) \quad [6.23]$$

6.1.2.5. Fourth strategy: stochastic dynamic programming

The model described in section 6.1.2.4 is extended in the following, to capture the "real option" of delaying the discharge of the CAES or PSHP storage. The stored energy is then used for electricity generation not only at the same day of charging, but also at following days, especially if higher electricity prices are expected in the coming days. More precisely, it can be optimal to use the storage volume for electricity production at day d, if the plant dispatch is optimized only for day d. However, if a longer period is considered, it can be economically more reasonable, to delay the discharge of the storage, if e.g. a higher income can be generated on the next day or later.

To consider this real option within the optimization problem, possible future returns are also considered in the objective function. The end storage state of each day d is optimized in a way that the return $CM_{d,ps,sb}$ of day d and the cumulative returns $CM^*_{d+1 \to D,ps',sb'}$ from day $d+1$ to D are conjointly maximized. The optimization will then result in that starting level "$sb' \cdot S^{max}$" of $d+1$ and end storage level of day d, that maximize the total return $CM_{d \to D,ps,sb}$.

The optimization steps are again carried out starting in D and moving backwards in the recombining tree, resulting in stochastic dynamic programming (SDP) model[12]. The new objective function covers the whole income from day d to the end of the model horizon D:

$$max\ CM_{d \to D,ps,sb}\left(S^{end}_{d,ps,sb}, ...\right) = CM_{d,ps,sb} + \sum_{ps'} Tpr_{d,ps \to d+1,ps'} \cdot CM^*_{d+1 \to D,ps',sb'}$$

$$[6.24]$$

---

[12]Xi and Sioshansi (2012) apply also an SDP model to cooptimize distributed energy storage. The developed model is especially able to cooptimize different uses of a battery in a home as a distributed storage device. Epe et al. (2009) apply a stochastic optimization model with recombining trees to analyse the influences of decentralized power generation and energy storage on cost-efficient power supply.

159

In the case of a diabatic CAES plant, the objective function can be formulated as follows:

$$
max\ CM_{d \to D,ps,sb}(X^{spot}_{d,ps,sb,h}, \dots) = \sum_{h=1}^{24}
\begin{bmatrix}
\left(
\begin{array}{c}
p^{EL}_{d,ps,h} - p^{FU}_d \cdot \frac{1}{\mu^{FU}} \\
-p^{CER}_d \cdot \frac{1}{\mu^{FU}} \cdot EF^{FU} - c^{turb}_{var}
\end{array}
\right) \cdot X^{spot}_{d,ps,sb,h} \\[1em]
-\left(p^{EL}_{d,ps,h} + c^{comp}_{var}\right) \cdot X^{comp}_{d,ps,sb,h} \\
-c^{turb,LC} \cdot X^{turb,LC}_{d,ps,sb,h} \\
-c^{comp,LC} \cdot X^{comp,LC}_{d,ps,sb,h}
\end{bmatrix}
$$

$$
+ \sum_{ts=1}^{6} p^{reserve}_{d,ts} \cdot X^{reserve}_{d,ps,sb,ts}
$$

$$
+ \sum_{ps'} b_{sb'} \cdot Tpr_{d,ps \to d+1,ps'} \cdot CM^*_{d+1 \to D,ps',sb'}
$$

$$[6.25]$$

This optimization problem again has to be solved subject to the time-coupled constraint 6.22 and subject to the other constraints described in 6.19. The backward computation from $D = 365$ to $d = 1$ again delivers for each starting price scenario ps and storage state sb the optimal annual return under uncertainty. In the final step the annual returns $CM^*_{d_1 \to D,ps,sb}$ are again chosen as the optimal annual return of the CAES, whose beginning storage state sb is equal to the end storage state of D, i.e. S^{end}_D (see Eq. 6.23). The resulting optimal annual return can be used for further economic evaluation.

Finally, it is worth mentioning that the difference between the annual return calculated in the day-by-day optimization and the one from the SDP model makes up the so-called "real option value (ROV) to wait" or "value of flexibility (VOF)". As mentioned above the day-by-day optimization does not consider the option that the earnings could be increased, if the discharge of the storage is delayed by one day or a couple of days. But as the SDP model captures this option incorporating possible future returns ($CM^*_{d+1 \to D,ps',sb'}$) into the objective function, the difference of both optimization results exactly corresponds to the ROV.

This model is again implemented in the software environment GAMS. The SDP model consists of 54750 single optimization steps. Each optimization corresponds to a mixed-integer linear programming model with approximately 400 linear variables, 20 binary variables and 400 constraints. The running time of the SDP model as well as of the day-by-day model depends on the number of price clusters ps. If the model is set up with 10 price clusters ps at each day d, the running time is approximately 2 hours. However, if 30 price clusters ps are applied, the total computing time equals to more than 10 hours. The running time is therefore not linear to the number of price clusters ps. This relationship can be reasoned by the fact, that the number of optimization steps triples, while the number of model variables also triples. Therefore, the complexity of the model possess a stronger growth than a linear growth.

In the following the results of all strategies and models are preseneted for different case studies. Futhermore these results will be used for the economic evaluation of investments in energy storage plants based on net present value (NPV) and ROV approaches.

6.1.3. Evaluation of CAES power plants under uncertainty

The developed models and strategies are applied firstly for the investment evaluation of a diabatic CAES power plant, secondly for the evaluation of a pumped hydro storage power plant (PSHP). The investment evaluations are carried out based on optimal annual returns, which are earned due to the different dispatch strategies introduced above. A further differenciation of the analysis is done for the markets that are available for the operators of energy storages. In the first step, it is assumed that the operators are only acting on the spot market, in the second step they can also bid on the minute reserve power market.

As mentioned above, the first analysed power plant is a CAES power plant with a storage capacity of 1000 MWh_{el}^{out} and a turbine size of 250 MW. The further applied plant data is illustrated in Table 6.1.

Based on this data, the economic feasibility of CAES investments is evaluated in the following, applying simulated electricity prices of the years 2011 and 2020. The 2011 evaluation is performed with the help of all strategies comparing their results. For the 2020 evaluation, only the SDP strategy is applied. Thereby, it is

Table 6.1.: Applied techno-economic input data of the CAES power plant (data source: Gatzen (2008) and own assumption)

specific investments	625 €/kW
annual O&M costs	9000 €/$MW_{TurbCap}$
storage capacity	1000 MWh_{el}^{out}
turbine capacity (min./max.)	90 - 250 MW
compressor capacity	70 - 150 MW
compressed-air factor (CAF)	0.66 MWh_{in}/MWh_{out}
gas heat ratio	1.13 $MWh_{in,gas}/MWh_{out,el}$
roundtrip effciency	56 %
economic lifetime	25 a
discount rate	5-10 %

discussed how different scenarios for the mean levels of gas and electricity prices in 2020 influence the evaluation results.

6.1.3.1. Results based on 2011 prices

Beside the techno-economic data described above, 1000 electricity paths, that are simulated for the base year 2011, are applied within the evaluation models. The electricity price model, which delivers the simulated price paths, is calibrated with the historical electricity spot prices between 2006 and 2011. Finally, historical CO_2 certficate prices, gas prices and minute reserve power prices of the year 2010 (and 2011 respectively) are directly incorporated into the evaluation models.

A first analysis of the storage dispatch shows that in all strategies the storage is filled with compressed air in the night hours reaching the maximum storage capacity early in the morning (see Figure 6.5), although the starting point of storage charging is different for each strategy. Another common characteristic is that all strategies discharge the storage at peak load hours following the high electricity spot prices. The main difference in the storage dispatch occurs in the evening hours of the analysed day: The more complex strategies "perfect foresight" and

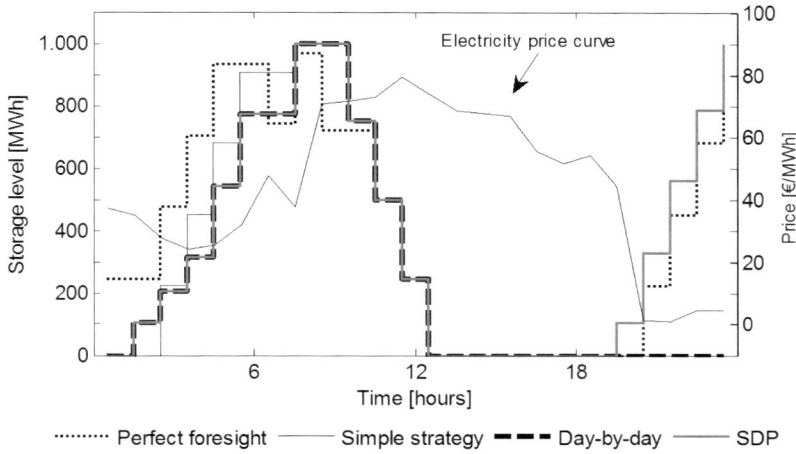

Figure 6.5.: Daily process of the storage level for an exemplary price path

the "SDP strategy" start filling the storage again in the evening hours, as they expect positive income in the following days. The simple strategy and the day-by-day optimization let the storage empty after discharging it. This results from the logic of these methods, which do not incorporate the prices and possible returns of following hours and days into the determination of the optimal strategy, as they carry out the optimization only for the analysed day.

Based on the optimal storage dispatch strategy, the evaluation of the CAES power plant is firstly done for the case that the plant is only operated on the spot market. An annual return of 13.89 MM€ is calculated for the CAES power plant, if the unit dispatch follows the "perfect foresight with MC simulation strategy". The "simple scenario under uncertainty" is far away from this result, achieving an annual return of only 9.06 MM€ (about 65 % of the perfect foresight strategy)[13]. The annual return of the SDP strategy (about 10.12 MM€) is considerably higher making up nearly 75 % of the perfect foresight strategy, the upper threshold (see

---

[13]The annual return determined with the perfect foresight strategy can be seen as an upper threshold for the yearly earnings of the CAES power plant, as the optimization is carried out under best conditions, i.e. a priori known prices, which are not given in reality.

Table 6.2.: Results of the CAES plant evaluation for the different plant dispatch strategies

	Perfect foresight / MC	Simple Strategy	Day-by-day optm.	SDP strategy
Annual return [MM€]	13.89	9.06	10.09	10.12
Spot market rev. [MM€]	43.32	24.61	39.62	39.57
Annual expenses [MM€]	29.43	15.55	29.53	29.45
Annuity (i = 8%) + O&M exp.	16.89			
Internal rate of return	5.5%	0.6%	1.9%	2.0%
Full load hours turbine [h]	2436	1461	2363	2359
Full load hours compr. [h]	2680	1605	2599	2590
Calculation time	8h	a few sec	∼ 10h	∼ 10h
	1000scen.		30 cluster	30 cluster

Table 6.2). Furthermore, it can be noted that the SDP strategy achieves a slightly higher annual return than the day-by-day optimization. This indicates that the "value of flexibility" or the annual value of the real option to delay the storage dispatch corresponds to only 0.03 MM€[14].

The spot market revenues and expenses of the perfect foresight strategy are significantly higher, which indicates that the CAES power plant comes into operation in more hours in the perfect foresight strategy than in the other strategies. This result is confirmed by the highest number of full load hours for both, turbine and compressor, in the perfect foresight strategy. The result is plausible, as in the perfect foresight strategy the unit commitment for a whole year is optimized at once, so that every positive spread between charging and discharging the storage is exploited. However, the SDP strategy, which is based on uncertain prices, achieves

---

[14]The real option value is defined as the difference between the annual returns of the SDP strategy and the day-by-day optimization strategy.

also a significantly higher number of full load hours than the simple strategy. The number of full load hours is increased by more than 60 % with the help of the SDP method compared to the simple strategy, but the annual return can be improved by only 11.7 %.

However, the increased annual return of the SDP strategy is still lower than the annuity of the investment + O&M expenses (16.89 MM€) based on an interest rate of 8 % and economical lifetime 25 years. If a discount rate of only 5 % is applied, the annual return does still not cover the annuity (11.08 MM€) of the CAES power plant. If the annual O&M expenses are also added to the annuity, the difference between annual return and annuity adds up to -2.19 MM€. This suggests that the investment is inefficient even by a low discount rate about 5 %. The only strategy, which exceeds the annuity at 5 % discount rate, is the perfect foresight strategy achieving a negligible higher value of 0.56 MM€. The internal rate of return of the investement reaches 5.5 % in this strategy and only 2 % in the SDP stratgy, which is another sign for the uneconomical investment, if the CAES is only operated in the spot market.

The economic efficiency of the investment can be increased, if the optimization of the unit commitment covers both markets, the spot and minute reserve market. The results based on the data described above show that the annual return is considerably improved by the option to take part on both markets (see Table 6.3). Thereby it is worth mentioning that the growth of the annual return is stronger in the SDP strategy (+1.12 MM€) than in the perfect foresight strategy (+0.51 MM€). This can be due to the fact that in the SDP strategy the reserve power prices are assumed to be known a priori, while spot prices are still handled as uncertain. Thus, the offers on the reserve power could be exploited rather by the SDP strategy than by the perfect foresight strategy. Hence, the SDP annual return increases from almost 75 % to 78 % of the return, which is calculated with the help of the perfect foresight strategy, if the CAES power plant is also operated on the reserve market.

Finally, the annual returns of the different strategies and markets are compared with the annuity of the CAES power plant investment applying different discount rates for its calculation. The comparison illustrates again that only if low discount

Table 6.3.: Results of the CAES plant evaluation based on different market participation

| | Perfect foresight / MC | | SDP strategy | |
	Spot market	Spot and reserve	Spot market	Spot and reserve
Annual return [MM€]	13.89	14.40	10.12	11.24
Spot market rev. [MM€]	43.32	41.26	39.57	36.62
Reserve market rev. [MM€]	—	0.91	—	1.44
Annual expenses [MM€]	29.43	27.77	29.45	26.83
Annuity (i = 8%) + O&M exp.	16.89			
Internal rate of return	5.5%	6.0%	2.0%	3.0%
Full load hours turbine [h]	2436	2294	2359	2167
Full load hours compr. [h]	2680	2524	2590	2378
Bids pos. minute reserve [h]	—	1348	—	1319
Bids neg. minute reserve [h]	—	827	—	1949

rates are applied, the investment can be evaluated as economically efficient. However, for discount rates beyond 6 % all strategies suggest to decline the investment (see Figure 6.6).

6.1.3.2. Results for the scenario year 2020

The evaluations above are carried out based on electricity prices simulated for the year 2011. However, evaluation results of the CAES investment can significantly change and the investment can probably be efficient, if the electricity price structure changes in future and the price volatility increases, which in turn could lead to higher short-term price spreads. This is expected, especially if the share of fluctuant power generation rises and the residual load becomes more volatile. Therefore, in the following the CAES investment evaluation is repeated for the

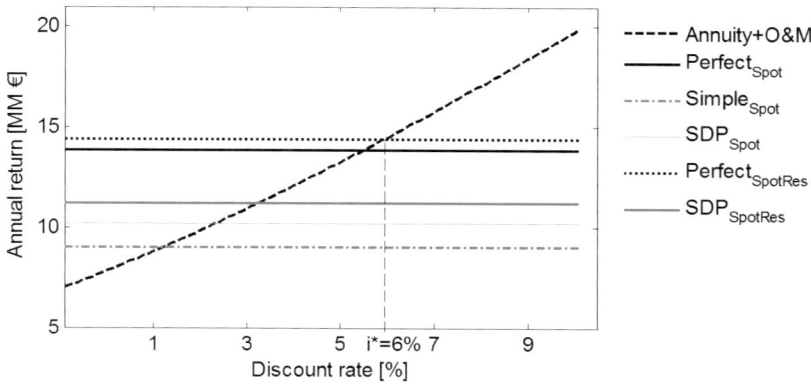

Figure 6.6.: Comparison of the annual returns of the different strategies with the annuity of the CAES investment

year 2020 assuming an overall installed wind capacity of 40 GW[15] for Germany. Based on this capacity assumption, wind power feed-in series and corresponding electricity price paths are simulated for the reference year 2020. The simulated price series are then used within the SDP model to recalculate the optimum annual return under uncertainty for the CAES power plant constructed in 2020.

Furthermore, different price tendencies and scenarios regarding the long-term development of electricity and gas prices are applied in the SDP model to compare the economic efficency of the CAES investment under different scenarios. In the first scenario "S1", a moderate growth of both, electricity and gas prices, is assumed until 2020. A moderate annual growth rate of the electricity price is also determined for the electricity prices between 2006 and 2011 at the EEX. This growth rate is used as trend parameter within the electricity price simulation. The simulated electricity price paths for the year 2020 possess a comparatively low mean (about 59 €/MWh) in scenario "S1". As for the gas prices historical data is

---

[15]39 GW onshore wind capacity are assumed for 2020 in the Leitstudie 2011 of the Federal Ministry for the Environment, Nature Conservation and Nuclear Safety (see BMU (2012)), while only 35.75 GW were assumed in the Leitstudie 2010. Hence, the author increased the value to 40 GW installed onshore wind capacity in 2020.

applied in the CAES evaluation models, the gas prices of the year 2010 are used in the first scenario representing a moderate gas price level.

In the second scenario "S2" a high gas price level is adapted, more precisely the gas prices of the year 2011[16], while the electricity prices are kept the same as in scenario S1. Scenario S3 corresponds to S1 and S4 to S2 respectively, but in these scenarios the electricity price period used for the calibration of the price models is reduced to 2007 to 2011. The reduced period is chosen, as a higher growth rate of electricity prices is determined for this period. The impacts of a high growth rate will be analysed in the scenarios S3 and S4. Summarily, S1 represents a low electricity and gas price level, S2 a low electricity, but a high gas price level in 2020. S3 assumes a high electricity price and a low gas price level, while S4 represents a high electricity and gas price level.

The SDP model runs for the different scenarios show that a higher annual return can be expected in 2020 compared to the results for base year 2011, if the overall installed wind capacity increases to 40 GW. However, the height of the annual return varies considerably in each scenario. The highest annual return can be earned in the high electricity price, low gas price scenario (S3) reaching the double of scenario S2, for which the assumptions are vice versa[17].

Analyzing these scenarios, it can be noted that in the scenario with moderate growth of electricity and gas prices (S1), the annual return reaches 16.32 MM€, which is still lower than the annuity of the investment, applying a discount rate of 8 %, plus the annual O&M-costs. Therefore, it can be stated that in the moderate price growth scenario the CAES investment is still away from beeing economically efficient in 2020. In the high price growth scenario (S4), however, the SDP model delivers an optimum annual return of 19.38 MM€, which is higher than the 8 %-annuity and which is almost as high as the 10 %-annuity. The CAES investment can be definitely evaluated positive in this case. Table 6.4 shows also

---

[16]The mean of the gas prices in 2011 (22.74 €/MWh) was significantly higher than the one in 2010 (17.25 €/MWh).

[17]The assumption of low gas prices and high electricity price or vice versa does not reflect the fundamental relationship between both parameters. Scenario S1 (low prices for both) or scenario S4 (high prices for both parameters) seem to be rather realistic than the others, as they consider the positive relation between both price parameters.

Table 6.4.: Results of the CAES plant evaluation for the different scenarios and year 2020

	S1	S2	S3	S4
mean electricity price [€/MWh]	59.94	59.94	77.32	77.32
mean gas price [€/MWh]	17.25	22.74	17.25	22.74
Annual return [MM€]	16.32	12.09	25.45	19.38
Spot market rev. [MM€]	57.32	39.38	103.14	76.56
Reserve market rev. [MM€]	1.17	0.99	0.73	0.72
Annual expenses [MM€]	42.16	28.88	78.42	57.90
Annuity (i = 8%) + O&M exp.	16.89			
Full load hours turbine [h]	2943	1920	4449	3088
Full load hours compr. [h]	3233	2107	4889	3393
Bids pos. minute reserve [h]	983	261	550	156
Bids neg. minute reserve [h]	1504	1938	765	1209

that the reserve market plays only a small role for generating revenues with the CAES plant.

Furthermore, net present values (NPV) of the CAES investment are calculated for different discount rates and economical lifetime assumptions. Assuming a discount rate above 8%, the NPV is negative in the low electricity price scenarios S1 and S2, independent from the applied economical lifetime of 20 or 25 years. For the high electricity and high gas price scenario (S4) a positive NPV is calculated in the case of a lifetime equal to 20 years and discount rates up to 9%. The NPV is even positive for discount rates up to 10% in the case of 25 years lifetime. In the less realistic scenario with high electricity prices, but low gas prices in 2020 (S3), the NPV is even positive for discount rates beyond 12% in any case (see Figure 6.7).

Thus, it can be concluded that the CAES investment is economically feasible, assuming an economic lifetime of 20 or 25 years, if a high growth rate for elec-

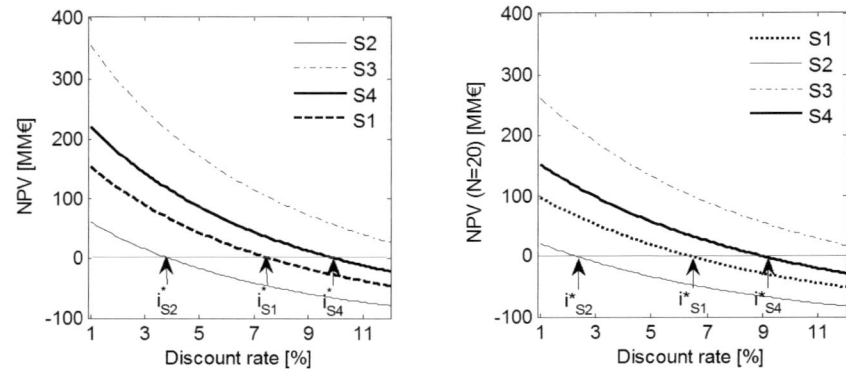

Figure 6.7.: a) NPV of the CAES power plant for different discount rates and different scenarios (lifetime=25a) b) NPV (lifetime=20a)

tricity spot prices (similar to that between 2007 and 2011) can be expected until 2020. In the case of low growth rates for the electricity price level, CAES investments will remain uneconomical, whether a higher (25 years) or a lower lifetime (20 years) is applied within the evaluation models.

6.1.4. Evaluation of PSHP plants under uncertainty

For the evaluation of PSHP plants a representative unit, i.e. the Goldisthal pumped storage hydropower plant, is chosen as a case study. The choice of this PSHP plant is motivated by the fact that it is one of the latest constructed PSHP plants and the investment was completely performed by a private company. Therefore, it is expected that this energy storage type is rather feasible than the CAES plant analyzed above. The model data of the Goldisthal PSHP plant is given in Table 6.5.

As it can be obeserved from the power plant data, the efficiency of the PSHP plant is much higher than the roundtrip efficency of the CAES plant, while the specific investments and the annual O&M costs are lower. This first analysis indicates that the PSHP plant is economically more attractive than the CAES plant analysed above. Indeed, running the SDP model with the PSHP plant data and the

Table 6.5.: Applied techno-economic input data of the PSHP plant (data source: Goldisthal PSHP)

specific investments	585 €/kW
annual O&M costs	4500 €/$MW_{TurbCap}$
storage capacity	8885 MWh_{el}^{out}
pumpturbine capacity	1060 MW
effciency	80%
economic lifetime	25 a
discount rate	5-10%

simulated prices for the base year 2011, a very high annual return (67.66 MM€) is achieved. This value significantly outranges the annuity of the investment at a discount rate of 5% (44 MM€) and reaches almost the annuity applying a 10% discount rate (68.31 MM€). The internal rate of return (IRR) of the PSHP plant investment consequently equals to 9.4%, which allows a positive evaluation of the investment. This is ecpecially the case, if the IRR of the PSHP is compared with the expected rate of returns of other investments in the energy sector and if it is compared with the discount rates applied in other studies (see Teisberg (1994), Roques et al. (2006) and King and Hall (2011)). Comparing the result of the PSHP plant evaluation with the one of the CAES power plant, it can be concluded that the investment in a PSHP plant should be preferred, if a appropriate location for a PSHP plant is still available in the Phelix area[18] and if the above applied techno-economic data is still given for PSHP investments.

After analyzing energy storage power plants as stand-alone investments, integrated power plants consisting of an energy storage and a wind power plant at the same location is evaluated next. The combination of both plant types to an integrated power plant is very interesting option to strengthen an energy system, as this new plant could produce and feed-in electricity into the grid in a more smooth way. The integrated power plants will be evaluated again on the basis of uncer-

---

[18]Phelix is the index for electricity spot prices at the EPEX for trades covering Germany and Austria.

tain electricity prices and wind power generation. However, the analysis will at first continue with the evaluation of stand-alone wind power plants based on the same uncertain parameters and the latest support policies for renewable power generation. This evaluation will help to present all analyses in a general context.

6.2. Mark-to-market evaluation of wind power plants under uncertainty

The German funding mechanism for renewable energy technologies has been based on fixed feed-in tariffs (FIT) for the last 12 years. However, since 2009 further mechanisms were introduced to bring the RES facilities closer to the deregulated market. These include the so-called "green power privilege"[19] and the "market premium" mechanism for directly sold RES power[20]. The market premium MP for electricity from a specific RES is equal to the difference between the corresponding fixed tariff and the weighted average of electricity prices during the hours in which the specific RES electricity is produced. For example, the wind market premium MP_m for month m is calculated as the difference between the FIT^{Wind} and the average market value MV of all units of wind power produced in the whole country in the previous month. The market value in turn is the total wind power production X_h^{Wind} in each hour weighted with the appropriate spot market price p_h^{EL}.

$$MP_{m+1} = FIT^{Wind} - \frac{\sum_{h=1}^{H_m} p_h^{EL} \cdot X_h^{Wind}}{\sum_{h=1}^{H_m} X_h^{Wind}} \quad \forall m \qquad [6.26]$$

$$MP_d = \sum_m (MP_m \cdot 1(d|d \in m)) \quad \forall d = 1..365 \qquad [6.27]$$

A wind power plant operator receives a market premium for each unit wind power directly sold on the spot market additionally to the electricity spot price. Thus, if his power generation perfectly correlates with the overall wind power

---

[19]Due to the latest renewable energy legislation Bundestag (2012) energy suppliers are partly exempted from the EEG charge (max. 2 €-ct/kWh), if they provide 50 % of their total electricity supply from renewable resources and if 20 % of this renewable energy comes from fluctuant resources, such as wind and solar.

[20]see Bundestag (2009) and Bundestag (2012)

generation, his income on the spot market and the market premium will add up to the earnings he would achieve in the fixed tariff system. However, if his generation occurs in times of peak load and high prices, his earnings are significantly higher than in the case of fixed FIT (see Schäfer et al. (2012)), as the market premium is constant throughout the day and does not depend on the earnings of a single wind power plant[21].

Since the introduction of the market premium at the beginning of 2012, the market premium mechanism has been more and more favoured especially by wind power plant operators. On average, this system enables higher incomes than the fixed tariff system. This is due to the fact that the market premium mechanism contains a further premium, the so-called management premium (see Förstner (2012)). The management premium helps to balance the costs for prognosis errors and increases the total revenues for a kWh electricity above the guaranteed fixed FIT (see Bundestag (2012)).

Because of that reason and due to the fact that it conforms better to a market evaluation than the other systems, the evaluation of wind power plants will be carried out based on the market premium mechanism in the following.

6.2.1. Evaluation method

A simple simulation method is developed for the evaluation of a wind power plant or park. According to this method the wind power plant is operated all the time, when wind is available, except in times in which the electricity prices become negative and fall below the negative value of the market premium. In these times/hours, the contribution margin would become negative and so the operation would be uneconomical.

Based on this dispatch method, the daily return $CM_{d,ps}^{Wind}$ of the wind power plant is calculated as the difference between all income components (spot price $p_{d,ps,h}^{EL}$, market premium MP_d and management premium $ManageP$) and the specific costs of wind power generation. These costs consist of the specific operation

---

[21]The market premiums are newly calculated at the end of each month for the following month depending on the spot prices and corresponding RES power production of all wind power plants in the elapsing month.

and maintenance costs c_{OuM} and the "specific costs for prognosis errors" c_{error}. The specific costs for prognosis errors are defined as the costs for balance power, which is needed for compensating wind prognosis errors, averagely portioned to every produced unit of wind power.

$$CM_{d,ps}^{Wind} = \sum_{h=1}^{24} (p_{d,ps,h}^{EL} + MP_d + ManageP - c_{OuM} - c_{error}) \cdot X_{d,ps,h}^{Wind}$$

$$\forall d = 1..D, ps \in PS$$

[6.28]

The applied electricity price paths $p_{d,ps,h}^{EL}$ are the same prices which were applied in section 6.1.3.1 for the evaluation of energy storages. Furthermore, the same recombining scenarios tree for electricity prices and the related transition probabilities from section 6.1.2.2 are used to add up the daily returns to the annual return of the wind power plant. The use of the same scenario tree is consistent with the evaluation of energy storages and makes a comparison between different investment options possible. Besides, it is worth mentioning that simulated wind power generation paths $X_{d,ps,h}^{Wind}$ are jointly clustered with the corresponding electricity price paths $p_{d,ps,h}^{EL}$ to keep the relationship between wind power feed-in and prices, which is described in chapter 5. Hence, the recombining tree represents both, the clustered electricity price paths as well as the appropriate electricity feed-in paths of the evaluated wind power plant.

Based on this recombing tree the returns $CM_{d \rightarrow D,ps}^{Wind}$ from d to D are recursively calculated with the help of the returns $CM_{d \rightarrow D,ps}^{Wind}$ from $d+1$ to D similar to the approach in Eq. 6.16:

$$CM_{d \rightarrow D,ps}^{Wind} = CM_{d,ps}^{Wind} + \sum_{ps'} Tpr_{d,ps \rightarrow d+1,ps'} \cdot CM_{d+1 \rightarrow D,ps'}^{Wind} \quad \forall d = 1..D-1 \quad [6.29]$$

Finally, the weighted average of all $CM_{d_1 \rightarrow D,ps}^{Wind}$ from the first day d_1 to D over all price paths ps_{d1} makes up the annual return of the wind power plant.

6.2.2. Evaluation of a wind power plant based on the market premium mechanism

Based on the simple approach described above, the value of a wind power plant can be calculated considering the uncertain development of prices and wind power generation. The evaluation method is applied for a case study consisting of a 100 *MW* wind power park. The specific investments of the wind power plant are assumed as 1247 €/kW according to Hirschl et al. (2010). The total investment sum amounts then to 124.7 MM€ for the entire plant. Furthermore, it is assumed that specific operation and maintanence costs c_{OuM} of the wind power plant equal to 1.2 €/MWh, while the "specific costs for prognosis errors" c_{error} correspond to 2.2 €/MWh (see Krohn et al. (2009)).

Considering this cost structure and the stochastic tree of prices for the analysed year 2011, the annual return of the whole wind park is calculated as 17.53 MM€. This value is only achieveable, if market premiums are included into the calculation. The market premiums are determined on the basis of the 2011 wind power feed-in tariffs for on shore wind, corresponding to 9.41 €-ct/kWh with all bonuses. The FIT for wind is reduced to 4.87 €-ct/kWh after five years. This period is extended, if the production of a wind power plant goes below 150 % of the reference production, which is seperately determined by a given wind speed for the location of the wind park/power plant and by the state of the art wind technology. The extension correponds to two month for every 0.75 % shortfall (see Bundestag (2012)). This suggests that if a wind power plant is analysed, whose power production corresponds to 125% of the reference production, the wind power plant would receive the higher FIT for an extended period that corresponds to the missing 25%. The extension would then ammount to 66 months or 5.5 years for an average wind power plant. Hence, the increased FIT of 9.41 €-ct/kWh would be paid for 10.5 years on average.

These 10.5 years are applied for the determination of the annual return in this case study. Afterwards, the market premium is removed, as it is would be negative, if the FIT is reduced to 4.87 €-ct/kWh after 10.5 years [22]. The annual return for the time after the initial 10.5 years is therefore calculated without the market premium. Based on the same price structure mentioned above, the annual return equals to only 7.35 MM€ without the market premium. This reduced annual return has to be taken into account, if the evaluation of the wind power plant is carried out assuming a higher economic lifetime than the 10.5 years. The annual returns are compared with the annuity of the investment, for which a discount rate of 8 % and a lifetime (N) of 10.5 years (and 15 years respectively) is applied. Table 6.6 summarizes the main results of the evaluation and the correponding input values for FIT, market premium, etc.

Table 6.6.: Main input data and results of the wind power plant evaluation

	first 10.5 a	after 10.5 a
FIT [€-ct/kWh]	9.41	4.87
market premium	9.41 - MV	0
management premium [€-ct/kWh]	1.2	0
specific O&M costs [€/MWh]		1.2
specific costs for prognosis errors [€/MWh]		2.2
expected full load hours		1721h
expected generation [GWh]		172.1
annual return [MM €]	17.53	7.35
annuity (i=8 %, N=10.5 a) [MM €]		18.5
annuity (i=8 %, N=15 a) [MM €]		14.6

---

[22]The current market value (2011) of electricity is about 5.1 €-ct/kWh. Therefore the difference between reduced FIT and market value would become negative assuming that the market value of wind power corresponds to the current value of electricity.

The results show that the full load hours of the wind power plant equals to 1721 hours, which correspond to an availability factor of about 19 %[23]. This indicates that the wind power plant is dispatched nearly all the time, if wind is available. This result is quite obvious, as electricity prices fell below the negative value of the market premium (minus the variable costs) only in a few hours of the year. Thus, it is economically feasible to dispatch the wind power plant nearly all the time.

A very high annual return can be achieved in the first 10.5 years, during which the market premium is paid. However, this annual return is still nearly 1 MM€ below the annuity of the investment at a discount rate of 8% and an applied lifetime of 10.5 years. But if the investment period is increased to 15 years, then the overall investment expenses of 219 MM€(=14.6MM€ x 15a), which are calculated based on the same interest rate of 8%, can be covered almost completely by the annual returns of the first 15 years, which add up to 217.14 MM€. Hence, investments in wind power plants are profitable under the new funding mechanism with market premiums, if a lifetime of 15 years and annual discount rate of 8% is applied, which are quite usual values for RES projects.

6.3. Combined evaluation of energy storage and wind power plants

Wind power plants and energy storages could be aggregated on a single site to a combined power station, which could be flexibly dispatched, delivering electricity for base or peak load contracts. However, due to the current market design in Germany, there is no financial incentive for a coordinated operation of energy storage and wind power plants, even if they are located on the same site. This results also from the fact that since 2011 new energy storages are exempt from net charges and from the EEG charge[24], which can be seen as an important incentive for energy storage investments. Thus, the energy storage operator has to pay only the price for the purchased electricity itself. The purchase costs of electricity

---

[23]This availability value is averagely calculated for wind power plants in the north of Germany.

[24]New energy storage plants are exempt from net and EEG charges for 20 years after their construction and existing plants for 10 years, if their power output is upgraded by 15 % and their storage volume by 5 % (see EnWG (2012)).

from the grid/market is now equal to the costs of electricity purchased from wind power plants[25]. A storage operator will therefore adapt the storage operation only to the current price structure. The availability of wind power from a nearby plant does not play a role for his decision on storage operation. This indicates that the operation of energy storage and wind power plants must not be coordinated, even if they are located at the same plant site. For this reason, the incentives for energy storage has to be rethought and changed in a way that a coordinated operation of wind power plants and energy storages leads to a positive portfolio effect. This could in turn lead to an adjustment of the storage operation to the availability of wind power[26].

Possible changes could be the introduction of a fixed payment (e.g. capacity payment) instead of the exemption from network and EEG charges. Another instrument could be the introduction of a "flexibility premium", which could be paid for shifting wind power production from offpeak hours to peak hours by using a nearby energy storage for this operation. In the following, the latter mechanism is implemented into an extended version of the SDP model introduced in section 6.1, which was used for the evaluation of energy storages. The extended SDP model evaluates an integrated power plant that consists of an energy storage and a wind power plant considering the uncertainty of electricity prices and of wind power production.

6.3.1. Model extensions for portfolio evaluation

The main extension lies within the objective function of the SDP model, which optimizes the sum of the daily returns between day d and the end of the planning period D. Thereby, further terms representing the daily returns of the wind power plants are added to the objective function. The first term $(p^{EL}_{d,ps,h} + MP_d + ManageP) \cdot X^{Wind,spot}_{d,ps,sb,h}$ illustrates the wind power sold on the spot market within day d, priced with the current spot price and the corresponding market premium

---

[25]The value of wind power in a specific hour corresponds to the spot market price for this hour, which is in turn exactly the price the energy storage operator has to pay for grid electricity if he is exempt of charges and taxes.

[26]The coordinated operation is desired, as it can relax possible congestions in the electricity grid

MP_d as well as the management premium $ManageP$ on day d. If some part of the wind power generated on day d is stored, the stored amount $X_{d,ps,sb,h}^{Wind,Storage}$ is valued with MP_d including the management premium and the flexibility premium $FlexP_h$ mentioned above. $FlexP_h$ is set to a positive value for offpeak hours and to "zero" for peak hours[27]. This approach promotes the storage of wind power surpluses in offpeak times. The objective function of the model for a combined plant, consisting of a CAES and a wind power plant can be formulated as in Eq. 6.30.

Beside the adjustment of the objective function, the constraint equations have to be also adjusted and new constraints have to be added to the SDP model to capture the restrictions related to the storage and sales of wind power. The main change is done in the first line of Eq. 6.19 to consider the amount of stored wind power $X_{d,ps,sb,h}^{Wind,Storage}$ within the determination of the storage level in hour h. Thereby it is worth mentioning that the storage level in h is calculated on the basis of the storage level of $h-1$. The previous storage level of the first hour h_1 corresponds to the beginning storage level of the day $sb_{d,ps} \cdot S^{max}$ leading to the second constraint in Eq. 6.32.

---

[27]In this approach the flexibility premium is only differentiated for two time slots (peak and offpeak). However, the impacts of a more differentiated flexibility premium could be analyzed in future analyses.

$$max \, CM_{d \to D,ps,sb}(X^{spot}_{d,ps,sb,h}, \dots) = \sum_{h=1}^{24} \begin{bmatrix} \left(\begin{array}{c} p^{EL}_{d,ps,h} - p^{FU}_d \cdot \frac{1}{\mu^{FU}} \\ -p^{CER}_d \cdot \frac{1}{\mu^{FU}} \cdot EF^{FU} - c^{turb}_{var} \end{array} \right) \cdot X^{spot}_{d,ps,sb,h} \\ +(p^{EL}_{d,ps,h} + MP_d + ManageP) \cdot X^{Wind,spot}_{d,ps,sb,h} \\ +(FlexP_h + MP_d + ManageP) \cdot X^{Wind,Storage}_{d,ps,sb,h} \\ -\left(p^{EL}_{d,ps,h} + c^{comp}_{var} \right) \cdot X^{comp}_{d,ps,sb,h} \\ -c^{turb,LC} \cdot X^{turb,LC}_{d,ps,sb,h} \\ -c^{comp,LC} \cdot X^{comp,LC}_{d,ps,sb,h} \end{bmatrix}$$

$$+ \sum_{ts=1}^{6} p^{reserve}_{d,ts} \cdot X^{reserve}_{d,ps,sb,ts}$$

$$+ \sum_{ps'} b_{sb'} \cdot Tpr_{d,ps \to d+1,ps'} \cdot CM^*_{d+1 \to D,ps',sb'}$$

[6.30]

$$S_{d,ps,sb,h} = S_{d,ps,sb,h-1} + X^{comp}_{d,ps,sb,h} \cdot CAF + X^{Wind,Storage}_{d,ps,sb,h} \cdot CAF - X^{spot}_{d,ps,sb,h} \quad \forall h = 2..24$$

[6.31]

$$S_{d,ps,sb,h_1} = sb_{d,ps} \cdot S^{max} + X^{comp}_{d,ps,sb,h_1} \cdot CAF + X^{Wind,Storage}_{d,ps,sb,h_1} \cdot CAF - X^{spot}_{d,ps,sb,h_1} \quad \forall d, ps, sb$$

[6.32]

Furthermore, the amount of wind power stored in the CAES $X^{Wind,Storage}_{d,ps,sb,h}$ and the amount sold on the spot market $X^{Wind,spot}_{d,ps,sb,h}$ has to be consistent with the overall electricity production of the wind power plant. Eq. 6.33 ensures that this constraint is taken into account within the optimization.

$$X^{Wind}_{d,ps,sb,h} = X^{Wind,Storage}_{d,ps,sb,h} \cdot CAF + X^{Wind,spot}_{d,ps,sb,h} \forall d, ps, sb, h = 1..24$$

[6.33]

A further consistency constraint affects the compressor operation, which guarantees that in total it cannot absorb more power from the wind power plant $X^{Wind,Storage}_{d,ps,sb,h}$ and from the grid $X^{Comp}_{d,ps,sb,h}$ than its maximum capacity X^{Comp}_{max}.

$$X_{d,ps,sb,h}^{Wind,Storage} + X_{d,ps,sb,h}^{Comp} = X_{d,ps,sb,h}^{Comp,total} \leq X_{max}^{Comp} \forall d,ps,sb,h = 1..24 \qquad [6.34]$$

To ensure that the flexibility premium $FlexP_h$ is paid only for shifting offpeak wind power to peak load hours using the storage, a further constraint is introduced. This constraint forbids the turbine operation of the CAES power in offpeak hours, if at the same time wind power is charged to the CAES. Otherwise the stored wind power could be simultaneously used for the turbine operation, as the technical characteristics of a CAES power plant enable the simultaneous operation of compressor and turbine. Therefore, this kind of operation has to be forbidden by regulation to avoid that the operator of the combined power plant receives the flexibility premium without really shifting offpeak wind power to peak hours. Mathematically, this constraint means that the turbine output, which corresponds to the sales on the market, $X_{d,ps,sb,h}^{spot}$ has to be zero, if $X_{d,ps,sb,h}^{Wind,Storage}$ possesses a positive value in offpeak hours.

$$X_{d,ps,sb,h}^{spot} = \begin{cases} 0 & X_{d,ps,sb,h}^{Wind,Storage} > 0 \wedge h = 1..8 \vee h = 21..24 \\ Y \mid X_{min}^{turb} < Y < X_{min}^{turb} \vee 0 & else \end{cases}$$

$$[6.35]$$

Beside these adjusted or added constraints, the other constraints of the SDP model are taken without any changes from the basic model into the extended model. In the following this model will be applied for the evaluation of an integrated plant, consisting of the CAES and wind power plant analysed in section 6.1.3 and 6.2.2 respectively.

6.3.2. Market-based evaluation of an integrated plant

The extended SDP model optimizes the dispatch of the energy storage and adjusts its operation to the wind availability due to flexibility premium payments. The optimization under uncertain prices and wind power generation is carried out for an integrated power plant, consisting of the CAES analysed in section 6.1 (turbine capacity of 250 MW) and of a wind power plant with a capacity of 100 MW. Based on further data for the power plant components introduced in Table 6.1 and 6.6, the annual return is optimized with the help of the extended SDP model for two cases: in the first case no flexibility premium is applied for shifting wind power from offpeak hours to peak hours, while in the second case a flexiblity premium of 1.5 €-ct/kWh[28] is applied.

The results show that the flexibility premium has a very little effect on the earnings of the integrated power plant. The annual return rises from 27.90 MM€ to only 28.43 MM€, which corresponds to a 1.8 % increase in total. The increased annual return is nearly at the same level of the annuity of the total investment (28.65 MM€) considering an economical lifetime of 20 years and an interest rate of 8 %. It should be mentioned that these annual returns are calculated on the basis of the market premium mechanism for directly sold wind power as it is applied in section 6.2. They are only achievable in the first 10.5 years after the construction of the integrated plant assuming that its specific wind power production corresponds to 125% of the reference production in Germany. However, if all the premiums are removed after 10.5 years due to the assumption that the market price will be higher than the reduced FIT (see section 6.2.2), then the annual return of the integrated plant equals to 18.25 MM€. Thus, the average annual return of the integrated power plant corresponds to 23.31 MM€ in the flexibility premium case and to 23.59 MM€ without this premium. As these average annual returns are below the annuity of the investment, an integrated power plant with the configuration mentioned above is not economically feasible, if investors expect an internal rate of return of 8 % per year.

Furthermore the applied flexibility premium (FP) of 1.5 €-ct/kWh causes that a total amount of only 244 compressor full load hours of wind power, which is generated by the 100 MW wind power plant, are shifted to the CAES plant and are brought to the market at peak hours. This number of compressor full load hours corresponds to 36.6 GWh. This indicates that 43.6 % of the total 83.90

---

[28]This value is chosen, as a similar flexibility premium is paid for biogas power plants due to the current renewable energy legislation, if a gas storage is constructed at the power plant site.

GWh wind power produced at off-peak times are made available at peak times. Table 6.7 summarizes the main results for the integrated power plant.

Besides, if the number of the turbine full load hours for the case with FP (2141 h) is compared with the case without FP (2161 h), it can be observed that the turbine is slightly less often dispatched in the case with FP. This can be seen as an inconsistency in the first. However, this outcome is caused by the constraint of no turbine operation during offpeak times, if wind power is stored in the CAES plant. Due to this model assumption the integrated power plant would not receive the FP, if it does not shift offpeak power to peak hours. If the compressor is run with wind power to shift this power into peak hours, no turbine operation is therefore allowed. The total number of hours, in which the turbine is allowed to be dispatched on the spot market, is reduced by this constraint compared to the case without FP. Thus, the reduced turbine full load hours are consistent with the FP assumptions. Furthermore, the full load hours of the turbine are reduced only by 0.9 % applying the FP and the constraint for shifting offpeak wind power. Nevertheless, almost 44 % of the produced offpeak wind power is shifted to peak hours, which makes the FP a successful policy in this respect and the insignificant reduction of the storage dispatch acceptable.

6.3.2.1. The impact of net charges on storage value

The analyses above are carried out without applying any net charges on electricity purchases of the energy storage from the grid. However, if net charges are applied, the annual return of such an intergrated power plant for the first 10.5 years would be reduced to 25.7 MM€ and 26.2 MM€ respectively, which corresponds to a decrease of the earnings by 8 %. The average annual return for the first 20 years would then be equal to 21.1 MM€ and 21.4 MM € in the case of net charges and FP[29].

Table 6.7 also highlights that the number of compressor full load hours resulting from wind power is increased from 244 h to 321 h, if net charges in the height of

---

[29] As a reminder: For the first 10.5 years the integrated power plant would receive market premium for directly sold wind power and other premia, after 10.5 years the plant would not receive any premia.

Table 6.7.: Results of the integrated power plant evaluation under different policies for the first 10.5 years

	without net charges		with net charges	
	without FP	with FP	without FP	with FP
Annual return [MM€]	27.90	28.43	25.65	26.20
Spot market rev. [MM€]	53.23	51.70	42.78	43.57
Reserve market rev. [MM€]	1.44	1.44	1.61	1.59
Annual expenses [MM€]	26.77	24.70	18.74	18.90
Annuity (i = 8 %) + O&M exp.	28.65			
Full load hours turbine [h]	2161	2141	1584	1606
Full load hours compr. (grid) [h]	2373	2111	1468	1445
Full load hours compr. [h]	0	244	273	321
from wind power [= GWh]	0	36.6	41.0	48.2
Directly sold wind power [GWh]	163.8	127.2	122.7	115.6
FLH pos. minute reserve [h]	1320	1390	1613	1575
FLH neg. minute reserve [h]	1950	1956	2285	2299

8.5 €/MWh[30] are again introduced. That means that the amount of stored wind power rises from 36.6 GWh to 48.15 GWh. Consequently, the amount of wind power directly sold on the spot market is reduced from 127.2 GWh to 115.6 GWh.

Besides, the number of full load hours, in which the compressor is driven by power from the grid, decreases by almost 32 % from 2111 h to 1445 h, if net charges are applied. The output of the turbine is analogously reduced, as the net charges lead to a further cost component that reduces the number of hours, in which the operation of the storage is economically feasible. Contrarily, an

---

[30]This figure represents the actual level of net charges in Germany for purchasing electricity from the high voltage grid (see Tennet (2012)).

increase can be observed for the full load hours on the minute reserve market, for both positive and negative minute reserve power, as the introduction of net charges does not lead to an additional cost component for bids on the reserve power market assuming that the bids on this market are designed in that way that reserve energy is kept ready, but it is in fact not requested and not delivered. Hence, the optimization of the power plant dispatch leads to an higher dispatch of the power plant components on the minute reserve power market, if net charges reduce the attractivity of bids on the spot market.

The analysis of the NPVs for the different cases shows also that the NPV becomes negative for interest rates from 4.7 % on (see Figure 6.8), if net charges are payable for the purchase of grid electricty, even if the FP mentioned above is paid for shifted wind power. If net charges are not imposed on energy storages, the NPV is negative for interest rates beyond 6 %. Investments in integrated power plants become more economic. The internal rate of return (IRR) of 6 % is also much higher than the one of the single CAES power plant investment evaluated with actual electricity prices (see section 6.1.3.1). Nevertheless, it is still too low compared with other investments in the energy sector, such as the pumped storage hydropower plant that is introduced in section 6.1.4. Hence, it is not to be expected that investments in such an integrated power plant will be carried out, even if energy storages remain exempt from net and EEG charges and a FP of 1.5 €-ct/kWh is paid for shifting wind power from offpeak hours to peak hours.

6.3.2.2. Changing the configuration of the integrated power plant

The IRR indeed increases from 3 % in the case of the single CAES power plant to 6 % in the case of the integrated CAES and wind power plant. However, this increase results mainly from the wind power plant component of the integrated power plant, which has comparatively higher annual returns thanks to the market premium mechanism. Therefore, it raises the question, how much the IRR can be increased and how much offpeak wind power can be shifted to peak times, if the configuration of the integrated power plant is changed in a way that e.g. the capacity of the wind power plant is doubled to 200 MW.

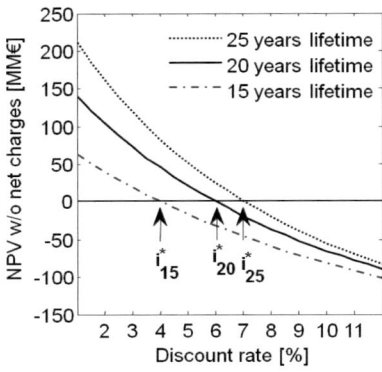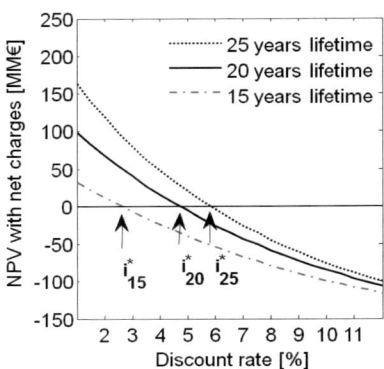

Figure 6.8.: NPV for different discount rates and lifetime considering flexibility premium (with and without net charges)

Due to the SDP model outcome under uncertain prices and wind power generation, the integrated power plant based on the new configuration (250 MW CAES and 200 MW wind power plant) optimally shifts 524 compressor full load hours from offpeak to peak hours. This number of full load hours corresponds to 78.6 GWh wind power, which in turn is up to 46.8 % of the 167.8 GWh offpeak wind power. Hence, the amount of shifted offpeak wind power can be slightly improved from 43.6 % (see above) to 46.8 % by doubling the wind capacity within the integrated power plant.

Besides, the new integrated power plant could achieve an annual return of 45.6 MM€ in the first 10.5 years, for which it receives the market premium for wind power output. The annual return of the further 9.5 years -assuming an economical lifetime of 20 years - is equal to 25.2 MM€, if all funding premiums (market and management premium) are removed. The average annual return is then calculated as 35.9 MM€, while the annuity of the modified power plant amounts to 41.3 MM€ applying the 8 % interest rate. There is again a discrepancy of approximately 5.4 MM€ between the annuity and the average annual return. Analogously, the IRR of this new investment equals to 6.15 %, which is only slightly above the IRR of the integrated power plant with 100 MW wind capacity. This suggests that the IRR and thus the economic feasibility cannot be increased just by increasing the capacity of the wind power plant component of the integrated plant. Hence, other funding or market mechanisms have to be established, if investments in such energy technologies are to be fostered.

6.3.3. Discussion of alternative policies

The flexibility premium introduced in 6.3.2 does not considerably improve the economic feasibility of investments in an integrated energy storage and wind power plant. Therefore, the question arises, how to design energy policy in a way that these kinds of energy storage investments can be fostered, as they seem to be necessary to balance the fluctuations of renewable power generation.

A first measure could be increasing the flexibility premium to a level, at which the average annual return of an integrated wind and energy storage plant becomes higher than the annuity of the investment calculated on the basis of a sector specific interest rate, e.g. between 8 % and 12 %. Another solution could be the redesign of the EEG feed-in tariffs (FIT) for fluctuant renewables. These renewable technologies could receive higher FIT, if they are built together with an energy storage system, which makes them flexible. A higher flexibility premium or higher EEG tariffs, however, would be a strong subsidy of a specific technology, which would lead to market distortions. Besides, it is politically very difficult to raise the FIT and thus the EEG charge for consumers, as there is strong opposition against further increases of the EEG charges within the population. The public discussion goes rather in the direction, how to reduce or at least to keep EEG charges at the level of the last adjustments (5.3 €-ct/kWh). Other funding mechanisms, which do not lead to a further increase of the EEG charge, have therefore to be found as an appropriate policy solution.

The introduction of a mechanism to promote flexible generation capacity, which has a high availability rate and which can balance the fluctuations of renewables, could stimulate investments in storage technologies. One of these mechanisms is the capacity payments mechanism[31], which guarantees flexible power generation

---

[31]The introduction of a capacity mechanism is currently discussed in Germany (see Maurer et al. (2012a) and Nicolosi (2012))

technologies a certain amount of income to cover their fixed costs, independent from their actual power generation.

In the case of the integrated power plant consisting of the 250 MW CAES and 100 MW wind power plant, the annual capacity payments would have to be as high as the difference between the annuity of the total investment and the average annual return. Without any other funding mechanisms, but considering the exemption from net and EEG charges, the average return was determined as 23.31 MM€ by the SDP model, while the annuity of the total investment was calculated as 28.65 MM€ applying an interest rate of 8 % and a lifetime of 20 years. This suggests that an investor has to receive an annual capacity payment equal to the difference (5.34 MM€), to cover his fixed costs and to receive an acceptable yield return of 8 % for the investment. If the 5.34 MM€ capacity payment are completely allocated to the 250 MW turbine output of the CAES, the specific capacity payment would correspond to 21360 €/MW*a [32]. This amount is similar to the capacity payment, which was paid in the last years and which is currently paid in Spain for conventional power plant capacities that have an availability rate of almost 100 % (see BOE (2012)). The capacity payments scheme seems to be a successful mechanism to promote investments in energy storage capacity. However, the introduction of a new mechanism, such as capacity payments, can have a strong impact on the energy market. For example, electricity price peaks can be avoided, if a capacity surplus is built up or if e.g. a price cap is also introduced, which is common in energy markets with a capacity mechanism. Hence, all aspects of such a mechanism has to be considered within the decision making process.

6.4. Conclusions

In this chapter different methods are introduced to evaluate bulk energy storages, such as CAES power plants or pumped storage hydropower plants, which can balance the inflexible power generation from fluctuant renewable energy sources.

---

[32]Almost the same number is calculated for the adjusted power plant with 250 MW CAES and 200 MW wind power capacity.

Among all introduced methods for the dispatch of energy storages, the perfect foresight optimization delivers the highest annual return for energy storage investments. However, this method is not applicable in reality, as prices, especially electricity spot prices, are uncertain and not really predictable. The results of the methods considering price uncertainty are more realistic. Among these methods the stochastic dynamic programming (SDP) model delivers the highest annual return. It achieves almost 75 % of the annual return of the perfect foresight strategy, while the "simple strategy under uncertainty" method ahieves only 65 %. The SDP model is therefore well suitable to optimize the dispatch of energy storages and to earn the highest contribution margins under uncertain parameters.

However, the annual return, calculated with the help of the SDP model based on 2011 prices, is not sufficient to cover the annuity of CAES investments, if an acceptable interest rate of 8 % is applied. CAES investments can become economically feasible in 2020, if electricity prices grow as strong as they did between 2007 and 2011 (see scenarios S3 and S4 in Table 6.4). Investments in PSHP plants, such as the Goldisthal hydropower plant, however, are economically feasible at the current price level and under the chosen framework conditions.

The analysis of the economic feasibility of wind power plants under the new market premium mechanism delivered a positive result, if on average, a wind power plant produces the same amount energy as all wind power plants in Germany. If the wind power production is evenly distributed over the day (peak and offpeak hours), an internal rate of return (IRR) above 9 % can be achieved. However, this result is only possible, if market premiums for wind power are paid at the current level. If the premiums are significantly reduced by policy makers in the future, the economical feasibility will not be given anymore assuming the investment expenses remain unchanged.

Furthermore, the economic feasibility of the combination of CAES and wind power plants has been also analyzed in this chapter. An integrated power plant, consisting of a 250 MW CAES power plant and a 100 MW or 200 MW wind power plant, has a higher IRR than a stand-alone CAES power plant. However, it still does not deliver the yield returns usually expected by investors in the energy sector. Even the introduction of an extra flexibility premium is not sufficient to increase the IRR of an investment in an integrated power plant to the level of PSHP plants.

Other mechanisms supporting investments in power plant capacity, such as capacity payments, seem to be more appropriate than a flexibility premium mechanism. A first analysis showed that investments in bulk energy storages, such as CAES power plants, can be economically feasible at the current price level, if capacity payments, as high as actually paid in Spain, are offered to CAES investments in Germany. However, the impacts of this mechanism on the electricity market has to be precisely analyzed by further work, before it can be introduced.

7. Conclusions and outlook

In this thesis uncertainties in liberalized electricity markets are analyzed and discussed in detail. An appropriate modeling approach for the main uncertainties, i.e. electricity spot prices and wind power generation, is developed and afterwards their integration into optimization models is demonstrated. Finally, investments in energy storage and wind power plant technologies are evaluated based on this integrated modeling approach.

The main conclusions derived from the analyses are clustered into two groups: the lessons learned from modeling uncertainties and the the most significant results for investors of energy storage and for policy makers. Finally, the modeling work and its results are critically reflected presenting possible improvements and future research areas for the evaluation of energy storage and power plant technologies under uncertainty.

7.1. Conclusions regarding modeling uncertainty

The electricity price modeling indicates that financial or time-series approaches on their own are not sufficient to simulate the main characteristics of electricity spot prices. To capture all characteristics, such as seasonal, weekly and daily cycles or price peaks, each has to be handled within a separate modeling approach. The separate modeling and removal of the deterministic seasonal cycles leads to a better performance of time-series and financial models, as their application to the stochastic residuals and their parameter calibration are not distorted by the deterministic components. The approach of seperate modeling of deterministic and stochastic components is also tested against an overall approach, in which all components are jointly modeled. The simulation results show that a seperate handling of deterministic and stochastic components leads to significantly better simulations results than the combined approach.

A further analysis is carried out to find the appropriate approach to simulate price jumps and peaks. The analysis suggests that a regime-switching (RS) approach delivers more reliable results than a single time-series model, although the time-series model is based on a heteroscedastic approach, such as a GARCH process, which can capture time-variable volatility. The root mean square error (RMSE), which is one of the main quality factors applied to compare model results with real data, is higher by a multiple in the case of models without an RS or deseasonalizing approach than in the case with an RS and deseasonalizing approach (see section 4.3.2). Therefore, it is strongly recommended to apply RS and deseasonalizing approaches within electricity price models.

Among the analysed financial and time-series models, applied to stochastic residuals of electricity spot prices derived from the EPEX, the mean reversion and the ARMA(5,1) models deliver smaller errors than more sophisticated models, such as ARIMA or GARCH processes. The results of these models can be further improved, if an approach for negative electricity prices is included additionally to the RS and deseasonalization approaches. The simulation results with negative prices fit real price paths better. These occur with a specific frequency since their permission in 2008 at the EPEX. Considering negative prices, the error term of the price simulation is indeed slightly lower, but even a few hours with negative prices are very important for energy storage operators. Operators can exploit these negative prices and increase the value of the storage by charging it in these hours. It can be concluded that an electricity price model should consider not only approaches for seasonal cycles and price peaks, but also for negative prices.

Beside electricity price modeling this thesis proposes an alternative autoregressive approach for modeling wind power generation and feed-in. According to this approach, seasonal and daily cycles, which could be determined within historical data, are again modeled seperately and removed, so that the autoregressive process can be applied only to the stochastic residuals. The proposed modeling approach adequately captures the structure and distribution of historical wind power feed-in values as shown by the lower RMSE between simulated and historical series.

There is a fundamental relation between wind power feed-in (WPF) and electricity prices, i.e. the merit order effect of renewable power generation. Therefore, the WPF simulation is integrated into the electricity price models to capture the merit order effect of WPF. This causes a reduction of electricity spot prices dependent on the amount of generated wind power. Consideration of the impacts of wind power on prices leads to a further improvement of the electricity price modeling. This is demonstrated by the smaller RMSE between simulated and historical electricity prices (see Table 5.3). In addition, the integrated modeling of WPF and electricity prices delivers consistent data for evaluation models, that rely on both parameters. This includes models that are developed to evaluate investments in wind power plants, or in integrated power plants consisting of energy storage and wind power facilities.

In the final step of the modeling work, several optimization approaches are developed for the evaluation of energy storages and integrated power plants under uncertainty. The optimization approaches considering uncertainty are compared with each other and with a perfect foresight optimization, in which electricity prices are assumed to be known in advance. The results show that the stochastic dynamic programming (SDP) approach delivers the best results among the approaches under uncertainty and that it achieves approximately 75 % of the annual return that is earned with the help of a perfect foresight strategy. As the uncertainty is taken into account within the SDP strategy, it represents an adequate methodology for the optimal dispatch of energy storages in order to gain maximum earnings under unknown electricity prices.

In summary it can be concluded that the developed models adequately describe uncertain parameters and that they can be used for the evaluation of energy storage and other power plant technology under uncertainty.

7.2. Recommendations concerning the viability of energy storage

The modeling approaches with the lowest errors are used to generate large numbers of simulated series of electricity prices and WPF for the years 2011 and 2020. These are then passed to a range of optimization models in order to determine the economic value of energy storages under uncertainty. The energy storage evaluation demonstrates that investments in diabatic CAES power plants are not economically feasible either in the approaches under uncertainty or in a perfect foresight strategy if the 2011 level of electricity prices is applied to the price simulation and to the evaluation models. The internal rate of return (IRR) of CAES investments is far below the rate of the latest investments in PSHP plants, even if a perfect foresight assumption is applied within the optimization model (see section 6.1.3). Therefore, investments in this technology are not recommended at the current price level.

However, the investment decision can be reassessed in the case of a price development with high growth rates until the end of this decade. Analyses for the year 2020 show that CAES investments can become financially viable, if electricity prices would on average grow as fast as they did between the years 2007 and 2011 and in the less likely event that gas prices stay at the 2011 level. In this case the annual return of the CAES power plant becomes higher than the annuity of the investment based on interest rates up to 8 %. Thus, the IRR of the CAES power plant comes closer to that of PSHP plants assessed at today's price level at the EPEX. PSHP plants, such as the Goldisthal power plant, can reach an IRR of almost 10 % under the assumed market parameters and given plant data. This IRR value is quite acceptable for investments in the energy sector. The construction of this type of energy storage can therefore be strongly recommended, if a location similar to the Goldisthal site can be found and techno-economic parameters remain unchanged.

The evaluation of wind power plants under the new market premium mechanism suggests that investments in these power plants are economically reasonable under this new funding policy, if the new wind power plant can produce power at the average efficiency level of all wind power plants in Germany. In this case the IRR is sufficient to cover the annuity of the investment, for which an interest rate of 8 % is used.

After analysing energy storages and wind power plants as individual units, the question arises, whether both technologies could be combined into an integrated power plant and how the economically feasibility of such an integrated plant could be achieved. Does this kind of integrated power plant represent an appropriate solution for an energy system based on renewable power generation? Initial analysis shows that IRR calculated for investments in such a plant considering uncertainty reach values slightly above 6 %. This IRR level does not significantly change, even if a flexibility premium is paid as a further support payment for the cordinated operation of both units of an integrated power plant. The applied flexibility premium of 1.5 €-ct for each kWh of wind power shifted from off-peak to peak hours is enough to shift move more than 40 % of the offpeak wind power to peak hours, but it is not enough for investors and operators of such an integrated power plant to earn the 8 % annuity of the investment.

The exemption of energy storages from net charges due to the latest Energy Economics Act (German: EnWG) can be seen as an important step into the right direction. With the help of this measure the annual return of energy storages or of integrated power plants can be increased by almost 9 %. However, the impacts of this policy on the financial resources of transmission lines has to be also considered, if energy storage is increasingly introduced into the market.

Furthermore, energy storages are exempt from EEG charges in Germany due to the same legislation. This regulation can be seen as essential for any economic operation of energy storages in the future if this charge is raised to nearly 5.3 €-ct/kWh from 2013 onwards, reaching the current mean level of electricity prices at the EPEX. If this amount of EEG charges is applied to energy storages, it will significantly increase the costs which an energy storage oprator has to pay for electricity purchases. This is because energy storages are mainly charged at times when electricity price is considerably lower than the mean electricity price. The total costs of electricity purchase therefore would be more than twice the costs without EEG charges, suggesting that an economic operation of energy storages would not be possible. It is therefore suggested that the EEG charge exemption could be valid for the whole lifetime of energy storages and not only, as in the current situation, for the first 20 years in the case of new investments and 10 years in the case of constructional expansions at the existing energy storage plants.

In this thesis, it is also shown that PSHP plant investments are economically feasible, if the framework and plant data of these investments are similar to the one applied in the case study within this work. It should be noted however that investments in other bulk energy storages, such as CAES, are performing poorly at the current price level. They can be positively evaluated only in a high growth scenario for electricity prices until 2020. However, as the technical potential for PSHP plants is limited, further storage capacities are necessary. Policy makers should consider additional incentive measures for CAES and other energy storages. Only then might a holistic concept be developed to transform the current energy system into a renewable energy based one. A short analysis also shows that the introduction of capacity payments, as high as they are currently paid in Spain for conventional power plants, would be sufficient to make CAES investments economically reasonable in Germany. The difference between the annuity of the investment (interest rate 8 %) and the annual return of a CAES power plant would in this case exactly correspond to the earnings derived from capacity payments. This support mechanism could be adressed and precisely evaluated in future work to derive robust policy recommendations.

7.3. Critical reflection and future research

Within this thesis only the main short-term uncertainties, electricity price and wind power feed-in, are considered for the evaluation of energy storages and integrated power plants. However, other uncertainties, such as power generation from photovoltaics (PV) or reserve power prices, should be also considered, as they affect electricity spot prices, which in turn directly determine the value of energy storages. PV power generation reduces peak prices, especially at midday, so that the earnings of energy storages decrease on days with high PV power production. The impacts of PV power generation can be incorporated into the existing models in the same way as done for WPF, if sufficient data is available to describe the stochastic distribution and other characteristics of PV power generation. This indicates an adequate integration of the PV effect is possible after several years, when sufficient time-series of data is available.

The other short-term uncertainty, i.e. prices for minute reserve power, can be added to the existing modeling approach, if the relationship of spot and reserve power prices can be clearly determined. However, this is a very challenging task, as the prices for minute reserve are not uniquely noted. Each bid, that receives a contract by the TSOs, is priced at its own offered price. Therefore, a series of prices exists for minute reserve power in each time slice. Hence, future research should rather concentrate on the short-term modeling of PV power generation and its impacts on spot prices rather than on modeling of reserve power prices. This latter parameter cannot be easily modeled.

Besides these short-term uncertainties, the long-term uncertainty of fuel prices also plays a role for the evaluation of diabatic CAES power plant. This CAES type does not only use compressed air from the storage, but also gas for electricity generation. Although a holistic approach could take this uncertainty into account, too, it is not necessary to regard it as a main aspect, especially if the evaluation of energy storages is carried out based on strategies for the short-term storage dispatch. The modeling approaches introduced above do not consider uncertainty of fuel prices. It could be incorporated in extended versions within future work, but it should be kept in mind that the greater the number of uncertain parameters that are added to a model, the more sophisticated and harder it is to solve. Hence, the inclusion of uncertainty should be limited to the main parameters.

The uncertain parameters this work focuses on are modeled with the help of a range of stochastic processes. New approaches are developed for specific characteristics of these parameters. Approaches are developed to capture new characteritics of electricity prices, for example negative values. The approach for the modeling of negative prices is a first step that can be further developed, when larger amounts of data with negative prices are available. Importantly, the stochastic distribution of negative prices can be replaced or adjusted within the modeling approach, if new data indicates changes in the distribution of negative prices.

Improvements regarding the integration of the electricity price and WPF models can be done, if the correlation between both parameters is analysed and described more precisely. The linear regression approach can be adjusted by increasing its dimension or by removing possible errors which distort a precise analysis of the relationship between electricity prices and WPF. However, the description of this relationship is already significantly improved in the existing model by applying a seperate linear regression for each hour of the day.

As described in section 5.2.3, the linear regression for each hour is developed to capture the load dependency of the merit order effect of WPF on electricity prices. If this load-dependency is directly incorporated into the model, its accuracy could be increased. Thus, the price reduction effect of WPF would be determined for each load interval and not for each hour of the day. The load intervals procedure would also describe the fundamental aspect of the merit order effect more ade-quately. This approach could be specified in future work, carrying out the linear regression for each load interval.

It is worth mentioning that the integrated model for electricity prices and WPF simulates hourly series for both parameters for a mid-term planning horizon, i.e. a whole year. But if the model is applied to the short-term simulation (single day), further information, such as wind speed prognoses, could also be integrated to the modeling approach. In this case a forecast could be set up for the day-ahead electricity prices based on the WPF expectation for the next day. However, the approach developed in this work is sufficient, if the simulated series are used for the evaluation of power plants or energy storages.

Energy storages are evaluated in this work with respect to the main technical aspects of storage operation. For example, the maximum turbine and compressor capacities are considered if bids are made on different energy markets for the same time slice. However, the technical details of each storage type could be modeled more precisely. Importantly though note that the relationship between changes of the storage level and the turbine output is assumed to be linear, as the storage level is roughly quantified as the amount of output energy. To specify the storage level in detail, the storage level could be metered by the pressure level of the compressed air in the case of a CAES or by the storage depth in the case of PSHP plants. This requires an adequate modeling of the nonlinearities between storage level and turbine output. Although a detailed description of the storage is always advantageous, it is in fact only necessary, if the focus of the analysis is set on the technical aspects of storage dispatch. For an economic evaluation, the modeling approaches introduced in chapter 6 seem to be sufficient.

The case studies, for which the evaluation models are applied for, are a diabatic CAES power plant and a PSHP plant with a specific configuration of their techno-economic parameters. Although the chosen case studies are already efficient in terms of their technical and economic operation, the models could be also used for other parametric configurations of these energy storage types. It would therefore be possible to check whether plants with another configuration can reach a better economic result than the ones analysed in this work.

The models could be used to evaluate not only other configurations of PSHP and CAES power plants, but also other bulk energy storages, such as hydrogen or electrochemical storages, if some smaller adjustments are made within the modeling approaches. However, as PSHP and diabatic CAES power plants are - in terms of actual investment expenses - the most economic ones among the different storage types, they have been the focus of the scope of this study. However, if a significant drop in investment expenses is expected for another storage type, this type could be adressed within future research using the developed models.

8. Summary

The liberalization of the electricity market and structural changes, that are also caused by strong support mechanisms for renewable power production, lead to new uncertainties including volatile electricity prices and fluctuant generation of wind and solar technology based power. Significantly, uncertain electricity wholesale prices have to receive increased consideration, if new investments are carried out on energy markets or if existing power plant technologies are dispatched on different energy markets. Similarly the expansion of renewable power technologies requires investments in energy storage technologies to balance the fluctuations of electricity generation. Energy storage technologies face the same market uncertainties suggesting investments in energy storages will only be made if they are economically feasible under the uncertain conditions. To carry out an appropriate assessment, new methods are necessary to evaluate energy storage and power plant technologies under conditions of increasing uncertainty.

Within this thesis the main uncertainties actors face on liberalized electricity markets are analysed. These uncertainties are electricity prices, energy commodity prices, fluctuant renewable power generation and political uncertainties regarding the further development of carbon and renewable energy legislation. Amongst these uncertainties electricity spot prices and wind power feed-in seem to be the most volatile and play a key role for the short-term planning of power plant operations. The power plant operation and the resulting cashflows in turn have to be taken into account, if investments in energy technologies are to be evaluated based on market prices.

The impacts of wind power generation on electricity prices are analysed and a method is developed for the combined simulation of wind power feed-in (WPF) and electricity prices. More precisely, the WPF method, which contains an autoregressive stochastic process, has been integrated into a regime-switching time-series model, which simulates electricity spot prices under consideration of WPF. The electricity price model also includes approaches to describe all characteristics of power prices, such as daily and weekly cycles or negative prices. The stochastic distribution of electricity prices is considered with the help of financial or time-series models. Nevertheless, the main innovation of the electricity models is the integration of WPF impacts on prices. The main advantage of this integrated modeling of electricity prices and WPF is that the merit order effect of WPF, i.e. the reduction of electricity prices by the feed-in of renewable power, is adequately captured.

The integrated model for the simulation of wind power and electricity prices is then used to generate a large number of price and WPF series. These series are in turn used to build a stochastic tree describing the distribution of the uncertain parameters. The stochastic tree is then applied within stochastic optimization models to evaluate energy investments and power portfolios under uncertainty. As there is hardly any prior published work evaluating PSHP and CAES plants under uncertain electricity prices and WPF, the focus is set on the evaluation of these storage types. Accordingly, a stochastic dynamic programming (SDP) model is developed, which optimizes the dispatch of energy storage plants and maximizes the annual return considering the real option value of energy storages. The real option analysed in this work enables the delay of the unit dispatch for a couple of hours or days, if later earnings are expected to be higher.

The developed SDP models are applied to the economic evaluation of both plant types mentioned above and the results are compared with each other and also with the results of other storage dispatch strategies, such as the Monte-Carlo simulation of the storage dispatch under perfect price foresight and a "simple strategy under uncertainty". The evaluation results show that investments in CAES power plants are not economically feasible under the current electricity price structure, while PSHP plants seem to fulfill the rate of return expectations of investors in the energy sector, if an appropriate location can be found and the applied market and plant data count for future investments. The SDP model achieves higher internal rate of return than other strategies that incorporate uncertainty, but this improvement is still insufficient to assess the investment in this technology as economically reasonable. However, CAES investments can become feasible in the future, if the mean level and volatility of electricity prices increase in the next decade. The volatility increase is very likely due to the growing share of renewables in the electricity mix, but an increase of the mean level is not certain, as the higher share of renewable power feed-in with marginal costs almost at zero leads to lower spot prices. The trend curve of electricity prices between 2006 and 2011 confirms this expectation.

In a further analysis the coordinated dispatch of energy storages and wind power plants is analyzed. It could be noted that after the exemption from grid charges for energy storages by the latest amendment of the Energy Economics Act, there is no direct incentive to coordinate the dispatch of the energy storage with the availability of wind power, even if both plants are located at the same site. A coordinated operation of both plants, however, is desirable to shift off-peak wind power to peak load hours and to balance fluctuant generation. Hence, the analysis focuses on the issue of whether the introduction of a flexibility premium for a combined plant, consisting of an energy storage and a wind power plant, would lead to a coordinated operation or not. The analysis shows that a flexibility premium incentive, as high as it is currently paid for biogas power plants, would not be sufficient to promote investments into energy storage at wind power plant sites.

Policy makers must therefore consider other support mechanisms, e.g. capacity mechanisms, to foster investments in energy storage power plants. This is especially important at locations with a high share of renewable power production. A first analysis shows that capacity payments, as high as currently paid in Spain, would be sufficient to facilitate the introduction of new diabatic CAES power plants into the German market. Further analyses can be adressed by future research to evaluate this mechanism and others, to determine a market design in which sufficient energy storage investments are undertaken.

A. Appendix

8. Summary

A.1. Equations

Volatility:

$$\sigma_\Delta = \sqrt{\frac{1}{\Delta t} \frac{1}{T-1} \sum_{t=1}^{T} (\Delta x_t - \bar{x}_t)^2}$$

[A.1]

$$\Delta x_t = \frac{p_{t+\Delta t} - p_t}{p_t}$$

Laplace distribution function:

$$F(x) = \begin{cases} \frac{1}{2} e^{\frac{x-\mu}{\sigma}} & x \leq \mu \\ 1 - \frac{1}{2} e^{\frac{x-\mu}{\sigma}} & x > \mu \end{cases}$$

[A.2]

Exponential distribution function:

$$F(x) = \int_{-\infty}^{x} f_\mu(t)\, dt = \begin{cases} 1 - e^{-\frac{x}{\mu}} & x \geq 0 \\ 0 & x < 0 \end{cases}$$

[A.3]

Root mean square error:

$$RMSE = \sqrt{\frac{\sum_{i=1}^{n} (\tilde{x}_i - x_i)^2}{n}}$$

[A.4]

Mean average percentage error:

$$MAPE = \frac{1}{n} \cdot \sum_{i=1}^{n} \frac{|\tilde{x}_i - x_i|}{x_i}$$

[A.5]

A.2. Tables

Table A.1.: Thresholds for triggering the second auction and main times for the day-ahead market (source: EPEX (2012a))

Market Area	Lower Threshold	Upper Threshold	Order Book Closure Time	Result Publication Time
Switzerland	0 €/MWh	500 €/MWh	11:00 am	from 11:10 am
Austria/Germany	-150 €/MWh	500 €/MWh	12 noon	from 12:40 pm
France	-150 €/MWh	500 €/MWh	12 noon	from 12:40 pm

Table A.2.: Estimated model parameters of the ARMA(5,1) and mean reversion model for electricity prices of different years

	Parameter	2004	2005	2006	2007	2008	2009
ARMA(5,1)	μ,σ	-2.2e-5;	8.6e-6;	-4.5e-5;	-3.7e-6;	-2.3e-6;	-3.7e-5;
		0.123	0.108	0.143	0.169	0.134	0.210
	α_i	1.553;	1.613;	1.527;	1.593;	1.645;	1.653;
		-0.601;	-0.545;	-0.499;	-0.534;	-0.614;	-0601;
		0.042;	-0.076;	0.050;	-0.028;	-0.007;	-0.058;
		-0.034;	0.036;	0.016;	-0.032;	-0.041;	-0.034;
		0.023	-0.032	-0.007	-0.005	0.011	0.034
	β_i	-0.826	-0.948	-0.864	-0.931	-0.942	-0.934
MR-Modell	μ	0.026	0.003	0.026	0.037	0.047	0.076
	σ	0.138	0.122	0.162	0.191	0.151	0.238
	κ	0.216	0.195	0.223	0.203	0.230	0.258

Table A.3.: Seasonality parameters calculated with the help of Equation (5.3) and (5.4)

month	$r_{m,a}$	$s_{m,a}$	$0.1q_{m,a}$	$0.9q_{m,a}$
1	0.0121	0.7431	0.0870	0.5532
2	0.0143	0.7354	0.0348	0.5485
3	-0.0012	0.8526	0.0584	0.4720
4	-0.0077	1.4710	0.0329	0.2911
5	-0.0067	1.1174	0.0354	0.3313
6	0.0099	1.0224	0.0249	0.2552
7	-0.0176	1.3401	0.0334	0.2704
8	-0.0133	1.7779	0.0279	0.2636
9	0.0003	1.1374	0.0349	0.3218
10	0.0024	1.0423	0.0336	0.3743
11	0.0018	0.6233	0.0664	0.5588
12	-0.0214	1.2238	0.0308	0.4863

A.3. Figures

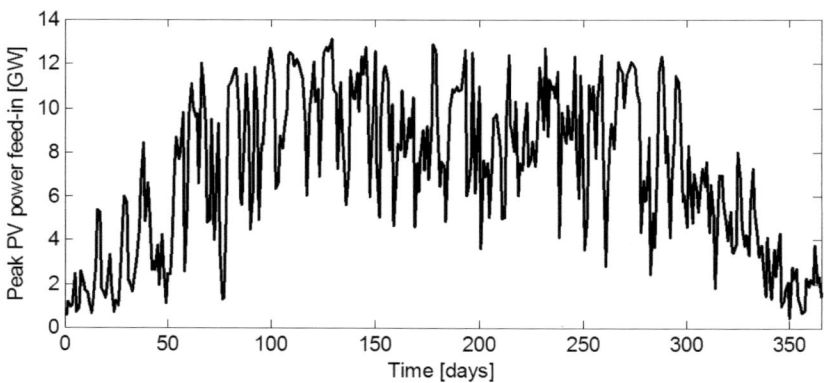

Figure A.1.: Maximum daily PV power feed-in for total Germany in 2011

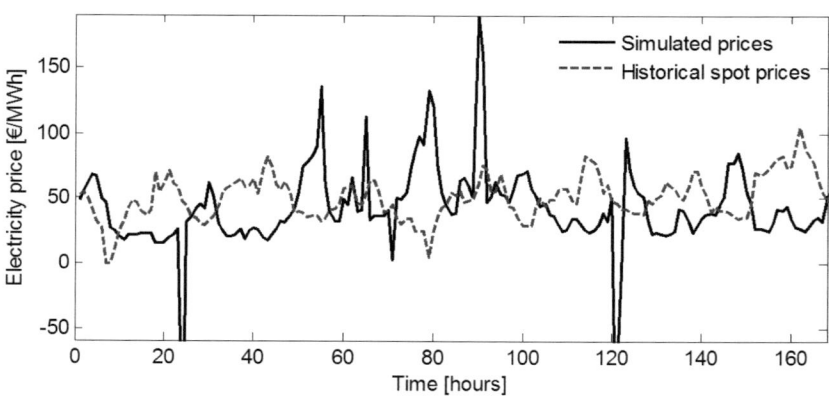

Figure A.2.: Real and simulated price paths for a week applying a closed regression for all seasonal cycles

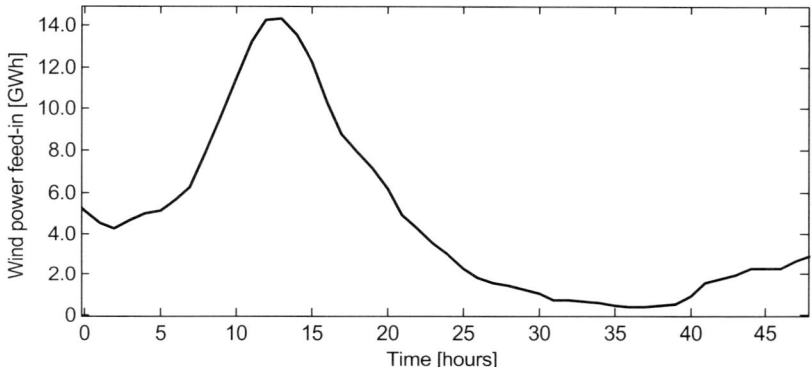

Figure A.3.: A typical pattern in the historical WPF curve: Progress of the hourly WPF at a windy day

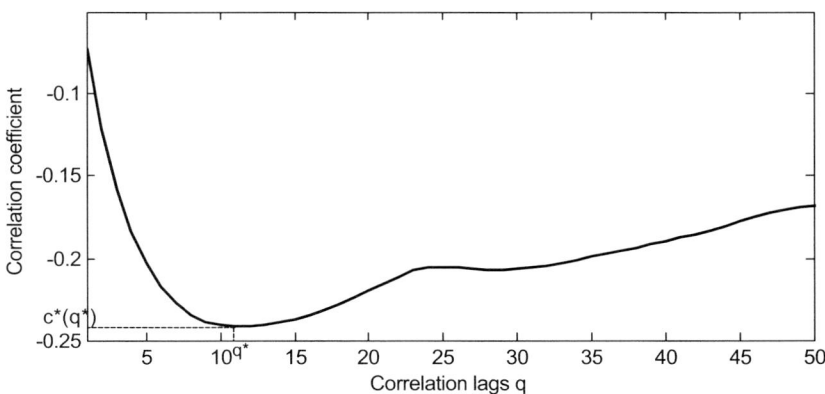

Figure A.4.: Correlation between change rates and capacity utilization levels with different lags (based on WPF data 2006-2009)

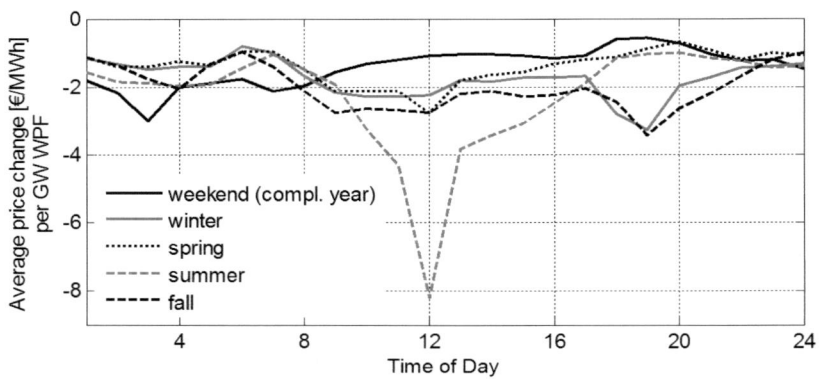

Figure A.5.: The hourly price reduction rates for each day type

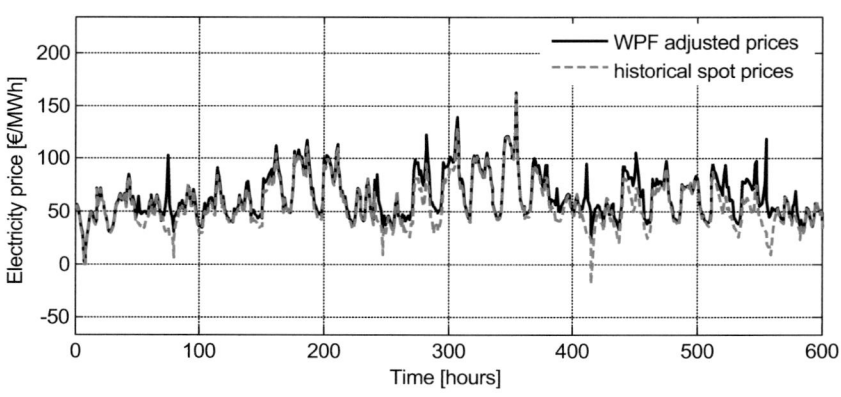

Figure A.6.: An excerpt of the historical and WPF adjusted electricity price series

B. Abbreviations

APX	Amsterdam Power Exchange
ARIMA	Autoregressive integrated moving average
ARMA	Autoregressive moving average
CAES	Compressed air energy storage
CAF	Compressed air factor
CAISO	California Independent System Operator
CDF	Cumulative distribution function
CHP	Combined heat and power
CM	Contribution margin
CO_2	Carbon dioxide
EEG	Erneuerbare-Energien-Gesetz, Renewable Energy Act
EEX	European Energy Exchange
EF	Emission factor
EGARCH	Exponential general autoregressive conditional heteroscedasticity
EnWG	Energiewirtschaftsgesetz, Energy Economics Act
EPEX	European Power Exchange
EUA	European Union allowances
FIT	Feed-in tariff
FOB	Free on board
FP	Flexibility premium
GARCH	General autoregressive conditional heteroscedasticity
ICE	Intercontinental Exchange
IEA	International Energy Agency
IDM	Investment decision
IRR	Internal rate of return
LSO	Long-term system optimization

MAPE	Mean absolute percentage error
MILP	Mixed integer linear progamming
ML	Maximum likelihood
MM	Million
MP	Market Premium
MR	Mean reversion
NAP	National allocation plan
NPV	Net present value
NYISO	New York Independent System Operator
O&M	Operation and management
OTC	Over the counter
OU	Ornstein-Uhlenbeck
PDC	Price duration curve
PEC	Primary energy carrier
PJM	Pennsylvania-New Jersey-Maryland Interconnection
PSHP	Pumped-storage hydropower
PV	Photovoltaics
RES	Renewable energy sources
RMSE	Root mean square error
ROV	Real option value
RS	Regime switching
SARIMA	Seasonal autoregressive integrated moving average
SDP	Stochastic dynamic programming
SMPP	Short/mid-term power production planning
SPE	Standard percentage error
TSO	Transmission system operator
VARIMA	Vector autoregressive integrated moving average
VOF	Value of flexibility
WPF	Wind power feed-in

C. List of Figures

2.1 Development of the trade volume at the main electricity spot markets (data source: EPEX, NordPool, APX) 13

2.2 Installed capacity and electricity generation of wind power plants and photovoltaics 19

2.3 a) Average daily price curves b) Weekly price curves for different seasons (based on 2011 EPEX day-ahead prices) 21

2.4 Boxplot of the electricity prices between 2006 and 2011 (data source: EEX, EPEX) 23

2.5 Development of the fuel prices between 2004 and 2012 (data source: Intercontinental Exchange ICE) 26

2.6 CO_2 price development in the second phase of EU emissions trading (2008-2012) (data source: EEX) 28

2.7 a) Wind power feed-in and system load on October 4th and 5th 2009 in Germany b) Exemplary weekly wind power feed-in (data source: German TSOs) 30

2.8 Average daily PV power feed-in and exemplary feed-in for summer weeks in 2011 (data source: German TSOs) 31

2.9 Daily inflow quantities on the Rhine river at the Rheinfelden hydropower plant (data source: BAFU (2012)) 32

3.1 Trinomial tree as an example of analytical scenario generation . . . 49

3.2 Scenario lattice with different states 51

3.3 Example of two-stage binomial decision tree 61

4.1 Occurrence of negative prices between 2008-2010 for different hours of the day (left) and weekdays (right) (data source: EEX (2012)) . 72

4.2 Occurrence of negative prices 2008-2010 at different hours and weekdays 73

4.3 Overview of the electricity price model 76

4.4 Autocorrelation of hourly electricity price logs before and after deseasonalising for 200 Lags 78

4.5 Transformation of the historical stochastic residuals of electricity prices to standard normal distributed residuals 82

4.6 The regime-switching algorithm for positive jumps 89

4.7 Historical and simulated price curves of the different price models for a week 95

4.8 Simulated price curves of ARIMA(1,1,1) model without deseasonalising and of a GARCH(1,1) process without regime switching . . 96

4.9 Real and simulated price duration curves of price models with and without negative prices 100

5.1 Right shift of the merit order and the supply curve particularly due to wind power feed-in 107

5.2 Average change of the deseasonalized electricity price per GW wind power depending on load interval 108

5.3 Price reduction per GW wind power feed-in depending on the load level and the German merit order curve (source: Erdmann (2008) and own calculation) 110

5.4 Overview of the WPF simulation model 112

5.5 Monthly 10% and 90% quantiles of the capacity utilization (based on WPF data between 2006 and 2009) 116

5.6 Hourly means of the capacity utilization (based on WPF data between 2006 and 2009) 117

5.7 Distribution of the hourly change rates of historical capacity utilizations 120

5.8 Estimation procedure for the distribution parameters of change rates for interval i 122

5.9 Overview of the WPF simulation model 125

5.10 Overview of the extended electricity spot price model 127

5.11 Comparison of simulated and historical wind power feed-in (top) and duration curves of capacity utilization (bottom) 130

5.12 Price simulation for a week based on 2009 data, considering WPF (left), without WPF impacts (right) 132

5.13 Simulated WPF and absolute price reduction series 132

6.1 Design of an PSHP plant (source: own illustration) 140

6.2 The structure of a CAES power plant (source: own illustration) . . . 143

6.3 Overview of model input/output and structure 145

6.4 Recombining tree for the price development 152

6.5 Daily process of the storage level for an exemplary price path . . . 163

6.6 Comparison of the annual returns of the different strategies with the annuity of the CAES investment 167

6.7 a) NPV of the CAES power plant for different discount rates and different scenarios (lifetime=25a) b) NPV (lifetime=20a) 170

6.8 NPV for different discount rates and lifetime considering flexibility premium (with and without net charges) 186

A.1 Maximum daily PV power feed-in for total Germany in 2011 208

A.2 Real and simulated price paths for a week applying a closed regression for all seasonal cycles 208

A.3 A typical pattern in the historical WPF curve: Progress of the hourly WPF at a windy day 209

A.4 Correlation between change rates and capacity utilization levels with different lags (based on WPF data 2006-2009) 209

A.5 The hourly price reduction rates for each day type 210

A.6 An excerpt of the historical and WPF adjusted electricity price series 210

D. List of Tables

2.1 Main properties of the German reserve power markets (source: Bundesnetzagentur (2011a) and Bundesnetzagentur (2011b)) 16

2.2 EEG funded electricity and funding quantities (source: BDEW (2012)) 20

2.3 Some basic statistics of electricity prices (data source: European Energy Exchange (EEX)) 22

2.4 Mean and number of outliers determined with the Grubbs' test . . . 25

2.5 Trend and volatility of fuel prices between 2004 and 2011 (data source: ICE) 27

2.6 Stochastic non-availability of power plants (source: EWI et al. (2004)) 33

2.7 Planned FIT for PV on roofs due to the different German EEG amendments 35

3.1 Stochastic electricity and commodity price models - Overview . . . 41

3.1 Stochastic electricity and commodity price models - Overview . . . 42

3.2 Overview of stochastic modeling approaches for energy markets . . 54

3.2 Overview of stochastic modeling approaches for energy markets . . 55

3.2 Overview of stochastic modeling approaches for energy markets . . 56

4.1 Estimated model parameters based on historical price logs 2002-2009 93

4.2 Expected MRSE, MAPE, R^2, mean and standard deviation for different stochastic models based on 30 simulations 98

4.3 Out-of-sample error measures of the different stochastic models for the period 2006-2009 99

4.4 Comparison of quality factors for models with and without the negative prices approach (based on 30 simulations for the year 2009) . 101

5.1 Estimated parameters of the regression functions for m, μ^+, μ^- . . 129

5.2   Estimated model parameters 131

5.3   Calculated error measures and other parameters of the simulated
      prices 133

6.1   Applied techno-economic input data of the CAES power plant (data
      source: Gatzen (2008) and own assumption) 162

6.2   Results of the CAES plant evaluation for the different plant dispatch
      strategies 164

6.3   Results of the CAES plant evaluation based on different market par-
      ticipation 166

6.4   Results of the CAES plant evaluation for the different scenarios and
      year 2020 169

6.5   Applied techno-economic input data of the PSHP plant (data source:
      Goldisthal PSHP) 171

6.6   Main input data and results of the wind power plant evaluation . . . 176

6.7   Results of the integrated power plant evaluation under different
      policies for the first 10.5 years 184

A.1   Thresholds for triggering the second auction and main times for the
      day-ahead market (source: EPEX (2012a)) 206

A.2   Estimated model parameters of the ARMA(5,1) and mean reversion
      model for electricity prices of different years 206

A.3   Seasonality parameters calculated with the help of Equation (5.3)
      and (5.4) 207

E. Bibliography

Amelin, M. (2004). *On Monte Carlo Simulation and Analysis of Electricity Markets*. PhD thesis, Royal Institute of Technology, Department of Electrical Engineering, Stockholm.

Arsie, V., Marano, M., Moran, G., and Rizzo, G. (2007). Optimal Management of a Wind/CAES Power Plant by Means of Neural Network Wind Speed Forecast. In *European Wind Energy Conference & Exhibition*, Milan. The European Wind Energy Association (EWEA).

BAFU (2012). Hydrologische Daten Rheinfelden (2091), Bundesamt für Umwelt, Schweizerische Eidgenossenschaft. http://www.hydrodaten.admin.ch/de/2091.html?#historische_daten, 10 Oct. 2012.

Baker, J. (2008). New technology and possible advances in energy storage. *Energy Policy*, 36(12):4368 – 4373.

Ball, M. and Wietschel, M. (2009). *The Hydrogen Economy*. Cambridge University Press, Cambridge.

Barlow, M. (2002). A diffusion model for electricity prices. *Mathematical Finance*, 12(4):287–298.

Barreto, L. and Kypreos, S. (2004). Emissions trading and technology deployment in an energy-systems "bottom-up" model with technology learning. *European Journal of Operational Research*, 158(1):243–261.

BDEW (2012). Erneuerbare Energien und das EEG: Zahlen, Fakten, Grafiken (2011). Technical report, BDEW Bundesverband der Energie- und Wasserwirtschaft e.V., Berlin.

BDEW (2013). Website of the BDEW, BDEW Bundesverband der Energie- und Wasserwirtschaft e.V. http://www.bdew.de/internet.nsf/id/energiemix-de, 15 Jan. 2013.

Billington, R., Chen, H., and Ghajar, R. (1995). Time-series Models for Reliability Evaluation of Power Systems including Wind Energy. *Microelectronics Reliability*, 36:1253–1261.

Binder, K. and Heermann, D. W. (2010). *Monte Carlo Simulation in Statistical Physics: An Introduction*. Springer, Berlin Heidelberg.

BINE (2007). Druckluftspeicherkraftwerke. Bundesministerium füer Umwelt, Naturschutz und Reaktorsicherheit (BMU), http://www.bine.info/fileadmin/content/Publikationen/Projekt-Infos/2007/Projekt-Info_05-2007/projekt_0507internet-x.pdf, 22 Oct. 2012.

Black, M. and Strbac, G. (2007). Value of Bulk Energy Storage for Managing Wind Power Fluctuations. *IEEE TRANSACTIONS ON ENERGY CONVERSION*, 22(1):197–205.

Blyth, W., Bradley, R., Bunn, D., Clarke, C., Wilson, T., and Yang, M. (2007). Investment risks under uncertain climate policy. *Energy Policy*, 35(11):5766–5773.

BMU (2006). NATIONALER ALLOKATIONSPLAN 2008-2012 für die BUNDESREPUBLIK DEUTSCHLAND. Technical report, Federal Ministry for the Environment, Nature Conservation and Nuclear Safety, Berlin.

BMU (2011). Erneuerbare Energien in Zahlen - Nationale und internationale Entwicklung. Technical report, Federal Ministry for the Environment, Nature Conservation and Nuclear Safety, Berlin.

BMU (2012). Langfristszenarien und Strategien für den Ausbau der erneuerbaren Energien in Deutschland bei Berücksichtigung der Entwicklung in Europa und global. Technical report, Federal Ministry for the Environment, Nature Conservation and Nuclear Safety.

BMWI (2008). Anreizregulierungsverordnung - Verordnung über die Anreizregulierung der Energieversorgungsnetze. Technical report, Federal Ministry of Economics and Technology, Berlin.

Bode, S. and Groscurth, H. (2006). Zur Wirkung des EEG auf den Strompreis. Technical report, Hamburg Institute of International Economics (HWWA), Hamburg. HWWA Discussion Paper.

BOE (2012). Real Decreto-ley 13/2012, de 30 de marzo. Num. 78, sec. i. pag. 26876, BOLETIN OFICIAL DEL ESTADO, Gobierno de Espana.

Bollerslev, T. (1986). Generalized autoregressive conditional heteroskedasticity. *Journal of Econometrics*, 31(3):307–327.

Börger, R. (2004). *Erweiterung eines Strompreismodells um GARCH-Prozesse.* Gesellschaft f. Finanz- u. Aktuarwiss., Ulm.

Bowden, N. and Payne, J. (2008). Short-term forecasting of electricity prices for MISO hubs: Evidence from ARIMA-EGARCH models. *Energy Economics*, 30(6):3186–3197.

Box, G., Jenkins, G., and Reinsel, G. (2008). *Times Series Analysis: Forecasting and Control.* John Wiley & Sons, 4th edition.

Brockwell, P. and Davis, R. (2002). *Introduction to Time Series and Forecasting.* Springer, New York, 2nd edition.

Bundesnetzagentur (2011a). Beschluss vom 18.10.2011, Az: BK6-10-097. Technical report, Beschlusskammer 6 der Bundesnetzagentur.

Bundesnetzagentur (2011b). Beschlüsse vom 12.04.2011, Az: BK6-10-098 und Az: BK6-10-097. Technical report, Beschlusskammer 6 der Bundesnetzagentur.

Bundestag (2009). Gesetz für den Vorrang Erneuerbarer Energien (Erneuerbare-Energien-Gesetz - EEG). Technical report, Erneuerbare-Energien-Gesetz vom 25. Oktober 2008 (BGBl. I S. 2074), das zuletzt durch Artikel 2 Absatz 69 des Gesetzes vom 22. Dezember 2011 (BGBl. I S. 3044) geändert worden.

Bundestag (2011). Dreizehntes Gesetz zur Änderung des Atomgesetzes Vom 31. Juli 2011. Technical report, Bundesgesetzblatt Jahrgang 2011 Teil I Nr. 43, ausgegeben zu Bonn am 5. August 2011.

Bundestag (2012). Gesetz für den Vorrang Erneuerbarer Energien (Erneuerbare-Energien-Gesetz - EEG). Technical report, Konsolidierte (unverbindliche) Fassung des Gesetzestextes in der ab 1. Januar 2012 geltenden Fassung.

Chatfield, C. (2004). *The Analysis of Times Series: An Introduction.* Chapman & Hall/CRC, London, 6th edition.

Commission, E. (2000). Green Paper on greenhouse gas emissions trading within the European Union, COM (2000)87. Technical report, European Commission, Brussels.

Conejo, A., Nogales, F., and Arroyo, J. (2003). Price-taker bidding strategy under price uncertainty. *IEEE Transactions on Power Systems*, 17(2):1081–1088.

de Miera, G. S., del Rio Gonzalez, P., and Vizcaino, I. (2008). Analysing the impact of renewable electricity support schemes on power prices: The case of wind electricity in Spain. *Energy Policy*, 36(9):3345 – 3359.

Defra (2008). Consultation on proposed EU Emissions Trading System from 2013. Technical report, Department for Environment, Food and Rural Affairs, London.

Delarue, E., Luickx, P., and Dhaeseleer, W. (2009). The actual effect of wind power on overall electricity generation costs and CO2 emissions. *Energy Conversion and Management*, 50(2009):1450–1456.

DENA (2010). Analyse der Notwendigkeit des Ausbaus von Pumpspeicherkraftwerken und anderen Stromspeichern zur Integration der erneuerbaren Energien. Technical report, Deutsche Energie-Agentur GmbH, Berlin.

Drury, E., Denholm, P., and Sioshansi, R. (2011). The Value of Compressed Air Energy Storage in Energy and Reserve Markets. *Energy*, 36(8):4959–4973.

Dupacova, J., Gröwe-Kuska, N., and Römisch, W. (2003). Scenario Reduction in Stochastic Programming - An Approach Using Probability Metrics. *Mathematical Programming*, Ser. A.95:493–511.

EEX (2007). Einführung in den Börsenhandel an der EEX auf Xetra und Eurex. Technical report, European Energy Exchange (EEX), Leipzig.

EEX (2011). EEX Product Brochure Power. Technical report, European Energy Exchange, Leipzig.

EEX (2012). Website of the European Energy Exchange. www.eex.de, 21 Jan. 2013.

Engle, R. (1982). Autoregressive Conditional Heteroscedasticity with Estimates of the Variance of United Kingdom Inflation. *Econometrica*, 50(4):987–1007.

ENTSOE (2012). Website of the European Network of Transmission System Operators for Electricity (ENTSOE). https://www.entsoe.eu/resources/data-portal/country-packages/, 10 Sep. 2012.

EnWG (1998). Gesetz zur Neuregelung des Energiewirtschaftsrechts vom 24. April 1998. Technical report, BGBl. Teil I S. 730, Berlin.

EnWG (2005). Zweites Gesetz zur Neuregelung des Energiewirtschaftsrechts vom 24. April 1998. Technical report, BGBI Teil I, S.1953, Berlin.

EnWG (2012). Energiewirtschaftsgesetz vom 7. Juli 2005 (BGBl. I S. 1970, 3621), zuletzt geändert durch Art. 2 des Gesetzes vom 16. Januar 2012. Technical report, BGBl. I 2011, S. 1554, I 2012 S. 74., Berlin.

Enzensberger, N. (2003). *Entwicklung und Anwendung eines Strom- und Zertifikatemodells für den europäischen Energiesektor*. VDI Verlag, Düsseldorf.

Epe, A., Küchler, C., Römisch, W., Vigerske, S., Wagner, H.-J., Weber, C., and Woll, O. (2009). *Stochastic Programming with Recombining Scenario Trees - Optimization of Dispersed Energy Supply, in: Optimization in the Energy Industry*. Springer, Berlin Heidelberg.

EPEX (2012a). EPEX SPOT NOTE - Day Ahead Auction Parameters. Technical report, European Power Exchange (EPEX), Paris.

EPEX (2012b). EPEX Spot Operational Rules - 07/05/2012. Technical report, European Power Exchange (EPEX), Paris.

EPRI-DOE (2003). Handbook of Energy Storage for Transmission & Distribution Applications. Technical report, U.S.Department of Energy, Washington.

Erdmann, G. (2008). Börsenpreise von Stromfutures und die drohende Stromlücke. http://www.prognoseforum.de/workshop/ws_17_04_08/Stromluecke.htm, 30 Nov. 2012.

EWI, IE, and RWI (2004). Gesamtwirtschaftliche, sektorale und ökologische Auswirkungen des Erneuerbare Energien Gesetzes (EEG). Technical report, Energiewirtschaftlichen Instituts an der Universität zu Köln (EWI), Instituts für Energetik & Umwelt gGmbH (IE) und Rheinisch-Westfälischen Instituts für Wirtschaftsforschung (RWI) im Auftrag des Bundesministeriums für Wirtschaft und Arbeit (BMWA).

Felix, B. and Weber, C. (2007). Bewertung von Gasspeichern mittels rekombinierenden Bäumen. *Zeitschrift für Energiewirtschaft*, 31(2018):129–136.

Fichtner, W. (1999). *Strategische Optionen der Energieversorger zur CO2-Minderung: ein Energie-und Stoffflussmodell zur Entscheidungsunterstützung*. Erich Schmidt Verlag, Berlin.

Fishbone, L. and Abilock, H. (1981). MARKAL: A linear programming model for energy systems analysis: Technical Description of the BNL version. *International Journal of Energy Research*, 5(4):353–375.

Fleten, S.-E. and Kristoffersen, T. (2008). Short-term hydropower production planning by stochastic programming. *Computers & Operations Research*, 35(8):2656–2671.

Fleten, S.-E., Stein, W., and Ziemba, W. (2002). Hedging Electricity Portfolios via Stochastic Programming. *IMA Volumes on Mathematics and Its Applications*, 128(Decision Making Under Uncertainty: Energy and Power (C. Greengard, A. Ruszczynski eds.)):71–93.

Förstner, U. (2012). Klima und Energie. In *Umweltschutztechnik*. Springer, Berlin Heidelberg.

Garcia, R., van Akkeren, M., and Garcia, J. (2005). A GARCH Forecasting Model to Predict Day-Ahead Electricity Prices. *IEEE Transactions on Power Systems*, 20(2):867–874.

Gatzen, C. (2008). *The Economics of Power Storage - Theory and Empirical Analysis for Central Europe*. Oldenburg Industrieverlag, München.

Genoese, F., Genoese, M., and Wietschel, M. (2010). Occurrence of negative prices on the German spot market for electricity and their influence on balancing power markets. In *7th International Conference on the European Energy Market (EEM)*.

Genoese, M. (2010). *Energiewirtschaftliche Analysen des deutschen Strommarktes mit agentenbasierter Simulation*. Nomos Verlagsgesellschaft, Baden-Baden.

Gibson, R. and Schwartz, E. (1990). Stochastic convenience yield and the pricing of oil contingent claims. *Journal of Finance*, 45(3):959–976.

Gieseke, J., Mosonyi, E., and Heimerl, S. (2005). *Wasserkraftanlagen - Planung, Bau und Betrieb*. Springer, Berlin.

Göbelt, M. (2001). *Entwicklung eines Modells für die Investitions- und Produktionsprogrammplanung von Energieversorgungsunternehmen im liberalisierten Markt*. PhD thesis, Universität Karlsruhe, Karlsruhe.

Gökcek, M., Bayulken, A., and Bekdemir, S. (2007). Investigation of wind characteristics and wind energy potential in Kirklareli, Turkey. *Renewable Energy*, 32(10):1739 – 1752.

Gourieroux, C. (1997). *ARCH Models and Financial Applications*. Springer, New York.

Greenblatt, J., Succar, S., Denkenberger, D., Williams, R., and Socolow, R. (2007). Baseload wind energy: modeling the competition between gas turbines and compressed air energy storage for supplemental generation. *Energy Policy*, 35(3):1474–1492.

Gröwe-Kuska, Heitsch, H., and Röemisch, W. (2003). Scenario Reduction and Scenario Tree Construction for Power Management Problems. In *Power Tech Conference Proceedings, 2003 IEEE Bologna*.

Hackl, P. (2008). *Einführung in die Ökonometrie*. Addison-Wesley, München.

Hahn, H., Meyer-Nieberg, S., and Pickl, S. (2009). Electric load forecasting methods: Tools for decision making. *European Journal of Operational Research*, 199(3):902–907.

Heidorn, C., Kalisch, F., and Hufendiek, K. (2009). Modellierung der Ölpreisentwicklung seit 2000 - Eine kritische Beurteilung stochastischer und fundamentaler Ansätze der Preismodellierung. In *8. Fachtagung Optimierung in der Energiewirtschaft*, pages 151–161, Duesseldorf. VDI-Verlag.

Heydari, S. and Afzal, S. (2008). Evaluating a Gas-Fired Power Plant: a Comparison of Ordinary Linear Models, Regime-Switching Approaches, and Models with Stochastic Volatility. In *31st International Conference of the International Association for Energy Economics*, Istanbul. IAEE.

Hirsch, G. (2009). Pricing of hourly exerciseable electricity swing options using different price processes. *Journal of Energy Markets*, 2(2):3–46.

Hirschl, B., Aretz, A., Prahl, A., Böther, T., Heinbach, K., Pick, D., and Funcke, S. (2010). Kommunale Wertschöpfung durch Erneuerbare Energien. Technical report, Institut für ökologische Wirtschaftsforschung (IOeW), Berlin.

Hobbs, B. (2001). Linear complementarity models of Nash-Cournot competition in bilateral and POOLCO power markets. *IEEE Transactions on Power Systems*, 16(2):194–202.

Hull, J. (2005). *Options, Futures and Other Derivatives*. Prentice Hall, New Jersey, 6th edition.

Hull, J. C. (2008). *Fundamentals of Futures and Options Markets and Derivagem*. Prentice Hall, New Jersey, 6th edition.

Hundt, M., Sun, N., and Swider, D. (2008). Modellunterstützte Investitionsentscheidungen fuer den Bau neuer Kraftwerke. In *Optimierung in der Energiewirtschaft*, number VDIBericht 2018, pages 157–173, Düsseldorf. VDI-Verlag.

IEA (2007). *World Energy Outlook 2007 - China and India Insights*. Number 600. International Energy Agency, Paris.

Jaillet, P., Ronn, E., and Tompaidis, S. (2004). Valuation of Commodity-Based Swing Options. *Management Science*, 50(7):909–921.

Jarass, L., Obermair, G., and Voigt, W. (2009). *Windenergie - Zuverlässige Integration in die Energieversorgung*. Springer, Berlin, 2nd edition.

Johnson, B. and Barz, G. (1999). Selecting Stochastic Process for Modelling Electricity Prices. In Jameson, R., editor, *Energy Modelling and the Management of Uncertainty*, volume Risk Books, pages 3–22. Risk Books, London.

Jones, D., Leiby, P., and Paik, I. (2004). OIL PRICE SHOCKS AND THE MACROECONOMY: WHAT HAS BEEN LEARNED SINCE 1996. *The Energy Journal*, 25(2):1–32.

Jonsson, T., Pinson, P., and Madsen, H. (2010). On the market impact of wind energy forecasts. *Energy Economics*, 32(2):313 – 320.

Kamal, L. and Jafri, Y. (1997). Time series models to simulate and forecast hourly averaged wind speed in Quetta, Pakistan. *Solar Energy*, 61(1):23–32.

Kanudia, A. and Loulou, R. (1998). Robust responses to climate change via stochastic MARKAL: The case of Quebec. *European Journal of Operational Research*, 106(1):15–30.

Karakatsani, N. and Bunn, D. (2008). Forecasting electricity prices:The impact of fundamentals and time-varying coefficients. *International Journal of Forecasting*, 24(4):764–785.

Karatzas, I. and Shreve, S. (2000). *Brownian Motion and Stochastic Cauculus*. Springer, New York, 2nd edition.

Kazempour, S., Moghaddam, M., Haghifam, M., and Yousefi, G. (2009). Electric energy storage systems in a market-based economy: Comparison of emerging and traditional technologies. *Renewable Energy*, 34(12):2630–2639.

Keles, D., Genoese, M., Möst, D., and Fichtner, W. (2012). Comparison of extended mean-reversion and time series models for electricity spot price simulation considering negative prices. *Energy Economics*, 34(4):1012–1032.

Keles, D., Möst, D., and Fichtner, W. (2011). The development of the German energy market until 2030 - A critical survey of selected scenarios. *Energy Policy*, 39(2):812–825.

Kennedy, S. and Rogers, P. (2009). A Probabilistic Model for Simulating Long-Term Wind-Power Output. *Wind Engineering*, 27(3):167–181.

Khalid, Q. and Langhe, R. (2010). Evaluation and monitring of energy consumption patterns using statistical modeling and simulation. In *6th International Conference on Emerging Technologies (ICET)*.

King, C. W. and Hall, C. A. (2011). Relating Financial and Energy Return on Investment. *Sustainability*, 3:1810–1832.

Konstantin, P. (2009). *Praxisbuch Energiewirtschaft: Energieumwandlung, -transport und -beschaffung im liberalisierten Markt*. Springer, Berlin, 2nd edition.

Kreiss, J. P. (2006). *Einführung in die Zeitreihenanalyse*. Springer, Berlin Heidelberg.

Krey, V., Martinsen, D., and Wagner, H. (2007). Effects of stochastic energy prices on long-term energy-economics scenarios. *Energy*, 32(12):2340–4349.

Krohn, S., Morthorst, P.-E., and Awerbuch, S. (2009). The Economics of Wind Energy - A report by the European Wind Energy Association. Technical report, European Wind Energy Association, Brussels.

Kumbaroglu, G., Madlener, R., and Demirel, M. (2008). A real options evaluation model for the diffusion prospects of new renewable power generation technologies. *Energy Economics*, 30(4):1882–1908.

Ladurantaye, D., Gendreau, M., and Potvin, J. (2009). Optimizing profits from hydroelectricity production. *Computers & Operations Research*, 36(2):499–529.

Lise, W., Lindeerhof, V., Kuik, O., Kemfert, C., Oestling, R., and Heinzow, T. (2006). A game theoretic model of the Northwestern European electricity market - market power and the environment. *Energy Policy*, 34(15):2123–2136.

Lu, N., Chow, J., and Desrochers, A. (2004). Pumped-storage hydro-turbine bidding strategies in a competitive electricity market. *IEEE Transactions on Power Systems*, 19(2):834–841.

Lucia, J. and Schwartz, E. (2002). Electricity Prices and Power Derivatives: Evidence from the Nordic Power Exchange. *Review of Derivative Research*, 5(1):5–50.

Lund, H., Salgi, G., Elmegaard, b., and Andersen, A. (2009). Optimal operation strategies of compressed air energy storage (CAES) on electricity spot market with fluctuating prices. *Applied Thermal Engineering*, 29(5-6):799–806.

MacQueen, J. (1967). Some methods for classification and analysis of multivariate observations. In *Berkeley Symposium on Mathematical Statistics and Probability*, volume 1, pages 281–297, Berkeley. University of California Press.

Maurer, C., Tersteegen, B., and Jasper, J. (2012a). Kapazitätsmechanismen in Deutschland und Europa: Wann gibt es wirklich einen Bedarf? *Energiewirtschaftliche Tagesfragen*, 62(3):32–37.

Maurer, C., Tersteegen, B., and Zimmer, C. (2012b). Anforderungen an den konventionellen Kraftwerkspark - wieviel und welche Kraftwerkskapazität wird benötigt? *Zeitschrift für Energiewirtschaft*, 36(2):147–154.

Menanteau, P., Finon, D., and Lamy, M.-L. (2003). Prices versus quantities: choosing policies for promoting the development of renewable energy. *Energy Policy*, 31(8):799 – 812.

Möst, D. (2006). *Zur Wettbewerbsfähigkeit der Wasserkraft in liberalisierten Elektrizitätsmaerkten - eine modellgestützte Analyse dargestellt am Beispiel des schweizerischen Energieversorgungssystems*. Peter Lang Verlag, Karlsruhe.

Möst, D. and Keles, D. (2010). A survey of stochastic modelling approaches for liberalised electricity markets. *European Journal of Operational Research*, 207(2):543–556.

Muche, T. (2007). Investitionsbewertung in der Elektrizitätswirtschaft mit dem Realoptionsansatz. *Zeitschrift für Energiewirtschaft*, 31(2):137–150.

Neubarth, J., Woll, O., Weber, C., and Gerecht, M. (2006). Beeinflussung der Spotmarktpreise durch Windstromerzeugung. *Energiewirtschaftliche Tagesfragen*, 56(7):42–45.

Nicolosi, M. (2012). Notwendigkeit und Ausgestaltungsmöglichkeiten eines Kapazitätsmechanismus für Deutschland - Zwischenbericht. Technical report, ECOFYS Germany GmbH, Berlin.

OakRidge (2010). Summary Report of the 2010 Technology Summit Meeting on Pumped Storage Hydropower. Technical report, Oak Ridge National Laboratory, Washington.

Öko-Institut (2010). Kostenlose CO_2-Zertifikate und CDM/JI im EU-Emissionshandel - Analyse von ausgewählten Branchen und Unternehmen in Deutschland. Technical report, Umweltstiftung WWF Deutschland, Berlin.

Olsina, F., Roescher, M., Larisson, C., and Garces, F. (2007). Short-term optimal wind power generation capacity in liberalized electricity markets. *Energy Policy*, 35(2):1257–1273.

Papaefthymiou, G. and Kloeckl, B. (2008). MCMC for Wind Power Simulation. *IEEE Transactions on Energy Conversion*, 23(1):234 – 240.

Parliament, E. (1996). DIRECTIVE 96/92/EC OF THE EUROPEAN PARLIAMENT AND OF THE COUNCIL of 19 December 1996 concerning common rules for the internal market in electricity. Technical report, European Parliament and Council, Brussels.

Parliament, E. (2003). Richtlinie 2003/87/EG des Europäischen Parlaments und des Rates vom 13. Oktober 2003 über ein System für den Handel mit Treibhausgasemissionszertifikaten in der Gemeinschaft und zur Änderung der Richtlinie 96/61/EG des Rates. Technical report, European Parliament and Council, Brussels.

Pilipovic, D. (2007). *Energy Risk - Valuing and Managing Energy Derivatives*. McGraw-Hill Professional, New York, 2nd edition.

Raczkowsky, B. (2008). *Lexikon Erdkunde - Geografische Fachbegriffe*. Stark Verlag GmbH, Hallbergmoos.

Ray, S., Munksgaard, J., Morthorst, P. E., and Sinner, A.-F. (2010). Wind Energy and Electricity Prices - Exploring the merit order effect. Technical report, A literature review by Poeyry for the European Wind Energy Association (EWEA), Brussels.

Regelleistung.net (2013). Internetplattform zur Vergabe von Regelleistung. www.regelleistung.net, 15 Jan. 2013.

Remme, U. (2006). *Zukünftige Rolle erneuerbarer Energien in Deutschland: Sensitivitätsanalysen mit einem linearen Optimierungsmodell.* PhD thesis, Universität Stuttgart.

Roques, F., Nuttall, W. J., and Newbery, D. M. (2006). Using Probabilistic Analysis to Value Power Generation Investments Under Uncertainty. Cambridge working papers in economics, Faculty of Economics, University of Cambridge.

RWE (2013). ADELE - ein Speicher für grünen Strom, Sechs Fragen zum Projekt in Strassfurt. www.rwe.com/app/Pressecenter/Download.aspx?pmid=4005594&datei=2, 23 Jan. 2013.

Ryu, S., Um, S., and Kim, S. (2010). The Impact of Wind Power Generation on Wholesale Electricity Price at Peak Time Demand in Korea. In Yao, T., editor, *Zero-Carbon Energy Kyoto 2009*, Green Energy and Technology, pages 79–84. Springer, Japan.

Safari, B. (2011). Modeling wind speed and wind power distributions in Rwanda. *Renewable and Sustainable Energy Reviews*, 15(2):925 – 935.

Schaal, P. and Kolshorn, J. (2005). Windenergie quo vadis? - Entwicklungspotenziale der Windenergie auf Binnenlandstandorten in Niedersachsen und Sachsen-Anhalt. *Raumforschung und Raumordnung*, 63(6):432–443.

Schäfer, A., WIENEN, B., and MOSER, A. (2012). Alternative Vergütungsmodelle regenerativer Erzeugungsanlgen. In *12. Symposium Energieinnovation*. Graz, Austria.

Schlittgen, R. and Streitberg, B. (2001). *Zeitreihenanalyse*. Oldenburg Verlag, München Wien, 9th edition.

Schmoeller, H. (2005). *Modellierung von Unsicherheiten bei der mittelfristigen Stromerzeugungs- und Handelsplanung.* Klinkenberg Verlag, Aachen.

Schneider, S. (2012). Power spot price models with negative prices. *Journal of Energy Markets*, online. http://mpra.ub.uni-muenchen.de/29958/.

Schoenung, S. and Burns, C. (1996). Utility energy storage applications studies. *Energy Conversion, IEEE Transactions on*, 11(3):658 –665.

Schulz, G. (1996). *Preisbildung in der Energiewirtschaft - Eine Analyse relevanter Preisbildungskonzeptionen unter preis- und wettbewerbstheoretischen Gesichtspunkten.* etv - Energiewirtschaft und Technik Verlag, Essen.

Schwartz, E. (1997). The stochastic behaviour of Commodity Prices: Implications for Valuation and Hedging. *Journal of Finance*, 52(3):923–973.

Seifert, J. and Uhrig-Homburg, M. (2007). Modelling jumps in electricity prices: theory and empirical evidence. *Review of Derivative Research*, 10(1):59–85.

Sensfuss, F., Genoese, M., Ragwitz, M., and Moest, D. (2008). Agent-based simulation of electricity markets - A literature review. *Energy Studies Review*, 15(2):19–47.

Sewalt, M. and de Jong, C. (2007). Negative prices in electricity markets. *Commodities Now*, pages 74–77.

Spliethoff, H., Wauschkuhn, A., and Schuhbauer, C. (2011). Anforderungen an zukünftige Kraftwerke. *Chemie Ingenieur Technik*, 83(11):1792–1804.

Sterner, M., Gerhardt, N., Saint-Drenan, Y.-M., von Oehsen, A., Hochloff, P., Kocmajewski, M., Jentsch, M., Lichtner, P., Pape, C., Bofinger, S., and Rohrig, K. (2010). Energiewirtschaftliche Bewertung von Pumpspeicherkraftwerken und anderen Speichern im zukünftigen Stromversorgungssystem. Technical report, Fraunhofer Institut für Windenergie und Energiesystemtechnik (IWES) Kassel, FuE-Bereich Energiewirtschaft und Netzbetrieb.

Stier, W. (2001). *Methoden der Zeitreihenanalyse.* Springer, Berlin Heidelberg.

Stoddard, L. (1996). Emerging Technologies. In Drbal, L., Westra, K., and Pads, B., editors, *Power Plant Enrgineering*, pages 781–808. Springer, New York.

Stoft, S. (2002). *Power System Economics - Designing Markets for Electricity.* John Wiley & Sons, New York.

Suomalainen, K., Silva, C., Ferrao, P., and Connors, S. (2012). Synthetic wind speed scenarios including diurnal effects: Implications for wind power dimensioning. *Energy*, 37(1):41–50.

Swider, D. (2006). *Handel an Regelenergie- und Spotmärkten: Methoden zur Entscheidungsunterstützung für Netz- und Kraftwerksbetreiber.* Deutscher Universitäts-Verlag, Wiesbaden.

Swider, D. and Weber, C. (2007). Extended ARMA models for estimating price developments on day-ahead electricity markets. *Electric Power Systems Research*, 77(5-6):583–593.

Tauer, L. (1983). Target Motad. *American Journal of Agricultural Economics*, 65(3):606–610.

Teisberg, E. O. (1994). An Option Valuation Analysis of Investment Choices by a Regulated Firm. *Management Science*, 40(4):535–548.

Tennet (2012). Website of the TSO Tennet. http://www.tennettso.de/site/Transparenz/veroeffentlichungen/netzentgelte/entgelt-fuer-die-netznutzung, 05 Oct. 2012.

Thome, H. (2005). *Zeitreihenanalyse.* Oldenburg Wissenschaftsverlag, München.

Torres, J., Garcia, A., De Blas, M., and A., D. F. (2005). Forecast of hourly wind speed with ARMA models in Navarre (Spain). *Solar Energy*, 79(1):65–77.

Troncoso, A., Riquelme, J., Aguilar-Ruiz, J., and Riquelme Santos, J. (2008). Evolutionary techniques applied to the optimal short-term scheduling of the electrical energy production. *European Journal of Operational Research*, 185(3):1114–1127.

Tseng, C. and Barz, G. (2002). Short-Term Generation Asset Valuation: A Real Options Approach. *Operation Research*, 50(2):297–310.

Uhlenbeck, G.E.;Ornstein, L. (1930). On the theory of Brownian motion. *Physic Review*, 36:823–841.

Umweltbundesamt (2011). Umstrukturierung der Stromversorgung in Deutschland. Technical report, Pressestelle des Umweltbundesamtes.

van der Linden, S. (2006). Bulk energy storage potential in the USA, current developments and future prospects. *Energy*, 31(15):3446 – 3457.

Ventosa, M., Baillo, A., Ramos, A., and Rivier, M. (2005). Electricity market modeling trends. *Energy Policy*, 33(7):897–913.

Villar, J. and Joutz, F. (2006). The Relationship Between Crude Oil and Natural Gas Prices. Technical report, Energy Information Administration, Office of Oil and Gas, Washington.

Wagner, M. (2007). *CO2-Emissionszertifikate - Preismodellierung und Derivatebewertung*. Universitaetsverlag Karlsruhe, Karlsruhe.

Weber, C. (2005). *Uncertainty in the Electric Power Industry*. Springer, New York.

Weigt, H. (2009). Germanys Wind Energy: The potential for fossil capacity replacement and cost saving. *Applied Energy*, 86(10):1857–1860.

Weron, R. (2006). *Modeling and Forecasting Electricity Loads and Prices: A Statistical Approach*. John Wiley & Sons, Chichester.

Weron, R., Bierbrauer, M., and Trueck, S. (2004). Modelling electricity prices: jump diffusion and regime switching. *PHYSICA A*, 336(2004):39–48.

Wietschel, M. (2000). *Produktion und Energie: Planung und Steuerung industrieller Energie- und Stoffströme*. Peter Lang, Frankfurt.

Xi, X. and Sioshansi, R. (2012). A Stochastic Dynamic Programming Model for Co-optimization of Distributed Energy Storage. *Energy Economics*, in Review.

Yang, M., Blyth, W., Bradley, R., Bunn, D., Clarke, C., and Wilson, T. (2008). Evaluating the power investment options with uncertainty in climate policy. *Energy Economics*, 30(4):1933–1950.

ZuG (2011). Gesetz über den nationalen Zuteilungsplan für Treibhausgas-Emissionsberechtigungen in der Zuteilungsperiode 2008 bis 2012 (Zuteilungsgesetz 2012 - ZuG 2012), Zuteilungsgesetz 2012 vom 7. August 2007 (BGBl. I S. 1788), das zuletzt durch Artikel 2 Absatz 23 des Gesetzes vom 22. Dezember 2011 (BGBl. I S. 3044) geändert worden ist. Technical report, Bundestag.

Zunft, S., Jakiel, C., Koller, M., and Bullough, C. (2006). Adiabatic Compressed Air Energy Storage for the Grid Integration of Wind Power. In *Sixth International Conference on Large-Scale Integration of Wind Power and Transmission Networks for Offshore Windfarms, Delft, Netherlands*.

PRODUKTION UND ENERGIE

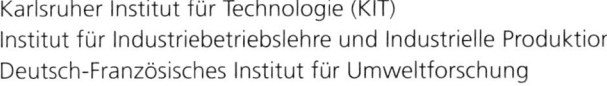

Karlsruher Institut für Technologie (KIT)
Institut für Industriebetriebslehre und Industrielle Produktion
Deutsch-Französisches Institut für Umweltforschung

ISSN 2194-2404

Die Bände sind unter www.ksp.kit.edu als PDF frei verfügbar
oder als Druckausgabe zu bestellen.

Band 1   National Integrated Assessment Modelling zur Bewertung
          umweltpolitischer Instrumente.
          Entwicklung des otello-Modellsystems und dessen Anwendung
          auf die Bundesrepublik Deutschland. 2012
          ISBN 978-3-86644-853-7

Band 2   Erhöhung der Energie- und Ressourceneffizienz und
          Reduzierung der Treibhausgasemissionen in der Eisen-,
          Stahl- und Zinkindustrie (ERESTRE). 2013
          ISBN 978-3-86644-857-5

Band 3   Frederik Trippe
          Techno-ökonomische Bewertung alternativer Verfahrens-
          konfigurationen zur Herstellung von Biomass-to-Liquid (BtL)
          Kraftstoffen und Chemikalien. 2013
          ISBN 978-3-7315-0031-5

Band 4   Dogan Keles
          Uncertainties in energy markets and their
          consideration in energy storage evaluation. 2013
          ISBN 978-3-7315-0046-9